Books by Susan Day:

Who Your Friends Are
The Roads They Travelled
Hollin Clough

Hollin Clough

Susan Day

Leaping Boy Publications

Published by Leaping Boy Publications
partners@neallscott.co.uk
www.leapingboy.com

Cover photo by Ken Rutter

A CIP catalogue record for this title is available
from the British Library.

ISBN 978-0-9935947-8-6

Main Characters

Sid and Dot Green

Glenys Midgeley (nee Green)
Frank (Midge) Midgeley
Beth Midgeley
Jen Midgeley

Elaine Fairlie (nee Green)
Keith Fairlie
James Fairlie
Patrick (Tricky) Fairlie

Neville Green
Mandy Green (nee Coldwell)
Troy Coldwell
Ashley Green
Honey Green

1

Jen: Excuses

'No excuses,' says my father over the phone.

'OK,' I say, because there have been excuses.

'Everyone,' he says.

'Even –?'

'Even –,' he says. 'Fingers crossed.'

'Fingers crossed,' I agree, knowing that you cross your fingers to hope that nothing goes wrong, and also to cancel out a lie.

Next thing, he's passed the phone to my sister. I didn't even know she was there.

'The thing is, Jen,' she says, and I just know she's going to be telling me something I've done wrong, or something I have to change about my life, and I'm nearly right, there's something she wants me to do. 'The thing is, God knows why, but Grampy Sid wants all the family there –'

'I'm coming,' I say. 'I never said I wouldn't.'

'– including –' she pauses longer than most people would for dramatic effect.

'Yes, partners, children, *Her*, the whole lot,' I say.

'Troy,' she says.

There's another long pause. I sense my father waiting in the background, half in and half out of the door.

'It's OK,' I say at last. 'He won't come. We're not even sure where he lives these days.'

'We have an address,' she says. 'We're pretty sure it's the latest one. But you're right, if we just send him an invitation he could just tear it up. It needs a personal approach.' Pause. I say nothing. 'Grampy can't do it, obviously, or NanaDot, they can't travel that far, and –'

'You want me to go round and see him,' I say, to stop her running through the excuses of the entire family down to the new baby ('and of course Xander would go

if I asked him, but he's still being fed on demand and I
don't think –')

'What about Honey?'

'Unreliable.'

'What about Nev?'

'You're nearer.'

'I'm the other side of London. Assuming he's still in
Clapham.'

'Catford. I'm not sure where that is, but you know
Jen, the Underground will get you there in no time.'

'Not to bloody Catford it won't.'

'Don't phone first, just go and see him. Element of
surprise.'

'And when he's not in?'

'Wait. Or go back another day. It's not till June. Stake
it out, like a PI.'

'A what?'

'Don't be thick Jen. Just do it. It's for Sid and Dot
after all. I'll text you the address.'

'OK then.'

'And Skype me, why don't you. You haven't seen
Xander yet.'

'OK,' I say, though I know it will not happen. I press
the button to end the call and I wish things were as they
should be with my sister. She's a bossy cow and I hate
her; and I hate myself for hating her when I used to love
her, bossy cow or not. It never used to be like this. But
things have changed and I haven't seen her for months.
I saw her some time in May last year, when she told me
she was pregnant. After that, work and holidays – hers
not mine – got in the way and by the time September
came things were different and I had no wish to see her,
no wish at all.

She is puzzled by my distance, I can tell, but she
won't ask me to explain. Just, on the rare occasions
when we speak on the phone she is brisk with me, as if
it doesn't matter, and I am irritated. We miss each other,

I think, but it is some previous version of each other that we miss.

Anyway. I have things to do this evening, before I head back tomorrow morning into the bedlam that is Year Four. And after I've finished planning my week, and cutting out display cards, and going over the online remedial reading programme for Yellow Group and making a set of written instructions for the Teaching Assistant (which she won't even look at, so sure is she that she knows what to do) and I should write a referral for that little Domenika who seems to me to have multiple difficulties, so far unnoticed by any agency outside school – but did I bring her file home? Damn – so I have to do it tomorrow evening, when I was hoping I could get to the gym for an hour. Still when I've done all that, then and only then will I think about Troy, and my mission.

Midge: Family

Yes, I was hovering in the doorway as my daughter Beth spoke on the phone to my daughter Jenny. On this day, the day of the phone call, Beth had brought the baby, our new grandson, our first grandchild, down for the day and naturally I took them to see my wife's parents. It was the first time they had seen him, and Sid especially was thrilled. Dot, though she held the baby and acquiesced in having her photograph taken with him, gave him back to Beth almost without looking at him. I had expected her to be more effusive, knowing how fond she always was of all her grandchildren.

When Sid and I went into the kitchen to make a pot of tea I asked if Dot was all right.

'A bit quiet do you think?' said Sid.

'Just wondered,' I said.

'It gets her down,' he said. 'You know, pills for this and pills for that, and the pills make her feel sick, so there are pills for that, and then she gets constipated – don't tell her I told you – and there's pills for that, and of course –' He tried and failed to rip open a packet of biscuits. I took them from him. – 'of course, by the time you're our age you know you're not going to get better, you know what the end of it is going to be.'

'Well, but –' I said.

'She misses the grandchildren,' he said. 'Every day, she wonders when she's going to see them again.'

'Beth's here,' I said. I too thought it was a long time since we had seen the others. 'And the baby.'

'I'd lay any money,' he said, 'if you was to be able to get it out of her, what she's feeling right now, it would be, she's never going to see this baby grow up, never even see him start school, learn to walk even. That's what it will be.'

'Surely –' I began to protest and thought better of it when I reflected that he could be right.

'But,' he said. He straightened up. He could still stand straight as long as he didn't try to move his legs. 'I have an idea,' he said. 'A party. In the summer. Dot's birthday. Something to look forward to, like a promise. Get us through the winter.' We both looked through the kitchen window at the colourless garden under a low colourless sky. 'What do you think?' he said.

I could not tell him what I thought. What I thought was that it was a terrible idea. I thought the prospect of it would probably cause Dot nothing but worry, the organisation of it would cause bad feeling between various members of the family each of whom would believe they were doing all the work and no one else was pulling their weight. I have to be honest here and say that I thought as well that it would probably be me that picked up much of the burden, and I felt I had, as always, enough to contend with.

We took the tea in and the phone rang. It was my wife – Glenys I suppose I should call her – wondering how soon we would be home. When I went back into the room Sid, unable to contain his idea, was telling Beth all about it. The baby was lying on the rug, concentrating hard on the light bulb. Dot was listening but saying nothing. I thought that maybe she would be able to talk him out of it when we had gone.

'We should invite everyone,' he said, 'the whole family, no one left out. Can you organise that Beth my love?'

She had her phone out already and was tapping in a list.

'Midge and my mother,' she said. 'Elaine and Keith. Nev. Me and Dan. Jen, and her boyfriend. Baby of course. Tricky and James and their plus ones. That makes – fourteen. Plus baby, plus you two. For NanaDot's birthday.' She was nearly as excited as Sid was.

'Honey and Ashley, don't forget,' said Sid. 'We'll have it at the campsite. Like old times.'

'Troy,' said Dot.

Beth looked at me. I imagine she had the same feeling as I did. Alarm, a slightly baffled alarm. Why now?

'No need to look like that,' said Dot. 'I loved that boy. He *was* a grandchild to us, for the time he was here, and even after. I would love to see him again.' She does not add, Before I die, but she doesn't need to.

'Fine,' said Beth, and tapped briefly on her phone.

Then she and I and baby Xander went back to Glenys and I phoned Jenny and spoke to her until Beth took over.

They are impressive young women, my daughters. Look at Jenny, down there in the badlands of the East End, even-handedly showering enlightenment and literacy on her clamouring, multi-faith, multi-lingual crew of eight-year-olds; Jenny with her boyfriend – nice enough chap, as far as I know – her new flat, her gym membership, her weekends away, her troops of friends; her busy life, so busy that she has not been to see us since early last summer.

Look at Beth, eight days after giving birth and still high on adrenalin, driving by herself all the way from Leeds. Listen to her telling me how she is going to train this baby to play by himself while she does some of her work from home.

'Is that possible?' I said.

'Just until he's old enough for daycare,' she said. 'With internet and email there's practically no part of conveyancing I can't do from home.'

'I meant, is it possible to train a baby?'

'We're all trained aren't we. It's just a matter of being aware of our objectives and our methods.' Her brown eyes – brown like mine – shone with purpose and confidence. She had given birth, hadn't she, and could therefore meet any challenge. She was a woman, wasn't she, and hers was the world and everything that's in it.

'But –' I said. What did I know?

Look at her quickly and competently changing his nappy, cleaning his little bottom with tidy swift strokes, snapping the poppers back together without once going wrong. She has no need (which is just as well) of a mother to show her how to do it.

'Before I go back,' she said, 'and while he's awake and clean, I'll just walk round to Elaine's. She'd like to see him.'

'She'd love it,' I said. 'I'll come with you.'

2

Jen: Him

Three weeks later, on a windy day, nearly spring supposedly, but more litter than snowdrops, here I am outside Troy's place. It's one of those big houses that have been divided into flats. His name is written – with an italic pen I notice – beside the bell for the top flat. Troy Coldwell. He is no relation of mine. I haven't seen him, none of us have, for more than twenty years, I don't even want to calculate how long. We have not seen his face ever, since he left. Not a wedding, not a birthday has called to him to show up. Will I recognise him? Will he recognise me? Will he even remember that I exist?

I think I will just tidy my hair while I think through – again – what I am going to say to him, and it is while I have both arms in the air and both hands twisting my hair – which is long – back into its knot that the door opens and Troy comes out. I haven't even touched the bell, only looked at it. How does he know I am here?

How do I know it's him? Well, I just do. It's him, not as he was as a teenager, but unmistakably him, skin light brown like milky tea, bright blue eyes, curly hair, darker than it used to be, escaping boyishly from a cap. Him.

I spring forward and my hair falls down on one side of my face making me look, presumably, demented.

'Troy,' I say, and it comes out too loud and startling. He is off down the road. Running away from me? Did he even see me? Did he recognise who I am? Who I was?

I watch him go. Then, as he is near the corner of the road he stops, looks back, waves, shouts something. Turns and goes on. What did he say? One word. Was it, Hurry? Or, Sorry?

Now what? Leave a note? Stand here on his doorstep like some sort of stalker? Might he come back? Might he have gone for ever, knowing that we're on to him? I wander off and sit moodily in a café, thinking I might try again later, but it starts to rain and I make a decision to go home. I have things to do after all.

I'm on the bus, idly watching what I think at first is an orange balloon but turns out to be a Sainsbury's bag blowing from doorway to doorway down one of those London high streets that are indistinguishable from each other, full of nail bars and kebab shops, and wondering why a balloon would make me happy but a Sainsbury's bag makes me feel the world is a careless and inhuman place. My phone beeps, and it's the text from Beth, the one she has been sending every two days. 'Have U seen him yet?' This time I text back. 'Been to the house. Not in.' Which is even sort of true.

There are more balloons – real ones this time, pink – tied to a gate post. A new baby? A little girl's party? The bus pushes on and I will never know. And an idea comes to me, so simple that I should have thought of it three weeks ago. Facebook.

Now I do not do Facebook. I am so busy and so unsociable and so tired that I can barely keep up with being an occasional friend to my real friends, never mind being a virtual friend to almost total strangers. And anyway, why would I want to find out what my ex-boyfriend is doing, and who with? But Honey, she could do it. Whatever Beth says.

I ran into Honey, who is a cousin of mine, at the end of a hot yoga session. She was coming out, wringing wet and with her hair wrapped in a towel as I was going in. She had to speak to me before I recognised her.

'Jen.'

'Oh hi. I didn't know you lived round here.'

'No, not really. But it's near my work. What about you?'

And I told her that I was sharing a house a couple of streets away, and we updated our phone numbers. I know that she temps in an office and I bet she checks Facebook and replies to a message in between every real work-related procedure she carries out. We should have let her do it in the first place. She will have Troy at her fingertips.

Three days later I am able to call Beth. She answers the phone in a whisper. 'Don't talk too loud, I've only just got him to sleep.'

'I thought he was a good baby. That's what Midge said.'

'Not any more. He'll be awake again by ten o'clock, wanting to be entertained.'

'Oh,' I say.

'Anyway, be quick.' she says. 'I was just going to have a little nap myself.'

'Troy,' I say. 'He says he'll come if he can.'

'Good,' she says. 'Bye then. Going to sleep now.'

Ha, I think. Not so smug now.

I think I will phone my dad then to show him that I do sometimes do things for other people, but he's out (of course, it's Wednesday, stupid me) and I get my mother.

'How are you?'

'Oh,' she says, coughing, laughing, 'creaky as usual. Haven't slept for weeks. Looking like an old witch. Nev's old dog looks better than me.'

'Been out?'

'Oh no. Sight of me would frighten people. But Elaine came and brought a cake. Sick as a cat afterwards. Threw up on the garden path when I was saying goodbye to her. I expect it's still there.' And again she laughs cheerily.

And there you have it. Ill, with a variety of changeable and indefinite symptoms, which she seems to relish. Cheerful, sometimes, in a chilling kind of way.

And too lazy to get a bucket of water to sluice away a pile of vomit. My father has to be a hero.

I look up 'hero' on my thesaurus app – this is something I like doing. 'Good man,' I find, 'demigod, seraph, angel, saint.' They are not words that call to mind my father's outward appearance – if he was a piece of furniture he would be a saggy old sofa, brown probably. But they are words that point in his direction. 'One of the best.'

I wonder, now that we have done the deed, how other people will take the appearance of Troy at our big celebration. How will my other cousins like to see him back, apparently, in the family? How will Nev feel? And me, how do I feel? I wish I was able to have a good long chat about it with Beth. She must have been thinking about all this too, surely. I decide that, come half-term, I will go and see her. I can cope. We can talk about Troy and I can keep the other things quiet.

Midge: Complicated

I had not felt altogether sympathetic to my younger daughter when she complained about Beth bullying her to see Troy, and I thought to myself that she could surely try a bit harder. I felt that she was getting off quite lightly, down there in London, compared to us up here in the north. Dealing with Troy might be difficult but it was only one job after all. We – by which I mean myself and Elaine, who is my sister-in-law – we had it all to do. Sid was on the phone every day, coming up with something new. We should have a band. There needs to be a vegetarian option. Make sure Nev knows that there are no bookings for the campsite that weekend. Elaine will need to clean the house, just in case it isn't up to Dot's standards, with Nev living on his own in it. About the band, maybe not after all.

'Of course I don't mind,' said Elaine to me. 'I only want them to be happy. But if only he could leave it to me to do it my way. It's the daily changes I could really do without.'

'But about Jenny,' I said, 'I really do think she gave up too soon. For her, what could be so uncomfortable about seeing him?'

'It's difficult for all of them,' said Elaine, 'in their different ways.' We rarely, if ever, have to explain what we are talking about.

We were in bed, as we often are on Keith's Samaritan shift evenings. She sat up to look at the clock. One of the endearing things about her is that she, a most intelligent woman, can't tell the time sideways. After some occasions of blind panic when she has misread nine o'clock for five past ten, and vice versa, I convinced her that she must always sit up.

'Time,' she said, and I kissed her bare shoulder and we began to get dressed. 'How's the baby doing?'

'Honeymoon's over,' I said. 'Poor Beth, she thought it was going to be easy, it started off so well, but she's found he's got a mind of his own, and a poor sense of night and day.'

'Poor Beth,' she agreed. Then, 'Patrick sent me a message today. His girlfriend's pregnant.'

'You didn't forward it straight to me.' I was hurt.

'Suppose Glenys saw it?'

'How could she? Do you think I leave my phone lying around?'

'Keith might see it on my phone.'

'Don't let him. Keep it with you. Delete your messages.'

She shrugged. She was never as careful about Keith finding out as I wanted her to be. 'Anyway,' she said, 'I knew I was seeing you tonight.'

'And you still didn't tell me till I'm on my way out of the door.' I was cross. There is a reason for my particular interest in Patrick – Tricky as the rest of the family calls him.

'I don't know why I didn't.' She never brushes off a complaint or criticism, but always listens seriously and thinks about her reply. Not that I have ever had many complaints about her. 'It felt complicated.'

'Complicated how?'

'How many reasons do you need? I'm just not sure how I feel about the whole thing. They haven't known each other that long, we've never even met her. And I'm not sure how Keith will cope with them having a baby so soon. He does like people to be properly married.'

'Does Keith know?'

'Not yet. I'll tell him when he comes home.'

'What else?'

'They don't even live together. You know how uncertain his income is.'

'What does she do?'

'I'm not sure. Something more reliable than acting though, I understand. But with a baby – and how much support will he be?'

'It might be the making of him,' I said, though that was clutching at quite a frail straw.

She was chewing the inside of her bottom lip, as she does when she is anxious. 'I'll let Glenys know tomorrow and then she'll tell you.'

'She won't tell me,' I said. 'It won't be important enough to her.'

'She will,' said Elaine. 'I'll tell her to.'

I left by the back door, went through the garden gate into the jennel and out into a parallel street. On my way home I called into the White Lion so that I would be smelling appropriately of beer. But it was unnecessary; my wife was already in bed and asleep. I never knew a woman who could sleep so much.

3

Jen: Family

Midge meets me off the National Express bus. As the bus pulls in I can see him standing under the light, short, round-shouldered, hands in pockets. He lifts his head as I come down the steps and smiles. Tired. Well of course he is, he's had it too, the worst half term of the year, dark in the morning, dark on the way home, the smell of wet children and, for him, teenagers hurling fistfuls of compacted ice down corridors.

He is like a little bear, my dad, quite cuddly – and yet we don't hug, just touch briefly on each other's shoulder, and I never call him dad. Ten-thirty in the evening and he smells, not unexpectedly, of beer. We are quiet in the car. This always happens when I come home during a school holiday. He is my favourite person in the world, now, even more than NanaDot, and yet we are strangers, and we don't know what to say.

When we get to the house the front room light is still on. 'Has *She* waited up for me?' Sometimes she does, sometimes she doesn't. I prefer it when she doesn't.

'Looks like it,' he says.

Yes, she's still up and even dressed, after a fashion. Obviously in quite a lively mood. She sends Midge to the kitchen to make hot chocolate and toast, she starts to ask questions. My journey? My term? My class? My boyfriend? How were they all? The weather in London, my friends, my home, she's covered them all before he comes back with the tray. And she's asking questions like a quiz show and not waiting for answers, and he's sitting there looking like some old orang-utan with his big sad eyes, and I'm sitting there in front of the gas fire in the same old armchair with its worn out cushions covered in the same old crocheted blanket.

This is the room I grew up in, just the same as it always was. Dust on every surface, a plate encrusted with baked bean sauce pushed under a chair, Midge's desk in the corner the tidiest thing in the room, three cardboard folders neatly piled with his laptop weighing them down. And my rusty, crusty old parents. I feel simultaneously, I've come home, and, Oh god, how soon can I get away.

Next morning I sleep late but I'm still up before she is. Waiting up for me will have taken it out of her. Midge, being an Assistant Head, has gone to school, where there is always work to do whether the children are there or not. But it doesn't matter, today I'm going to see my grandparents.

My other grandparents, the Midgeley ones, died long ago, and anyway, they lived far away, on the coast, where they ran a guest house and could never leave it enough to be a significant part of our childhood. But Sid and Dot, they were a massive part, and not just for me and Beth, for James and Tricky too.

I take our old route down the hill. Visibility is poor today, the trees coming out of the mist like developing photographs. This is the way we always came, me and Beth, or sometimes all four of us, pushing each other, or racing each other, till we got there and Nana opened her door and said, 'Look who's here. Your Grampy's out. Go and find him and tell him the kettle's on.'

In my earliest memories, they still ran the campsite. They bought it before I was born, before any of us children were born. They lived in a caravan while they modernised the farmhouse, and then set about improving the site, and setting it up as a business. And then James was born, and then Beth, then me and then Tricky and it was our playground. School holidays, weekends, after school, some or all of us would be there, just playing, and NanaDot would feed us and if we hurt ourselves Grampy Sid would pick us up and carry us into the house and put a magic plaster on the knee, or wherever, and if we fell out with each other and went in wailing they would never ask who did what to who, they would just give us a biscuit and leave us to get over it.

They were energetic, busy people, Sid and Dot, in those days. The grey stone house, called Hollin Clough, was set sideways on to the road and facing down the hill. Inside it was like a stage set of a house of grandparents – family photographs on polished sideboards, exotically embroidered cushions on green chintz armchairs so big that all four of us could sit in one of them, and lots of brass bowls full of flowers or pot pourri, and inlaid boxes and odd bits of furniture that had come from Africa or somewhere a long time ago before I was born. I used to imagine them searching in jungles for these pieces, before it dawned on me that Africa must have factories just as we did.

The back of the house was dark and sunless because of the hill behind. The kitchen light was always on and the pantry was as cold as a fridge. We sat at the table and cut out pictures or coloured while Nana cooked. Our hands reached for the felt tips, we argued over who had used up the black one so that it was faint and grey, we heard without listening the radio talking and the metal on metal sound of her scraping every last bit from the saucepan on to the plate. The condensation ran down the windows.

But mostly we were outside. Outside the back was a yard full of things that might be needed on the campsite – wheelbarrows and tools, mallets for tent pegs and rope for tying people's trailer loads down. People were always forgetting to bring essential items like gas canisters, but equally, they were always forgetting to take things away with them, so the back yard was a sort of swap shop where Sid would solve their equipment problems. 'Never fear,' he'd say, 'Sidney's here. No need to traipse into town. I dare say I've got something that'll be just the ticket.'

The front garden was the only place we were not allowed to play. It was only a strip in front of the house but it was dizzy with flowers. She taught me and Beth all the names (boys, she thought, wouldn't care to learn them) and I still remember them though I've never had a garden of my own in my entire life. Begonias in hanging baskets, all red and orange like flamenco dancers, fuchsias like ballet dancers, snapdragons that we called bunny rabbits and squeezed to make them open their flowery mouths. Sunflowers and dahlias. Apricot and flame and scarlet and gold – the hot half of the spectrum was what she loved, and so did I.

That garden, that field and the little wood that we called the Forest are where I locate my childhood. And I tell myself that in my memory it is always summer, and the sun is shining and we are running across the field to the Forest and the light is coming down through the leaves and we are shouting and laughing and getting scratched by brambles and there is childhood without end.

I've seen photos of Sid and Dot, all dressed up at some dinner dance or something, Sid in a suit and bow tie, grinning like a monkey, Nana in quite a slinky dress with a fox fur thing round her neck. I don't think they ever wore such things after they came north.

'You see,' she said when I asked her, 'in those days we had to mix with all these business people. Your Grampy was in the Rotary so we had to go to the dinners. You had to show your face. Our business depended on getting orders from other businesses. That's how it works.'

'Did you dance at a dinner dance?'

'Of course we did,' she said. 'He was a lovely dancer. Oh yes.'

It seemed to me that she must have been a different sort of person then, that maybe everyone who lived in London was a different sort of person from Yorkshire people. In Yorkshire, she would have to go out in wellies and push a car out of the mud, or help a family put up their tent when an autumn storm was blowing up the valley and twigs and leaves were coming off the trees like hail. At the beginning of the season she would work with Sid to clear away the winter rubbish and cut the grass and repair the fences and gates, and then, when we all turned up after school, she would cook for us while Sid sat in his armchair and watched television with us.

She had no time for God or Jesus but she was always doing things with the church, because, she said, that's where the life was in a village. She organised the carol singers at Christmas and had a plant stall at the spring fete. She did things with the WI, and was on the well-dressing committee. She was the sort of person who joined in whatever was going on, our NanaDot, and for me and my sister she was a shield and a safety net.

And now every time I see her she is older. I do know that's a ridiculously obvious observation but it's how it is. Throughout my childhood she didn't change, she was always a smallish woman with a bun of hair, grey as clouds, and a big wide smile full of teeth, tidy but never flashy in her dress and brisk and busy in her life. Now she's more and more drawn and stretched, every visit, and I haven't even seen her since May last year, and yes, I'm beating myself up about it, because I deserve it.

I let myself in through the back door so they don't have to get up out of their chairs. Of course they are not in the campsite house now, but in a bungalow further up the hill. Dot is sitting in her chair, but not looking comfortable, not leaning back. Her walking stick is in her hand and she's twitchy, fidgety, tapping the stick on the floor and jiggling it from side to side. Her mouth is hanging open as if it's too much effort to hold it closed. When she sees me she makes that effort and gives me a sort of smile and lets me kiss her but her forehead stays creased as if she's in pain.

'Hello Junie.' She has pet names for all of us; mine is Junie.

'Are you all right?'

'I ache all over,' she says, and I think it's the first time I've ever heard her complain.

Maybe she thinks it too, because she smiles a more determined smile and says 'It'll clear up when I get moving.' And I smile too because 'Clear up' is and has always been one of her maxims. It was what the weather was bound to do if we were patient, it was what a cold or cough or grazed knee would do if we stopped thinking about it. And, 'I can't play with you, I've got to clear up this mess, ask your Grampy.'

So although I offer to put the kettle on she creaks into the kitchen. No homemade cakes of course, these days, just biscuits. Sid comes in from the bathroom, pink from shaving, and kisses me and calls me 'Jennifer' in a silly voice that is some joke that only he knows the meaning of. Nana makes a pot of tea in a sort of one-handed way, and then I load the tray and carry it through. I can see various splashes on the cupboard doors that seem to indicate some hot-drink-related mishaps, and I wonder, maybe for the first time, just how awful their day to day existence might be. And it feels as if my own heart has me by the throat and is strangling me and I find that I am hanging on to the thought of Dot's birthday party. That's a promise, we'll get that far, I'll see them again.

Midge: Substitute

Of course Jenny and Beth never knew Sid and Dot in their pre-campsite days. Glenys and I were only just married when her parents made the move North. They were not country folk at all. When I first met them they were still London business people, running an import business that supplied the new fancy kitchen shops of the nineteen-seventies with African cooking pots and Turkish rugs and Moroccan pierced ironware lamps. Once or twice a year one or other of them – usually Sid but sometimes Dot – would set off on a month's journey to North Africa and the Middle East, to look up new suppliers and check up on old ones, and the rest of the year they were managing import licences and invoices and payments and problems and complaints, and making money.

Glenys was their younger daughter and I met her in my first week at teacher training college. For me, who had grown up in Filey, a town where you could stand on the cliff and see the whole place in its entirety without moving your head, Sheffield was a rousing and ravishing place. It had night clubs. Plural. Cinemas, department stores, art galleries, people of different colours. For Glenys it was a dirty provincial city whose night clubs were tacky and whose shops were behind the times. She'd come there because her sister was at York University and she'd thought it was close enough that they would be able to share accommodation. It was typical that she didn't look at a map, or even ask her sister, but to me it served to make her amusing, spontaneous, insouciant. And she was pretty.

She was on the primary teaching course and I was on the secondary so we never shared lectures or teaching placements. And she was not like me. She had an intensity about her. She wore bright colours, shawls and scarves and beads, though all around us the hippy thing was pretty much over. She didn't care. She dyed her hair different colours, or rather, she dyed bits of her hair; it was never the same colour all over. I gathered that headteachers, when she was on teaching practice, often commented on it.

She never seemed to be part of a group that included girls, but hung around with boys, or else would be noticeable by being on her own. I was not the sort of someone she would go out with; I was only someone she knew. Someone she would go out with would be from the University not the College, probably reading English, and at least one year older than we were. A year is significant when you've only lived through eighteen of them. So it was not until well into our third year, and then only as a substitute, that I was introduced to her parents.

I was enchanted. So calm, so engaging, so humorous and relaxed. So sophisticated and worldly, and so different from my dull and harassed mother and father whose lives were spent worrying about the roof or the price of back bacon for the guests' breakfasts.

'Gregory?' said her mother, in a voice that may have held a tinge of disappointment, politely covered up.

'I'm Frank,' I said.

'Midge,' said Glenys. 'We all call him Midge. Greg's stood me up Mum so I brought Midge. I didn't think you'd want to waste the ticket.' We were going to the theatre, which in itself seemed very cultured to me.

'Nice to meet you Midge,' said Sid, and handed me a glass and a bottle of beer, without asking whether I wanted it. There were pictures on the walls and lamps on tables and olives in bowls. Their television was twice the size of ours at home, and they had a hi-fi system with a speaker placed high in each corner of the room.

Dot had taken Glenys aside and they were discussing something in low voices. I saw Glenys shrug, and agree to whatever it was. She soon explained to me. 'You have to sleep with me tonight.' I have wondered since what my face looked like when she said that. 'She thought Greg was coming so she put us in together in the guest room. But don't worry' – worry had not been my only emotion at that point – 'she's moved us into my little brother's room. We'll have a bed each.'

'Where will he sleep?'

'In my sister's and my room. And my sister and her friend will double up in the double bed. Mum says it's the best she can do.' I have tried to work this out in the years since, and it has never yet made sense.

It was some sort of anniversary celebration and each of the three children were bringing a friend – this being the way to accommodate the fact that Glenys was bringing her serious boyfriend Greg Johansen, to dilute, so to speak, the weight of his being the only outsider. But he had taken fright anyway and refused to come. I never knew the bloke, I don't know if Glenys was lucky to escape from him, I only know that he made a good call for himself that weekend. Even that may not be fair. With a different husband Glenys might have been a different wife. As they say, there are always two sides.

So she had hastily recruited me, probably because I was docile and had a car, of sorts, and my first night with Glenys was spent in the room of a thirteen year old boy, under a squadron of model planes hanging from the ceiling, and permeated by a whiff of socks and underpants from the mound of clothes hastily kicked under the bed. My head was spinning and pounding from alcohol and the impact of the play – What was it? I haven't remembered – and I was confused as to what was expected of me. I remember I lunged at Glenys when we got into the room, and she hugged me briefly and then pushed me away.

'You go in the bathroom first,' she said.

I was still standing in the middle of the floor, dressed, when she came back into the room wearing what looked like her father's dressing gown.

'Not asleep?'

'Where shall I sleep?' I said.

'Take whichever bed you like,' she said, so I undressed down to my pants and got into one and she turned out the light and got into the other.

'Goodnight,' I said, and she made a noise which could have meant anything.

Some time in the night she got into bed beside me, and wriggled against me. 'I'm cold,' she said. 'I don't want you to do anything, all right? Just keep me warm.'

Which pretty much set the pattern.

4

Jen: Baby

I borrow my father's car to go to Leeds. I've got presents for the baby and a bottle of Prosecco for me and Beth to drink. I am almost looking forward to it. She will still be herself, I think, having a baby won't have changed her that much. She is still Beth. Sure, she is always going to be older than me, she has always been cleverer, she will always tell me what to do, and I have always resented it a little. I will not resent her, I tell myself. It's not her fault. I can handle it.

On the way there I think what I will say to her about Dot and Sid. How worried I am about them. I know they are looked after, by Elaine and Nev, and Midge when he has time, and a whole bunch of neighbours in the village, they are visited and supported and included and it could not be better in any way, except I wish they didn't have to get old. Dot said that to me – 'Don't get old Junie, it's no fun.' I have never heard her complain before. And they were quiet. It was hard work getting them to chatter away in their usual style. Except for a brief mention of the party, and how they were looking forward to seeing everyone – 'All under one roof, the whole family,' said Sid – apart from that it was hard for them to get going conversationally. Not like them.

Because usually they talk all the time about their lives, past and present. Tales of their youth, their escapades, throwing fireworks through letterboxes, tying door knockers with string. The war in the desert, the heat, his friends (Rusty and Jim), their deaths. From Dot, the factory, its heat and noise, and the people she sat with.

Shops, they loved talking about shops – 'Don't talk to me about Tesco, I knew Jack Cohen when he had a barrow on Edmonton Green.' The shops they had run, the mistakes, the successes, the staff, good and bad.

Their first car, their dogs, their children as babies, their neighbours going back fifty years, their parents and grandparents, their uncles and aunts and cousins; stories big and small, pointless and major, those that we know by heart and those that surface once and never come back again. Recent ones as well. They would be as likely to tell you about someone dropping their purse in the post office and the pennies rolling under the ice cream freezer as about their uncle dying of appendicitis before the days of free doctors.

Will I, I wonder miserably, ever have children to bore with my stories, grandchildren that I can entertain with my history. What would I tell them anyway? What will Beth choose out of her life to tell Xander? And I park as near as I can get to her house, and knock on her front door.

She looks awful, thin in the face and kind of pulpy in the body. She opens the door to me dressed still in pyjamas and her lovely hair is all gone except for a covering like a doormat that has been chewed by an animal. My big sister, my big control-freak sister, as sensible as a fitted kitchen, looks as if she's the one who needs looking after. Well I hope she doesn't expect me to step up.

'What happened to your hair?' It's sticking out at all angles round her head.

'I cut it off.' She says this as if somebody has died and I try to pretend it doesn't matter.

'Just needs a bit of conditioner,' I say, and tears start flowing down her face.

I put the bottle I've brought down on the floor inside the door – it seems quite inappropriate now – and follow Beth into the kitchen where I watch her fill the kettle and switch it on, rubbing her eyes with her hands.

'All right?' I say.

'Fine,' she says.

'Where's Xander?'

'Just gone to sleep. He'll be awake in about twenty minutes.'

'Still not sleeping well then?'

She doesn't bother to elaborate, or even reply. She makes two cups of coffee and hands one to me.

'Thanks. Do you want to go and get dressed?'

She looks down at herself. 'Not really.'

'Beth.' I am filled with a sudden alarm, like when you realise that it's true, your house *has* been burgled, your boyfriend *is* seeing someone else. 'Beth. You're not going like *Her* are you?'

'Her? I'm just tired Jen, that's all.'

I am feeling a tightness in my chest that I don't understand. 'You're scaring me Beth. This isn't like you.' Then I think this is probably not helpful, so I change the subject. 'I went to see Sid and Dot yesterday. They send you their love.'

She nods, she smiles slightly, she sips her coffee. The baby starts to cry. 'Fuck,' she says.

So now I'm walking through the streets of an unknown town, pushing an unknown baby in a pram. This is so surreal I can't believe it. Beth put up so little resistance. I would have expected her, even if she's agreed to me taking responsibility for anything, to have spent the time hoovering the front room or planning her next month's meals, but in fact, when I last saw her, as I came out of the bathroom, she was already lying down on the bed. She might even have been asleep.

How it happened was that while she went upstairs to see to the screaming baby, I went into the garden and phoned my Aunt Elaine. She is boringly sensible, but it is sometimes wonderful to have someone in the family who is competent.

'What shall I do?'

Elaine was at work but she stopped what she was doing and concentrated hard on what I've said. Over the airwaves I could feel her thinking. 'OK,' she said. 'This is the plan. First aid. She needs some sleep. You take the baby out.'

'Me?'

'What can go wrong? He's in a pram, he can't run away. Take a bottle with you in case he screams. And a dummy. Put him in the pram, go out, walk round. Stay out for three hours while Beth sleeps. She can phone you if she needs to check up on you. If you have a problem you can phone me. It's not raining is it?'

'No. Sun's out.'

'He might sleep in the pram he might not, but at least Beth will have time for a nap. Don't let her be doing housework.'

'Is that it?'

'Well, I think she needs to see her health visitor or GP, but you might not want to be the one to suggest it.'

'Not kidding.'

'I'll talk to her about all that. Then – when you bring the baby home, do some housework for her. Get the kitchen clean at least, empty the bins, that sort of thing. Don't ask her, just do it.'

'All right. But Elaine – it feels like she going like our mother. Do you think –?'

'No I don't,' she said. 'Your mother was always crackers. I have to go now. Call me if you need to, but you'll be fine. Good luck.' Crackers. One of Midge's words.

The baby, my nephew, lies on his back gazing up with what looks like interest at the hedges and street furniture of Chapel Allerton. 'Oh yes,' Beth said to me, 'he's better if I take him out, but how can I, it takes me so long to get dressed, then he needs feeding again.'

'I thought –'

26

'So did I,' she said. 'I thought I could manage. I don't have a brain any more Jen, I just can't do it. When he starts to cry I just hate him, I don't even want to go and pick him up, but I have to, that crying, it just draws you, like a spell, you can't do anything to resist.'

'What about Dan?'

'Never here,' she said. 'Working all hours. You know if he doesn't get this PhD finished by – well I don't know exactly, but he has to get it done.'

'You said that last year.'

'There you are then. Last chance.'

'It matters?'

'I suppose so.' She started to cry again, and that's when I decided to take Elaine's advice and take the baby out. I made a bottle of formula; the tin had never been opened before and she watched me tearfully, as if I was a kidnapper, or a poisoner.

'Dummy?' I said.

'Oh no. Dan hates them.'

So as we pass a small chemist's shop in a pleasant looking parade of shops I go in and buy a pack of three dummies. Bollocks Dan, I think, bollocks to your ideas about feeding on demand and not letting poor little babies have a bit of comfort, to say nothing of their poor little mothers. When he starts to get a bit restless I snap open the pack – hoping they are sterile – and pop one in. He gives it an exploratory suck, decides it contains no nourishment and neatly ejects it. I pop it back in and this time he seems to see the point of it. It must be, I think, like the first time you drink beer. Yuck, it's horrible, why do people drink this stuff? Followed by, can I have another taste, oh yeah, it's not so bad, get us a pint will you.

I start off walking like a maniac, manoeuvring like it's a speed-buggy race, but gradually I slow down. I recognise this optimistically red Stokke pram from a photo Beth sent me back before Christmas. She was thrilled to bits because she'd got it cheap as slightly shop-damaged but I was uninterested in her pleasure. It ambushed me from my phone before I had the wits to delete it and it pointed out yet again how far I was from what she had and what I wanted. I never replied.

The sun is on my back, this year's new leaves are the tiniest points of fire scattered through the bushes. There are snowdrops and crocuses and buds on the daffodils. People smile at me, partly I'm sure, because I'm pushing a baby in a pram and partly because I'm back in the North, where smiling at strangers doesn't necessarily mean you are deranged.

I drive back home in a glow of virtue and love. Beth has let me help her. This time I was the sensible one. I took charge. Beth has been left rested and refreshed, for a little while anyway, and with a clean kitchen. She cried some more and then we managed to have a bit of a laugh about the insane amount of stuff you have to have as soon as you have a baby. How he has more chairs than I have and he can't even sit up. I piled up a skipload of toys and mats and padded bags into a corner and gave the floor a quick hoover while Beth fed him.

'Let me burp him,' I said, surprising myself, and I sat with him on my knee, propped against my arm and his head was so close to my cheek that I just bent a little and found out how soft he is, such new skin, such fluffy little hairs.

And I thought to myself, Don't worry kid, I'll look out for you, which is a ridiculous thing to think, when I live something like two hundred miles away, but I do feel something for him which must be the beginning of love, and at the same time I don't feel what I thought I would, which was raging jealousy. I feel unexpectedly fond of little Xander, but he is not the baby that I want to be mine. That baby, the one I want, is *mine*, not someone else's. This is a relief to me.

Midge: Treat

'That's a hungry cry,' said Elaine. How does she know these things? 'That baby is hungry. There comes a time when you are allowed to throw in the towel, and this is it. This breastfeeding is not doing either of you any good.' And we told Dan that Beth had done her best and it was time to move on, and he needed to do more to help. To be fair to the lad I think he was being what he thought a good husband should be, all for naturalness and Breast is Best, and the holiness of the bond between mother and baby.

'He's six weeks old now,' Elaine said to him. 'He's bonded with Beth. Now he's ready to bond with you.' Diplomatic but brisk.

I was happy to be seeing Beth and the baby, of course I was, but I was also impatient to get away. Elaine and I were going to spend the night together, secretly.

Keith had quite understood that Glenys couldn't or wouldn't go to see her own daughter, and would not have been any use if she had. There never was a woman less interested in babies; if it didn't sound over-dramatic I would say she hated them. So he was entirely happy for Elaine to go and check out how Beth was getting on. What *he* didn't know was that I was going too.

Jenny was at home with her mother, not looking after her exactly, because Glenys doesn't need looking after, as such, but we have always been nervous about her staying on her own in the house for too long, especially overnight. Why this is and how she got us to believe it, I really do not understand. To explain away my overnight absence I told Jenny I was going on from Leeds to see my great aunt who was in a Home in Selby.

To make that plausible I had to say that Elaine and I were going in separate cars, and so I had had to arrange with Dave the school caretaker to park my car out of sight behind the gym. Even with all this forethought I was worried that we would be found out.

We didn't go to Selby of course. Nor to York, or Hebden Bridge, or anywhere there would be even a possibility of meeting someone from work on a half-term day out, or some neighbour or acquaintance who might find it strange to see us together far from home. We stayed overnight in Dewsbury, not known for its tourist attractions, in the anonymity of a Premier Inn, but before we went there we found a nice quiet pub with secluded corners, and had a nice quiet dinner. Together. Just having dinner together and talking was a rare treat.

'And this party. Troy. I can't stop wondering what will happen.' She knew what I was talking about. We sometimes think of it as a disaster, but really it was a small incident, small in comparison to things that happen to other families. Nobody died. Beth and James were twelve then, and the other two just a bit younger, and they are all still alive, and functioning grown-ups. So not a disaster, not a cataclysm, but an event certainly, and one that changed things for the whole family, except maybe Glenys. 'Could it even make things better?'

'No, I don't think so.'

I ordered a treacle sponge with custard and Elaine had profiteroles. Our waistlines were telling us, and we were telling each other that we should restrain ourselves, but on occasions like this, which are rare, I believe we both try to make the most of it. 'We restrain ourselves most of the time,' Elaine said on one occasion. 'I think we're entitled once in a while.' She may not have been talking about food.

There is a long list in my head of things that Elaine and I have not been able to do in all the years we have loved each other. We have never held hands in public. We have never carried a photo of the other. We have never, except for one previous occasion, woken up in the morning together.

Yes, just one night in all those years Elaine and I spent together. I'm talking about a whole night, through the evening, into bed, waking up together, having breakfast. That was about ten years ago, when one of Keith's many weekend conferences coincided with a rare hospital stay for Glenys, coincided with none of the children being home, coincided with Dot saying she would visit Glenys on the Sunday so that I could get on with my work.

A whole night, and most of the next day, of pretending we lived together. 'Do you know,' I remember saying, 'that Beach Boys' song, Wouldn't it be nice?'

'Of course,' she said. 'And do you know the ending of it?' And she sang it, slightly flat, as she always does.

I recalled that conversation as we sat in the corner of the pub, waiting for our coffee, the empty wine bottle in front of us. I said, 'Wouldn't it be nice if we were younger.'

She knew immediately what I was talking about, she remembered too that one previous occasion, and she put her hand over mine and said, 'Don't. Remember the good times.'

'I am doing,' I said. 'And I'm wishing there'd been more of them. And I'm wishing we had more of them to look forward to.'

'Don't,' she said.

In the car next day, on the way back to Sheffield, she told me that she was being offered redundancy from her job with the library service, and had decided to take it. Keith too, a couple of years older than her, was about to retire from his local government job, though not – yet – from his many committees and organisations.

'What he really wants us to do,' said Elaine as she drove down the M1, 'is to go abroad.'

I felt a kind of punch to my stomach but managed to say nothing. Elaine doesn't like scenes.

'He's thinking of somewhere in Africa. It's something like VSO for old people.'

'How long for?'

'I think that's fairly open-ended. Can you imagine them wanting to get rid of Keith once they found out what he was like? That man will work twenty three hours a day for nothing if only there are disadvantaged people to be picked up and dusted off.'

'And he wants you to go with him?'

'Of course he does. I would worry about leaving Sid and Dot. But Nev is there to keep an eye on them.'

What about worrying about me, I think.

'Do you want to go?'

She was driving steadily down the inside lane. She signalled to turn off at Junction 36. She said, 'If I could have what I wanted here, then I wouldn't want to go anywhere else.'

I waited until she had exited the roundabout and was accelerating away. 'We can't,' I said.

'I'm beginning to think,' she said quietly, 'that we've given enough of our lives to looking after Glenys.'

I had been thinking that for the greater part of my life.

5

Jen: Cousins

While my mother is sleeping the afternoon away I go out for a walk. Our road is called Hollin Road. It leads as it always has, to the village of Hollin, but where it was once a country lane it is now and has been since 1937, a road of semi-detached houses. All of them have been extended and improved since then. Carports and kitchen extensions have been added, block paving drives are on every front garden, attic windows have been put into loft spaces. Several of the front gardens have skips in them, as if a rather trashy sort of space invasion has started. The broken up kitchens in them are way newer than the one still in use at our house.

Our house – my parents' house of course – is just as it was in 1975, when they bought it. Imagine that though. Less than two years out of college and able to buy a house.

I wander down to the village, thinking I will see Sid and Dot again. I go again the way we always used to go, the long way, through our suburban streets as far as the fields, then along the footpath, in spite of the mud, to what used to be called the village, but now is a tiny stone flounce on the edge of Sheffield.

The pub is closed and boarded up and for sale, the Methodist church has been converted into a desirable residential property. The smaller cottages have mostly been knocked through, making one house out of two, the bigger ones have been extended at the back, or in the loft, or they have garden rooms visible from the driveways. You never see the new people – no one comes out of their front door, it's out the side, into the car and off to Waitrose in town.

When I get to the bungalow the door is locked and I remember they will have gone to the lunch club so continue on to Hollin Clough, where Nev will be at home.

Two caravans, a motorhome and a tent are on the field, though it must be pretty cold at night for sleeping in a tent. Nev is at that moment letting another caravan in, taking the deposit and pointing out which pitch they should use. Sometimes, when we were kids, we would be allowed to take the money and guide the customers to their pitches. In theory anyway; in practice I never got to take the money because Beth liked to do it, and sent me into the field to wave my arms as they parked and point out the electric hook-ups.

My uncle Nev is a nice man. Everyone likes him. He doesn't make any noise but he will always help people. In the village he is known for his helping, does jobs for old people in the season when the campsite is closed, is always part of any social event, lets them have the November bonfire on his field, and lets them use the field for the summer hog-roast, even though he loses a little income because of it.

Since his wife left him all that time ago he has lived in the house on his own, apparently peacefully. He has kept in touch with Mandy, I believe, and his children, though so far away, have always visited, though less and less as they have grown older. When they were little he used to drive all the way down to pick them up, and then, when Ashley was about twelve or thirteen and Honey was about seven or eight, they used to come by train or bus.

We wondered, Beth and I, whether, and how much they were still in touch with Troy, but I don't believe we ever asked. His name just never came up.

Nev puts an arm round my shoulder, briefly. 'How are you then?'

'Fine.'

I don't often come down here now. The garden still has snowdrops in it – you can't destroy snowdrops, Dot always says – and tulips pushing through, and bluebells, for later in the year, but I can see dandelions coming up among the bulbs and last year's plants have not been cut down so there are too many dead sticks. 'Nev's not a gardener,' Nana would say.

He offers to put the kettle on and we go inside. Whenever I am in his house I can't help remembering that it was my grandparents' house before it was his.

And I always remember how it felt after Sid and Dot moved out and Nev moved in, with his wife and baby, and Troy. The house was the same, even some of the furniture was the same, big sideboards and tables that wouldn't fit into the bungalow, but it smelled different. Beth would say that was because of Ashley, who was a toddler then, just walking, tottering around and smearing sticky fingers and dribble on every surface, but it felt to me as if the new smell was something to do with the parents, Nev and Mandy, with them being younger than the other adults we knew, and cooler and more colourful. Mandy had dyed black hair and lots of eye make up. The first time I saw her she was wearing a big bat-winged jumper in stripes of orange and purple and brown, and Nev, who of course I had seen a million times before, was wearing a slouchy sort of hat and a waistcoat.

He asks again how I'm doing and I say I'm fine. I tell him I met Honey, briefly, and I ask how Ashley is getting on, and he tells me that they are both thinking of settling down but somewhere to live is a problem, and he thinks they should come back north.

'Maybe I should as well,' I say, and he says that Sheffield knocks the south into a cocked hat, and he smiles his particular Nev smile, that grows slowly on his face, and stays there long after the moment has gone.

It was winter when they arrived, so that they could get settled in before the season started, and there was snow on the ground, deep snow so that the removal van had to park at the top of the lane and the men had to carry all the stuff down. We – James and Beth who were in the same class, and me and Tricky – came out of school and ran all the way to the campsite, sliding and floundering, so eager to see the new state of affairs that we didn't even pause to throw snow at anyone.

We passed the big van, met Nev on the lane, going up as we were going down, who waved to us briefly and carried on, snow over the top of his boots, to carry on unloading. NanaDot was in the kitchen and you would hardly have known it was a kitchen in the middle of a removal, still orderly, still smelling warm. Two kettles were boiling and a row of mugs was ready for the next cup of tea. She sat us down and gave us hot orange squash and biscuits – out of a packet on this occasion because she had been a bit busy. We could hear Grampy Sid in the passage telling men where to put things.

'Where's Troy?' said James.

'Is he here?' I said.

'Of course he's here. He's helping unload the van. You must have passed him on the way down.'

'We didn't see him,' said Beth.

We had so far never seen this new sort-of cousin of ours.

'Well, he must have been there,' said Nana. 'He's only just this minute gone out. You must have just not recognised him.' But, as it turned out, it was Troy's talent to be invisible when he wanted, to be not noticed, to be – like Macavity – not there.

Now I think that moment, the four of us sitting at the kitchen table, the light on and the door shut and the day fading swiftly into night and NanaDot with her hair tied up in a scarf to signify that it was a specially hard-working day – that was the last time we were just us four and things were as they always had been and always would be. Because after that they weren't.

Mandy came in with a small child on her hip. Strange to say, we had never met Mandy before. We'd seen a few snapshots of their wedding, and pictures of the baby when he was born, but they had never come North until now. So here she was, and looking different from her wedding photos, though still tall and thin and pale, with blue eyes, and extravagantly bouffant hair. The baby had a look of Nev and was decidedly ginger. NanaDot stopped what she was doing – unpacking cutlery from a box into a drawer – and lifted him out of his mother's arms, as if she was unwrapping a birthday present.

'Look at all these children, Ashley my little bud,' she said to him. 'Come and meet your cousins. What a lot of cousins. Come and say hello.'

Mandy didn't speak, to us or to Nana. She picked up a dustpan and brush and went towards the door. She nodded to us, as much to say, Talk to you later, things to do now, and Ashley stretched out his arms to go back to her. As they went out of the kitchen Dot stood and stared after them, as if she was disappointed. Then she sent us off home, saying that they were too busy to have extra people, come back at the weekend, it should have cleared up a bit by then. What should have cleared up, the weather, or the removal chaos, or the mood, she didn't say.

Troy. Beth and I talked about him endlessly. We were both besotted. He was like no one else. He came to our school for a few months but then he moved up to the comprehensive, which added to his attractions. He was nearly grown up, in our eyes. We knew, slightly, other boys who went to the big school, but none of them had the mystery, the difference, the pull, of Troy.

Troy Coldwell-Green he was called, a surname he shared with Ashley, and later with Honey, till he dropped the second part of it, renouncing Nev and all our family. But before all that, some of his glamour reflected on us, and we enjoyed that. 'He's your cousin?' they would say, disbelieving, and we would say, 'His stepfather is our uncle. We're not related to him by blood. We could marry him, he's not the sort of cousin we couldn't marry.' Because of course, that was what Beth and I both looked forward to, in our junior school sort of way.

He was tall, Troy, like his mother, and he had blue eyes like her, made startling by the toasty brown of his skin. His nose was long and thin and his mouth was wide and thin and his hair – this was the thing that made him stand out – was the same colour as his face. Light brown, maybe a touch of gold, softly curling, so that he looked as if head and hair both were sculpted out of some lovely warm stone. No one else looked anything like him.

My mother is awake when I get home but still in bed. She has been like this, by Midge's account, since shortly after I was born. Not that anyone, not even Her, has ever suggested that I caused it. She was eccentric before she had children, even before she somehow enticed Midge to marry her. Eccentric is Midge's word for what she is: our words – Beth's and mine – are a bit harsher. We decided long ago that it's all put on. We *know* there is nothing wrong with her. She is just in the habit of being bone-lazy, expecting all responsibility to be taken by other people, lolling about in a dressing-gown for weeks at a time, letting children – me and Beth – do age-inappropriate jobs with boiling water and hot grill pans, making Midge do all the shopping and cooking and then complaining because he goes to the pub once a week.

I had a friend at college – Karina she was called – who said her mother was just the same. 'Just not cut out to be a mother,' she said, and laughed affectionately as if it was something to be easily forgiven. But I found out later, when I visited her at home one summer, that her mother was an artist, a painter, who spent hours drawing, painting, having lessons, giving lessons, trying to produce something she could be satisfied with. *My mother produced nothing.* Just irritation, despair, resentment, estrangement. As soon as my sister and I learnt the word we called her, between ourselves, the Bitch. If my father was around we said 'Witch' instead, so that he would not look quite so hurt. Even now, he wants to believe that deep down we love her, as he presumably must do, in spite of the awful life she leads him.

So I stand in the doorway of her room and she smiles pleasantly and distantly at me, as if I'm a nurse maybe, or a paid help. And the words come out of my mouth – a habit, without the slightest thought behind them. 'Would you like a cup of tea?'

'Oh yes,' she says, as if she's entitled to be waited on.

And I'm trapped. 'What sort?' I say. And what do you know, she's on some special sort of green tea, or white tea, or something, and when I look this is the last teabag in the box, so it has to be put on the shopping list that I will be taking to Morrison's tomorrow. After that I will be catching the last bus back to London.

She gets up and comes downstairs, wrapped in a dragon-printed kimono, and I put the gas fire on to warm up the room. She curls her feet under her and when she's finished sipping her tea, hugs a cushion to her, like a teenager in a TV soap.

She starts on the questions again, without waiting for replies, as if it's a trick she's learnt to make herself appear human. 'Did you see Nev? How did he seem?

Was the campsite busy? Did he say anything about Dot? Is she keeping all right?'

'He said he hadn't seen you lately.'

'I haven't been down there all winter. I couldn't walk all that way' – it's less than half a mile – 'in the cold.'

'It's not cold,' I say. 'It would do you good to get out.'

She smiles indulgently, as if I'm a child suggesting that she might ask Santa Claus for better health. 'That's what Beth said to me once. I did it – she made me do it, she is such a bully – and I was in bed for a week.'

'Surprise,' I say, but not so that she can hear me.

We have said to Midge – Beth and I, at times when we've been worried for him – that he should have a holiday. Just go away and leave her. She would have to do things for herself, she would surely survive, she wouldn't starve, she might even recover. He always says the same. 'I couldn't risk it. She might die, if only to show us how ill she is.'

'But she's not ill.'

'Who's to say?' he says.

'The doctor has never found anything wrong with her.'

'Ah,' he says, 'but we know, don't we, that there's nothing right with her. So there must be something wrong, mustn't there?'

'Don't be clever. How will she ever learn to do things for herself, if she has you – and us, and Elaine – doing everything for her? It's time she grew up. Isn't it?'

'Your mother,' he says, 'will never grow up. I don't waste my time hoping for it. It might not be that comfortable after all if she did. Let's just muddle along with the way things are. Let's not try to make anything better, just in case it makes it worse. We manage.'

Now, I tell her how the campsite is looking, how Nev is looking, how the blackthorn is just beginning to flower. Then, 'Do you remember when they arrived,

Nev and Mandy? How much snow we had that winter, do you remember?'

She shuddered. 'I don't know which winter that was, but I know this winter I've been colder than I've ever been.' She always says that.

'Do you think Troy will come to the party? Do you think he'll make it?'

'Party? Oh, you mean Nana's do. Well, how would I know what Troy might do? I hardly knew him even when he was a child, let alone now he's what? – getting on towards forty. And I might not get there myself.'

'You have to be there.' So many sentences I say to her should have 'Mum' at the end, and I cannot – *cannot* – bring myself to put it there. 'Sid and Dot will be devastated if you don't come.'

'They might be a little put out,' she says. 'But really, it's the young ones Dot wants to see. She can see me any old time.'

'I don't think she would get up the hill these days.' I think about what I have just said. 'When did you last see her?'

'I don't know. I don't keep a record of what I do.'

'Did you see her at Christmas? I don't think you did, did you, you were in bed all the time.'

She agrees. 'So cold, wasn't it.'

'So, before Christmas? Did you see them in the autumn?'

'Don't get at me,' she says. 'I'll go when the weather warms up. They don't miss me, and if they did, they could come here and see me. Nev would bring them.'

She takes no responsibility. I know Nev is on the doorstep, more or less, and I know Elaine is nearby too and often calls in on them on her way home from work, and I know Midge and Uncle Keith help out sometimes, getting shopping, or taking them to the doctors, but *she*, the Witch, the Bitch, is here, not even

41

half a mile away, doing nothing, not even making a phone call as far as I can see.

'You can't rely on other people all the time,' I say to her and she does not reply but looks at me with that insolent stare that hard kids use, that means, I can do what I like.

I pick up Midge's old Thesaurus from his desk and look up 'resentment.' 'Umbrage, huff, miff' – these are too mild for what I feel. 'Bitterness, gall' is a bit more like it. 'To pour out the vials of one's wrath.' That's what I'd like to do. I don't know what vials are, but mine are full of wrath, and it does me no good I'm sure.

Midge: Change

I was never party to the ins and outs of just how Nev and Mandy came to take over the campsite. I would have quite liked to have taken it over myself, and if I had known Sid and Dot were thinking so seriously of giving it up I would have suggested myself as the next manager – though I suppose I have to concede that Glenys was never really the right sort of wife for the job. Anyway, I never asked and they never brought the subject up, and then one day it was presented as a done deal. What they said was that the work was getting too much for Sid – he was over sixty by then after all, and deserved to retire, and could afford it. And it would be nice for Dot to have all her children nearby.

'It's natural,' said Elaine to me. 'She wants all her family near her. It's to make up for missing out on our early years.'

'Well why did she?'

'Work,' she said. 'You've seen how hard she works now, and that's nothing to what she used to be like.'

I thought Nev and Mandy were lucky, to be offered the chance of a job, nice house, rent-free, in the country, babysitting provided, fresh air and freedom for the children, near his family.

I don't know whether I grasped at once that there was a certain coldness from Mandy towards Dot, and maybe vice versa too. Looking back, maybe Mandy never really wanted to move out of London. Maybe she left behind some sisters or friends that she missed. Maybe she was dubious about settling so close to her mother-in-law, an almost unknown mother-in-law at that, and one who clearly liked to be in charge. I did not know why Nev wanted to come, but maybe he had lost a job, I never asked. Maybe he thought he should be closer to his parents as they grew older. He never said.

As the months went on I noticed that Mandy and Dot were polite to each other, in a way that might conceal a lack of liking. I noticed that Dot was not as easy with Troy as she was with her own grandchildren. Not surprising, I thought. He was older, she wasn't used to older children yet. And he was not an easy boy to get to know, quite secretive, guarded, careful.

He was careful about rules. He didn't come with an attitude that suggested he expected to be liked. He was slow to say whether he agreed with something or not; he tried to guess the right answer from the faces of others, which made him appear untrustworthy. He did not have the openness and merriness that she was used to in children. Mandy – she told me this herself – wanted to make it up to him that he had had to leave his school and his friends, and she wanted to be able to protect him from anyone who would make fun of his accent, or make him feel unwelcome.

'See Midge,' she said to me, 'it's all right for Nev, and me, we've chose to come here. Troy never chose this, we've made him come, I've told him it will be all right, so I've got to make it all right.'

'Has he complained?' I said. 'Has anyone been bullying him?'

'He wouldn't complain,' she said. 'He'd die before he snitched on someone. There's only me who can tell when he's unhappy.'

'So is he?'

She moved her hand stiffly side to side, up and down, indicating a state of precarious equilibrium.

'He'll make friends,' I said. 'At least' – watching Ashley toddling about on the field – 'the littl'un seems happy enough.'

'Yes, well,' said Mandy.

Dot adored Ashley and he was indeed a sweet boy, cute as a pie. And Mandy did not like it when she carried him away and gave him biscuits and cake and allowed him to have his own way at the bungalow. Even I, noticing, thought that Dot had not been so indulgent to the other four. More difficult, for me and Elaine, was that Patrick lost his place as the youngest and therefore Dot's favourite. I watched sadly as he became babyish and mardy, absurdly trying to outdo Ashley and win back his top spot.

My daughters and Elaine's sons still went to see their grandparents several times a week, they could still play on the camping field and in the wood. I believe that at first Troy remained aloof. They were so much younger than him it was not surprising. But there was no one else that end of the village – and the campsite was even outside the village – that he could conceivably want to hang out with.

As the spring came and lighter evenings, the children spent more time down there at Hollin Clough and gradually I think Troy let himself become part of the group. And his was a presence that unpicked the fabric, so to speak, of their tight little group, so close in age that there was barely more than two years separating the four of them. I expect he hung around, keeping a dignified distance until James – probably – said 'Come and have a go.' Or something like, 'Help us get this rope

44

over this branch.' Troy pushed James off his perch as oldest, tallest and first in command, but James, without too much trouble, made an alliance with him, and they seemed to become good friends.

James was Elaine's elder son, and he was big for his age, and confident, having always been the one in charge. Eight years old, just right for worshipping a boy of ten. He would be encouraged to greater feats of climbing and swinging and whatever else by having a big boy to impress. The two of them, if I'm remembering correctly, began to pull away from the other three, gradually, not suddenly. I would say imperceptibly perhaps, if I didn't remember Beth coming home in a temper. 'He's taking James away from me,' she whined. Her face was twisted with trying not to cry.

'You see James all the time at school,' I said to her. 'He's allowed to have other friends you know.'

I am sure that my memories of that first year or two are unreliable because they are affected by what happened later. Probably if I'd been able to watch the five of them in the wood – they called it The Forest – making dens and throwing sticks and stones into the stream and getting muddy and torn – if I'd seen them I would have seen just five kids, just mucking about. Having fun.

6

Jen: Honey

News from Beth. Xander, entirely bottle-fed now, is sleeping three hours at a time, more at night, and except for an evening exercise of his yelling muscles is a different baby. She is so much better now that she can think again, and what do I know of Troy? How was he when I saw him? Is he bringing anyone else to the party? Tell me all about it Jen. How did it feel to be seeing him again?

If I tried to lie she would suss me out so I have to tell her about Honey and how it turns out that she and Ashley are in touch with Troy, always have been though it was never mentioned to us all this time, and how she simply asked him and he simply said yes. And I never spoke to him at all.

I think a lot about Troy these days. Coming out of a long-term relationship, willingly or not, leaves you with this space to fill. I could go on fretting about Russell or I can fasten my attention on some other man. (And yes, I could say that I find enough joy and fulfilment in my career and my friends, but it would not be true.) Troy is the perfect fantasy object. Childhood crush, unjustly banished, silent for so many years, and then briefly glimpsed on that cold afternoon in Catford.

After an evening plodding through recording and preparation it's only reasonable I believe, to go to bed and have someone to think about as I crash into sleep. Once the alarm goes off in the morning and I gather my folders and bags and queue at the bus stop, once I'm at school and concentrating – as I have no choice but to do – once I'm back in the real world I don't think of him at all.

This weekend, I call Honey to see if she wants to go for a coffee. It means me schlepping out to

Walthamstow, but hey, she has to do that journey every day to work and back so it won't hurt me to do it once, and I owe her for getting hold of Troy for me. I admit that it's also an opportunity to talk about him, legitimately, to someone.

Honey is one of those thin pale sandy girls, but she's one who works it to her advantage. Perky, alert, like one of those meerkats, and a trained dancer. She was a tiny baby when she was taken away from Yorkshire, so she was a visitor rather than a fixture in our lives. And the big age difference meant that we had very little in common. By the time she was old enough to have proper conversations my sister and I, and James and Tricky, were less often at home, and the distances between all of us had grown, but she was still our baby cousin and Ashley was still our cousin. Naturally, as they have got on with their own lives – jobs and partners and that – we have seen much less of them; the last proper time was the Christmas before last.

We meet in a little Turkish café, and she asks after Sid and Dot, and about Beth and the new baby, and I ask politely after her mother and Ashley.

'Ashley's getting married,' she says. 'I guess Nev must have told you.'

'No, he didn't mention it.'

'Typical.'

'What does Ashley do for a living?' I ought to know this, but I don't.

'He's a fireman now.'

'Wow. You need to be fit for that.' I'm licking baklava off my fingers and wondering how to get on to Troy when she does it for me.

'Did Troy get in touch with you?'

The very idea causes the air to rush away from me, but, 'No he didn't. Why would he?'

'I thought he might. As he has your number.'

'Did he ask you for it?'

'No, but I gave it him. Do you know how you're getting up there for the party?'

'I'll go by bus, that's what I usually do. What about you?'

'Going in my boyfriend's car. I'd offer you a lift, but Ashley and his fiancée' – she laughs at this word as if it's a private joke – 'they might be coming with us.'

'Thanks anyway. I'll be fine. It's Spring Bank holiday so I'll probably be there already. I'll have all week off.'

'Lucky you,' she says. 'I wish I was a teacher.'

'Why aren't you then?'

She laughs again. 'I couldn't stand it really. Dad told me that your mum trained as a teacher but she never actually did it. Why was that then?'

'Who knows? I think she got a job but had a lot of time off and failed her probationary year. She wasn't suited to it, that's the truth.'

'Dad says she's still a bit of a recluse.'

'You could say that.'

'Sorry,' she says, 'if you don't want to talk about it. It's not easy, is it, worrying about your mother.'

'Do you?'

'Oh I do.' She sighs and looks at her phone as if I've reminded her of her duty. 'No, really, we do, Ashley and me, we do worry, but Troy takes most of it on.'

'What is it then?'

'Drink partly. Depression we think as well. She's all right really, most of the time. I mean, she goes to work, she's not that out of it. Lonely I think, that's what it mostly is. Since I moved out.'

'I thought she had a new partner. Didn't she?'

'She went through one or two. But none of them stuck around. She always said Nev was the best man she'd ever known, but she could have just been saying that. Because he's our dad.'

'Why didn't she go back with him? After you all – well, Troy I guess, mainly – left home.'

'Who knows,' she says. 'I've never asked her.'

'Would you like it if she did?'

'Of course,' she says, and then there's a bit of a pause while we sit in the sunshine and wonder – at least I do – whether to get another coffee and go on with this, or whether the meeting has run its course.

'Tell me about Troy,' I say, and I wave my hand through the window for the lad to bring us more coffee. 'What does he do?'

'Some sort of youth work,' she says. 'Arty stuff is his area mostly. I think he goes into prisons – you know, young offenders – and does stuff with them.'

'Do you see much of him?'

'Hardly anything. It's such a long way to the other side of London. I can get to Yorkshire in less time.'

'I know.' I've got what I came for now, except I suppose for the most important piece of information – girlfriend? wife?

'Oh hey,' says Honey, 'are you doing anything next Friday night?'

'Not that I know of.'

'I'm in this dance thing.' I don't know why she's embarrassed to ask me, but that's how she seems. 'Would you like to come and see me?'

'Of course I'll come. What is it?'

Midge: Wrong

I know exactly when I realised I'd married the wrong sister. It was one Sunday afternoon when Beth was about a month old and I was pushing her pram through the draughty streets so as to let Glenys have a rest from her crying. I already knew – I had known since before I even did the deed – that I should not have married Glenys. I hadn't meant it to happen, whatever I might have said, but it had seemed a good enough thing to do, we seemed to get on together well enough, and I was hopeful that being married might improve the amount of sexual activity I was getting. How I would mock and pity my younger self if he was here in front of me now. I was flattered as well. After two or three years of casual friendship she suddenly appeared to want me. It did not come to my mind at the time that her sister had just married and that this had left Glenys behind in the status race.

Similarly, she didn't want children – which was OK by me at the time – until Elaine announced she was pregnant. That caused Glenys and I to have a frenzied two months of never to be repeated twice daily sex until we achieved the right result. Except it wasn't right because Elaine and Keith had a boy and we had a girl. I don't know if Glenys felt that girls were inferior in themselves, or if it was just that failure lay in getting a different result from Elaine. I no longer wanted to know what she thought.

Anyway, on this Sunday afternoon, passing the local Rec, I saw Elaine and Keith, pushing James in his buggy. I saw her stop pushing and pick up something the baby had dropped on the floor. I saw her bend over him and rub his tummy to make him laugh and shake her hair over him to tickle him, and then put her hand over Keith's on the handle of the buggy and look up at him while he stared across the field at the deserted goal posts as if she wasn't there at all. I didn't call out or wave, I meandered on through the new estate and past the infants' school where the children would one day go together and thought to myself that if I had had the intelligence and luck to notice Elaine before Keith did, then I would be a happier person, and – it came to me – so would she.

I ought, after that, to have made a point of avoiding her. She often visited Glenys in the afternoons and I could have stayed late at school, as I usually did, catching up on things. I was never that keen to get home in the ordinary way. So yes, I could have found more useful things to do, straightened the maps on the wall, cleaned the graffiti off the desks, even marked some books. But I was drawn home as I never was on other afternoons. Sometimes I phoned Glenys in the middle of the day to check whether Elaine was expected, and if she was I would say, 'Well then, I'll make an effort to get home a bit earlier' and be out of the classroom almost before the kids were.

They would be sitting together in the front room, and the babies would be sleeping, or rolling, or crawling around, and the smell of baby wee and baby milk, and puke and poo would hit me as I walked in. The women never seemed to notice it. I would make more tea and sit with them and maybe tell them if something interesting had happened in my day, and Elaine would tell me something about my daughter, how her toenails had needed cutting, perhaps, or she had tried to roll over, or she had been laughing at something James had done. Glenys would look out of the window.

Then I would drink my tea, pick up a baby at random and tickle it, or bounce it about a bit, and then Elaine would say that she needed to go home. Even though Keith was often not expected home till much later, she had to cook his dinner and bath James and put him to bed. When she went the room felt colder. I would pick up my daughter and hold her, just to be holding on to something. Glenys would say that she was going to her room – it was still our bedroom at that time but she called it her room even then.

I had a fantasy that Keith and I could simply swap partners. It was a fantastic idea in every way. Brilliant, except that it wouldn't work. Glenys would have been even less happy with Keith than she was with me. At least I did some of the housework and looked after the baby when I was at home. At least I came home, evenings; I didn't go out to interminable meetings and I didn't spend my time at home on the phone to other worthy folk or going through minutes and reports.

I came to realise that as a husband and companion Keith was a washout, as, I suspect, his father was before him. The idea that Elaine had been at home all day looking after his children – and often mine too, I have to admit – did not seem to bother him. Well, that was what women often did, and still do, but there was beginning to be a feeling around that fathers should have a bigger part in their children's lives than they had in the past. She was a reasonable enough woman and no kind of militant feminist but she could see that she was being ignored and taken for granted.

As well as his day job, as some sort of manager in the elderly residential care sector, he was on every charity committee and steering group he could find. Though only a couple of years older than me – not yet thirty – he was making a name for himself in the city, as someone who knew everyone, could introduce and persuade and form alliances and get money out of organisations.

As time has gone on he has known everyone who mattered in both the voluntary and statutory sectors in South Yorkshire and beyond. His name has been on countless minutes of AGMs, numerous funding applications, a profusion of reports, a multiplicity of feasibility studies, a host of letters of support, or enquiry, or commendation. A crowd of people answered to him, deferred, referred and were responsible to him. There has been talk, as he approaches retirement, of some sort of honour being bestowed upon him.

He was always the total opposite of anything I could hope to be. Tall, for a start. Sporty-looking, though as far as I know he never played any kind of sport, competitively or not. Handsome. A man that a woman could have been proud to be seen with. Their sex life, she always told me, was minimal; no, less than that even, almost non-existent.

Well, so was mine, although – and I am not proud to say this – once I began to yearn after Elaine I perversely became much more demanding towards Glenys. It was much too soon in so many ways. I had the idea that Glenys could not possibly conceive so soon after having Beth, and I was wrong. By the time I recognised that it was Elaine who I loved and needed to be with, and my marriage was over, Glenys was pregnant again. She, no more than Keith did, ever showed us a sign that she knew what was going on in other people's hearts and minds.

'He must suspect,' I have said to Elaine. 'Why does he keep quiet about it if he suspects? It's not normal.'

'Maybe it's part of turning the other cheek,' she says.

I should have mentioned that he is a Christian, though not in his family tradition. Rather, he spreads himself around all the churches he can find, appearing in a different one each Sunday (or Thursday) as if conferring a benefit on them.

He still sleeps in the same room as Elaine, though in a separate bed, which was, she says, his idea, to alleviate his bad back. Which gives me the pain of jealousy as I imagine them lying in the dark, chatting gently about the events of the day, or waking together every morning to another day of being married.

How can he not know about us? Is it just so unlikely that a woman like Elaine, chosen by him to be an asset – intelligent, placid, well-spoken – should have been drawn into caring for someone like me, someone without grace, or success, someone who needs, but does not deserve, someone like her.

Or does he know but refuse to contemplate the knowledge. Or does he like it this way, so that he gets his house looked after and his meals cooked, and his occasional dinners catered for, without any scandal of divorce or adultery being visited on his family. Does he prefer men, we have wondered, but if he does he gives away no clues. Is it to protect his children that he keeps quiet about a situation he knows about?

But he is a good man, as everyone knows, and I am, probably, not.

7

Jen: Spring

On this fine, crystalline Sunday I get up and go downstairs to find Annie sitting on the back doorstep, still in shade, and crying quietly. I can tell from the shape of her back. She's a tall, well-built woman, a reassuring presence normally. I think about sneaking back upstairs before she knows I'm here but I know I shouldn't. I might not want to hear her troubles, I might be impatient already at the thought that I'm not the only star-crossed one in this postcode. Still, I like what I know of her, I want her to like me, I know I have to do the right thing, and that will be to put the kettle on and ask her if she is all right.

'I'm fine,' she says. I hand her a cup of coffee. I know so little about her that I don't even know how she takes her coffee. I sit on the stool in the kitchen so that we don't have to look at each other.

'No really,' she says. 'You know you just wake up some mornings thinking, is this it? That's all it is.'

Annie owns this house. She advertised for someone to share with to help pay the mortgage and that person turned out to be me.

'You doing anything today?' Sunday is always the most difficult day of the week.

'Not really. Might clean my room.'

'We could go to the park,' I say. 'You know, get a sandwich, buy a paper, sit on the grass.'

'OK.'

So this is the first occasion Annie and I have ever spent time together in any appreciable quantity. She is a hospital doctor and her shifts and my hours rarely coincide. We pass on the stairs, text each other to apologise for failing to do chores, leave polite notes about using up all the bread or needing more milk; we get along just fine.

It's a new experience, being together. I have to be conscious of how long I take to get ready – don't want her to feel I am hurrying her, don't want her to have to wait for me – have to stop myself saying, Won't you be too hot in those boots? Have to wonder what she thinks of my clothes, of my choice of sandwich, of my choice of newspaper. I tell myself there is nothing hanging on this, it's not like she's a date, if we don't get along as friends we don't have to do this again. When we take the wrong turning and fail to find the gate in to the park – we can see the damn thing, there, behind the railings, green grass and blue space – we don't have to blame each other, we don't have to apologise. At the same time we are cautious, we are not taking anything for granted. I have noticed that we each brought our own door key, in case we need to go home, and each of us has our phone handy, in case we get a better offer.

The clocks don't go forward for another week, but it feels like spring. She takes her shoes and socks off as soon as we find a place to sit on the grass. She has big slender feet, very white after a winter of socks and boots, and she wiggles her toes in the grass. Well, my feet are white too – no child of my parents would ever have skin that tanned easily – and I slip off my sandals and feel the coolness and slight dampness against my soles.

'Maybe we should have brought something to sit on.'

'It'll be fine,' she says.

We divide up the paper and plunge into the horrors. But this is one of those stunningly lovely first spring days that make you feel everything must be all right with the world and that everything in the Sunday paper must be happening on some other planet. She puts her section aside and leans back on her elbows, watching people go past.

We both start to speak at the same time.

'Sorry. Go on.'

'No, you.'

'It's all right, it was nothing. What were you going to say?'

'I was just going to ask you – where did you live before you moved in with me?'

'Not that far. Hackney. But I was sharing and –' There's silence between us. Which way will we go? 'What about you?'

'I was in Birmingham,' she says. 'Well, near Birmingham anyway. Dudley.'

'And you fancied coming to London?'

'Not really. I needed a new job. I didn't mind really where it was. How long have you been in London?'

'Ages. I came to University here. Just never went back home.'

'Which is where?'

'Sheffield. Ever been there?'

'Don't think so.'

More silence. 'Do you like London?'

'I can't tell really,' she says. 'It feels like all I do is go to work, and sleep. Like you I guess.'

I used to have more of a life. I consider telling her this but it will end with telling her more, and I consider long enough to stop myself. Maybe she is thinking the same sort of thing. After a while she says, 'I'm thirty five.'

'Thirty six, me.'

She pulls the Observer magazine towards her and turns a page. 'By now,' she says, 'I thought I would be married. Or – not married exactly, but settled. Even –'

'A baby?'

'Well yes. Something like that.'

'My sister is thirty-seven. She's got a baby. He must be about three months old by now.'

She turns another page and looks at an advert for a car which I am sure is of no interest to her. She turns to look at me, and smiles – warmly, appealingly. 'Do you mind,' she says, 'if I tell you about myself?'

I do hesitate, I can't help it, but there is no possibility of saying, No, actually I don't want to hear it, and remaining under her roof. 'Go on then,' I say, and hope it hasn't come out in a way that betrays how I feel.

'You must have guessed,' she says, 'I'm sure it's written all over me, I split up with my partner.'

'No,' I say. 'It's not obvious, at least not to me. Anyway –' I risk a bit of self-disclosure, I can't help it – 'you wouldn't be the only one.'

She does not look at me now but pauses, politely, in case I want to continue. Then she says, 'We'd been together ten years. Almost. Then, last summer –'

I wonder what it's going to be. He turns out to be gay? Turns out to have a wife? Or another woman? Doesn't want children?

'– he said it was all over.'

'Just like that?'

'Pretty much. I didn't have a clue this was in his head. It just –'

'So. What did he give as his reason?'

'Well, we never got to that bit.' She's let her hair fall forward, to hide her face.

'He just walked out?'

'I knocked him out.'

'What do you mean?'

She looks up, and her face is impossible to read; satisfaction, a kind of horror, a wish for me not to be shocked?

'I hit him. I punched him as hard as I could and he went down.' The look leaves her face. 'I couldn't believe I'd done it. I'm not a violent person. I didn't even think, it happened without any thought process going on.'

'What happened next?'

'I was sick.'

'Sick? You mean actual vomit?'

'I know. How stupid is that? You know, I've watched operations, I've seen the most gruesome sights, I've seen awful deaths and I've sewed people up, their faces and stomachs and everything, and I don't know what happened. He was there on the kitchen floor, looking absolutely fine except he was unconscious, and I looked at him and just vomited all over him.'

I can't think of anything to say. I have to stop myself from laughing. I want to know, was she actually sick on his face? On his feet? Did she mop him up before she woke him up? Did she call an ambulance, and what would she say to them? Did he get her arrested? But all the questions seem a little impolite to ask someone I'm only just getting to know.

'I'm not a violent person,' she says again. 'In fact, I was brought up a Quaker, my parents are in, you know, the Society of Friends. I've never done anything like that before.'

'It's all right,' I say. 'I trust you not to do it to me.' Our eyes meet, we smile.

Midge: Normal

Elaine and I always agreed that we had married too young. If we had waited we might have been able to marry each other.

But then there would be no James, no Beth and Jenny. How can a parent write their children out of their fantasy history on the grounds that it was a mistake to marry their other parent? But I longed for Time to go back to my early days of teaching. My classroom in what we called the Rosla huts, the piles of exercise books that I was always mixing up, the boys in their baggies and Kevin Keegan perms, the girls all hiding behind great falls of wavy hair trying to look like Lynsey de Paul, or some such. The field trips – standing in the coach at the end of the day, counting a bunch of kids who would not keep still, counting the clipboards, waiting for the ones who had got themselves lost, or who were still snogging in the woods. Then the singing on the bus ('We're from Sheffield, Mighty mighty Sheffield') and trying to make them pick up all their litter and ending by picking it up myself. And going back to the staff room where people in those days sat around chatting at the end of school, gossip and shop talk and banter and complaints, before I headed off to my room in the house that I shared with two blokes I had been at college with. And we might have a kickabout in the park if it was still light, and get a pie and chips from the BakeandTake and maybe watch the telly while marking a few books. And then sometimes – we didn't have a phone – Glenys would come in.

Yes, that was it, Glenys would come in, just walk in as if it was her house, and sit down and someone – me usually – would make her a cup of tea and she would sit with her hands round the mug as if she was in an advert for soup, and cry. At this Pete and Rick would sidle away – sometimes even to do the washing up – and I would be left wondering what I was supposed to say or do. Or, if they were watching something important, like the cricket, I would respond to their fretful glances by taking her upstairs to my room, where she would subside on to the bed and cry harder. I remember standing in the doorway like an idiot wondering where to put myself, but after the second or third time of this I used to lie down beside her and kiss her. This usually made her moan, as well as cry, which I found exciting. 'Just hold me,' she said, and I tried to obey but my hands kept moving of their own will, not mine.

One evening she told me her sister was getting married.

'You're invited,' she said. Apparently I was considered to be Glenys' boyfriend and we were enough of a couple to be invited together.

Since the day I had met her sister Elaine, at their parents' house a couple of years earlier, I had not seen her again. That day it was taking me all my time to deal with the idea that Glenys had asked me to spend the weekend with her. And Elaine was with another girl (whose name and face I could never remember) and that made me wonder if they were lesbians, and that made me recoil and go quite shaky with too much forbidden curiosity.

By the time I heard about the wedding I felt much more a man of the world so I said, 'I often wondered if she was a lesbian you know.'

'Ha,' said Glenys. 'Not likely. That would make her interesting. That's the last thing she wants to be. I've told you before, she has to be the same as everybody else. You wait, marriage, two children, nice house, that's all she wants.'

'What's he like?'

'Another cold fish,' she said.

When I wonder, now, what made me actually marry Glenys, her sister's wedding has to take some of the blame.

Keith's parents, being strong church people, insisted on a church wedding. Sid and Dot, who were not religious but liked to do things properly, made sure that properly was how things were done. There was the white dress, the best man, ushers, flowers everywhere, relatives with regulation buttonholes, the organ, the photographs. I had never been to a wedding before. I had no function there except to sit next to Glenys when she was available. The rest of the time I stood awkwardly, usually getting in the way of someone with a job to do, and I marvelled at the amount of difference there could be between an ordinary Saturday, and this one. I was at the back of the church when Elaine came in, with her flowers and her father, followed by Glenys, also with flowers. I wish I could say that I fell in love with Elaine there and then but I would not have dared. She was far above my cowardly aspirations. She looked composed, and untouchable.

I looked at Glenys instead. She was not crying. Her parrot-coloured hair had been dyed brown all over on the instructions of her mother – this had caused some anguish and a threatened rebellion, but she had given in. She was wearing a pale blue long dress and was prettier than I had ever seen her. I was often scared of Glenys – her tears her tempers, her demands, and as much as anything else, her clothes. Wildly thrown together garments in colours that made you wince and a special mania for scarves and shawls made people look at her in the street. The senior staff at her school had asked her to moderate the way she looked but she didn't know how. But now, tamed and demure in that soft blue colour, she looked like a normal person and the idea that I could say she was my girlfriend, *my* girlfriend, took my breath away.

Later, when Elaine appeared in her going away outfit – these were the days when such things happened – she threw her bouquet and Glenys caught it. It was clearly a put up job. And later still, when we slipped out through the fire doors for a bit of fresh air, and the music followed us out, and I lit her cigarette and she leaned against me and smiled up at me, I asked if she would like to get married.

'To you?' she said, and I said, 'Yes,' and then she said, 'Yes,' and after that we seemed to be engaged.

8

Jen: Trust

'What about you then?' says Annie. 'Did you split up with someone?'

'Of course. Just the same. Though different.'

I tell her how Russell and I had been together four years, we'd lived together for two and a half. 'It seemed like time to start thinking about buying somewhere together. We were saving, we were both putting money into a savings account, we were even looking at properties, not that seriously but as research, you know.'

She murmurs sympathetically. 'So many of my friends –'

'I know. It just made us argue. When we wanted to go on holiday, or even out for an evening, we'd be thinking of the money we'd be spending instead of saving. It was like an addiction, we were addicted to self-denial, both of us, we couldn't have any nice times, no meals out, no drink. It shouldn't even be necessary. We have decent enough jobs, we're not like these poor kids like my cousin who are just resigned to living in some rented dump – I don't mean yours is a dump – for ever. It was a compulsion. I was calculating all the time, how long till we'd saved enough, how long till we could buy and move in, how long till we could afford to have a baby. And he was the same. Trying to do extra jobs, cycling to work, giving up his season ticket. And his season ticket to the Arsenal.'

'You stopped living. And your sister was getting on with having a baby.'

'I don't think I was being influenced by that.' I play that back to myself and decide maybe it's not true, but I'm not about to go back and contradict myself.

'So what happened?'

'He packed up and left. In some ways, not a surprise. We'd done nothing but row all summer. Then one day, he'd gone.'

'Without saying?'

'Well yes. Failed to return home from work. At first I thought he'd been working late, then I got cross because he hadn't let me know. Then I got worried that he's been in an accident or something. Rang round people. He'd not even been to work. Someone said to me, had I checked his clothes? Like, had he packed his stuff? And I looked and I thought, No not taken anything. Suitcase still there on top of the wardrobe, suit and shirts in wardrobe. I thought he must have had an accident. This is last September, first week of the new term, I didn't have time to think, never mind go out searching for a missing person. Didn't sleep all night. Went to school next day, what else could I do? Anyway, then he sent me a text.'

'He was all right?'

'He was in Morocco, that's how all right he was.'

'What did the text say?' She is more open about asking questions than I am.

'It said, Sorry I have gone away for a bit to sort my head out.'

'That's all? Not, Love you?'

'No, just that. So I texted back of course – I was on playground duty at the time – Where are you? And got this one word back. Marrakesh.'

'And you haven't seen him since?'

'No. Not him, or our savings. He took the lot.'

She says nothing for a full minute. Then, 'And no more texts?'

'Oh plenty. He said I could go and join him. Said he would pay me back the money. Said he just needed some space. You know.'

'And you said?'

'Told him to go fuck himself.' Out of some sort of shame I don't tell her about the texts I sent him saying I understood completely, please come back, I would always love him, I was sorry I'd made him go away, I would always be here for him.

'So that was it?'

'He sent me some of the money. He went to New Zealand and got himself a job. I got back a bit of what we saved. I haven't heard from him since. But then, I never thanked him. For the money you know.'

'Me too,' she says, looking across the grass at a group of boys playing cricket, thin Pakistani-British boys, maybe twelve, the youngest, up to maybe sixteen, taking it very seriously, their voices coming to us, yet not meaning anything to us, debating as they are over rules and decisions that we know nothing about. At least I don't.

'You too?'

'In that I haven't seen him since that day. I rang his brother and told him, you know, what I'd done. He came over and took him away, to hospital actually. I thought he'd be all right but he hit his head on the floor, he was concussed. I haven't seen him since. His brother sorted everything out. Told me again it was all over – well, I knew that by now – and I had to leave the flat. It was Jonathan's flat you see.'

'Jonathan's the brother?'

'No, he's Michael. Jonathan was my boyfriend. He was the one who wanted out, then I put myself in the wrong with what I did.'

'You didn't hurt him though.'

'Oh I did. He was off work for a couple of weeks. He could have got the police on me. Assault you know. I don't know why he didn't.'

'You haven't spoken to him?'

'I wanted to.' She shrugs. 'But he didn't.'

We eat the provisions we bought at the corner shop.

'God, I'm getting fat,' she says, cramming in her Brie and bacon baguette. 'I used to be thin. I just can't stop eating.'

It must take people different ways, I think. I can barely face a plate of food these days, unless it's composed solely of sugar.

The sun has just come out behind her, dazzling me as I look at her. Against the light her deep eyes are inscrutable dark wedges and I think I will never get the measure of her. Mercury, is what she reminds me of, slipping through your fingers, though if she was an animal she would be something big and awkward, an elk or a moose, something like that, not slippery at all.

Annie and I have a nice day. We read the paper a bit more, and go for coffee in the park café and look at the families whose mothers are our age. And if they look at us it's probably with envy that we can still do as we like. And on this day we are calm, having dropped our burdens on each other and found that we can bear them, and we can look at the pleasant young mothers and fathers and believe still that it might happen for us.

Later we wander back to the house and Annie goes out to practise her flute with someone and I'm sitting on the back step, where she was this morning, but now it's in sun and I know I should go and prepare tomorrow's work but I just want to have this last warm slice of sun before I do.

What I did not include in the story I told Annie was that on Christmas Day, when she had gone home for a dull and dutiful parental Christmas and I had stayed in London being a martyr, my phone had rung early in the morning and it was Russell.

'Where are you?' I said.

'New Zealand,' he said. 'South Island. It's beautiful Jen. Why don't you come?'

'How can I?' I said, not even stopping to think whether I wanted to.

'I'll pay,' he said. 'It's our money anyway, there's plenty. Just get on a plane and come. It's summer here.'

'All right,' I said.

But after he'd hung up I began to think sensibly. He was probably drunk, though he hadn't sounded it; he would certainly be feeling seasonally sentimental. I couldn't trust him to want me there with him, really. I hadn't given notice at school, I would not be able to get away until Easter. And abroad. I never wanted to go abroad. Even when it seemed that everyone I knew was having a gap year and climbing up Machu Picchu – or whatever you do with it – I was not moved to want to go. Even Beth did a little trip – not round the world, but she did Thailand and Laos and Cambodia – and I didn't feel jealous. It did not seem to me a sensible thing to do.

I have a passport of course. I've been to Spain and Greece. But the idea of going to a whole other continent makes me afraid. I know it's silly, I know people are people all over the world, I know some of the children in my school, in my class, have made journeys more difficult and terrifying than anything I would have to do if I went to China or India. But the thought of doing that only brings to my mind an image of Sheffield, and the hills beyond, and a wish to be back there. Russell and I have discussed it many times. I used to think he understood.

It would be stupid to chuck everything and take off, just like he had. I emailed him a long explanation, pressed SEND and drank a whole bottle of red wine, then the last quarter of Annie's bottle of whisky. It was disgusting, it made me feel shit, but it was better than sitting sober and sobbing while the Christmas programmes took over the TV until I wanted to put a brick through it.

I think of it often, and I think of it now sitting on the step in the sun. I haven't heard from him since, he didn't even text me on my birthday, and time is passing.

It will be moving towards winter there now and he will not have forgiven me.

My phone rings. I look at the number but don't recognise it. 'Hello.'

'This is Troy.'

'Who?' Though I know perfectly who.

'Troy. Honey's brother?'

'Oh. Yes. Hello Troy.' I don't know what I'm feeling. Butterflies, excitement and a sort of disappointment. This is what I wanted to happen and now – it's almost ordinary. It's a phone call from someone I'm distantly related to, so what.

'How are you?'

'I'm fine thank you. You?'

'Yeah, good. Lovely day today.'

'Lovely.'

'Well.' He really doesn't have anything to say to me. 'I just thought I'd call and say thanks for getting in touch and I'll be there at the party. Looking forward to it.'

'OK. See you there.'

'Bye then.'

I am so glad Annie is not standing by listening to me being as incompetent as a girl of fourteen. I can think now of a thousand – a dozen at least – things I could have said, and even one or two that I wanted to say. How is he getting there? Is he taking anyone? Will he be staying with Nev? Surely these are legitimate and non-intrusive questions to ask. But he has gone, and the sun has slid away over the wall and I drag myself to my room to get ready for the following week.

Midge: Kiss

Elaine and I first kissed one warm summer afternoon in our kitchen. It was the school holidays and for the previous three weeks I had been trying to decorate our small bedroom ready for the new baby. I said I didn't see why it – he/she – couldn't go in with Beth, but Glenys said it was going to be a boy and we might as well put it in a separate room straight away. It should have been an easy job but I had never even seen painting and papering being done. My parents, running a guest house as they did, had always used proper decorators, in January, while they themselves went off to Cornwall for their annual break. But also, I never seemed to get a run at it, so to speak. Glenys would call me down because the baby was waking up, or we had run out of rusks, or sterilising fluid, or cigarettes, or because Beth was wriggling too much for Glenys to change her and I had to go and hold her still. How she managed when she was on her own I never understood; maybe she summoned Elaine or Dot every time there was a minor crisis.

Anyway, on this particular day I had finished the decorating, or at least I had stopped. There was no gloss coat on the door or skirting board, and the paper was not trimmed at the bottom; there was quite a lot of paint adhering to the glass of the window and I could not get the handle back on the door in its proper way, so to this day you have to push the handle up instead of down. To this day, as well, the door has its matt finish and the paper behind the bed remains untrimmed, but it doesn't matter, I only use the room for sleeping in. The wallpaper has faded to quite a pleasing pattern and you have to look carefully now to see that there were once pale blue cartoon elephants on it.

'That will have to do,' I said to the two sisters, when I came into the garden. Beth was in a playpen on the grass, James, about a month off his first birthday, was on the outside, on his feet, holding on and cheerfully retrieving the toys that Beth was throwing out of her prison.

'Finished?' said Glenys. She had never once been into the room to see how I was getting on.

'Nearly,' I said. 'A little bit here and there but I'll finish off at half-term. I really need to get on with some lesson prep before September. Do you want to come and look?'

'Later,' she said, and Elaine said she would wait until it was completely finished before she saw it, and added that I must need a cup of tea and she would go and put the kettle on. Beth – I think we still called her Elizabeth in those days – was getting fed up, and I lifted her out of her playpen, managing to smear her with wallpaper paste as I did.

'Will that hurt her?' I said and Glenys, without really looking, said that Elaine would clean her up if I took her inside. So our first kiss, Elaine's and mine, happened as I held my eight month old daughter and Elaine mopped at her with a dishcloth which was probably much less hygienic than a whole bucket of paste.

'You've got it all over you too,' she said, and rubbed at my front. Beth grabbed hold of her hair, and now there were sticky dabs of paste in her long pony tail. And her face was so near mine, her smooth soft cheek – I can see it now, the even curve of it – that I just leaned towards it, I hardly had to move at all, and kissed it. I was formulating an excuse even as I did it – it didn't mean anything, it was just brotherly, it was just a thank you for mopping me up, that was all, but she turned her head quickly towards me and kissed me. On the lips, deliberately, lightly, briefly, and just then James began to realise she had gone out of sight and began to shout for her. She went and picked him up and then there in the kitchen, each of us holding a small child, we put our

70

spare arms round each other and held on tight, while the kettle, which was faulty and would not switch itself off, poured steam into the air, and Glenys, four months pregnant, lay with her eyes closed outside on the sun lounger, knowing nothing.

I knew – so did Elaine – at least two things straight away. I knew that this was right, it was good, it had all the promise of a new and wonderful life. And I knew that it was useless, it was doomed, no happiness could come of it. I could see a whole future encompassing the four of us, Elaine and me, James and Elizabeth, a family, and I could see a disastrous, fragmented future of mess and muddle and upset.

A little later, when Elaine was going home, I thought of some things I should buy at the shop, and went with her. But of course I had to take Beth in her pushchair, and the pavement was too narrow for us to walk side by side and both children were getting towards that late afternoon stage of being hungry and petulant. And so was I. I was hungry for more hugs, more kisses, but someone might see, and how could we, in the middle of the street, with a buggy apiece. And I was petulant because when Elaine walked in front of me I couldn't see her face and wondered what she was thinking, was she smiling, was it all right, and when I walked in front of her I couldn't see her at all. Before we got to the shop, when we were side by side waiting to cross a road, I said, 'This is no good.'

She looked at me, sadly I think, and said quietly, 'You're probably right,' and I turned round and came home and thought I could empty her out of my mind, as if my mind was a teapot half full of cold tea.

9

Jen: Toast

Modern dance is definitely not my thing but I was touched that Honey asked me, so I'm going. The weather has turned back to winter again but the evening is light as I make my way to North London and the far flung University building where it is taking place.

She's not getting paid for this, she told me, it's a student drama production where her job is to be some sort of non-speaking spirit, communicating the horror of global destruction through dance while the characters harangue each other about politics.

'They're so unprofessional,' she said. 'Always late, miss rehearsals, want to change things and then change them back again. They say there's an agent coming to watch, but I don't know whether to believe them. But I tell you, if I was sure they were lying I'd be out of there. I just don't want to quit, in case –'

Being in this audience makes me feel old. I look around in the hope of seeing someone who looks like a theatrical agent, but what would I know – big camel overcoat? cigar? as in old black and white movies – and anyway all I see is students and a few parents.

It's not until after the interval that I notice, on the far side of the hall from me, someone who could well be Troy. Honey didn't say he was coming but it looks like him and furthermore, the person the other side of him, who I can only just see, looks like Ashley, and the other side of him is a very pretty Asian girl who could well be Ashley's fiancée.

I wait with impatience for the end. Actually I suspect that everyone in the room is waiting impatiently for the end. Honey was very good though, mobile and willowy and expressive as she conjured up the deserts, the floods, the starvation, the wars and the desperation. We are all, I think, ready for a medicinal and cheering drink after that.

I am making an effort to get to the far side to intercept my cousin and Troy, who I'm sure will be waiting for Honey, when I am intercepted in my turn.

'Jenny.'

It's my friend's mother, Julia's mother. Julia has, after what seems half a lifetime, married Moody Matthew and they have left dirty busy old London and gone to live far away. I no longer see her every day of term, flying down the corridor late for her class and I miss her greatly. Of course she, and other friends of mine, know about me and Russell, and that is why I do not want to see any of them.

What her mother is doing here I cannot imagine but here she is all the same, and wants to tell me all about Julia, their little cottage, their chickens, Matthew's silversmithing, their neighbours and her hopes that they will start a family. She's a nice woman, of course she is, and I'm filled with guilt for not replying to Julia's communications to me.

'Tell her,' I say, 'I'll go and see her at half term – oh no, I can't, I've got to go home, my grandparents are having a big family do – tell her I'll see her in the summer.'

'Why don't you tell her?' says this woman, Jean she's called, and I flounder about and tell her things are a bit difficult at that moment.

'Well, you're here tonight,' she says. 'It's always important to keep going.' I know she is right. I do try, honestly, to get off my arse and do stuff, but it's with my jaw painfully clenched. Joyless.

I tell her that my cousin was the dancer in the piece (to call it a 'show' makes it sound too frivolous) and we discuss how good she was and I save up the comments to tell her. And then, by the time I've heard all the news about Julia I look round and Troy and the others have gone.

And I make my way on my own through the windy streets back to Leyton.

Annie, for a change, is in, eating toast and watching TV. It feels lovely all of a sudden, to have a friend to come home to. I tell her all about it, and about seeing Troy in the distance.

'You'll see him at the party,' she says.

'We used to think he was amazing, when we were little. My sister had a big teenage crush on him, even before she was a teenager.'

'Imagine,' says Annie, 'if we only had one chance and you had to spend your whole life with the first person you fancied. I'd be chained for ever by now to a hoodlum called Wayne.'

'Are you making that up?'

'Not at all. Wayne Whiteside. Year above me, used to get on my bus. Black baseball cap, scarf over most of his face, beautiful eyes.'

'Oh yes, eyes.'

'And you see,' she says, 'I can tell you about it because you weren't there. If I told one of my friends from school, even now, they'd be going, You didn't, how could you?'

She never makes a person talk, there's just something about her that draws it out of you, and I find I want to tell her things I'd never told Beth, even. It's a real effort, keeping things to myself, working out what I can say and what I would regret telling. I tell myself I must never get drunk with this woman.

She sets us off by telling me about this dream she had. I hate it when people tell me their dreams – like you're supposed to have something to say about all this nonsense – but there is no stopping her.

'I dreamed,' says Annie, 'that I was punching Jonathan but my fist was going right through him. I didn't even touch him because he wasn't there. You don't think he's dead do you?'

'Why should he be?'

'From his concussion.'

'Someone would have let you know.' Probably the police, I think but don't say. 'And anyway, it was a dream, it doesn't mean anything.'

'You don't know that. Dreams can speak to us.'

'I thought doctors were supposed to be rational.'

She laughs at that, and pushes her dark red hair off her face. 'Rational, you're joking. Loads of doctors are even Christian.'

'I thought you were too.'

'Not on your life. Oh my god though – have I offended you? You're not – are you?'

'Who is, nowadays?'

The smell of her toast is so enticing that I go to the kitchen to make some for me and when I come back in she has turned off the TV and I can feel, in the warmth and cosiness of the room, and the air of expectation she has, that we are in for an evening of confidences, and suddenly that is what I want.

I could tell her about my dreams – half-waking dreams, not deep sleep ones – the noise and the towering shadows and the fear inside my hiding place and the burden of the secret after it. But I stop short. I am not going to reveal too much. She knows already about Russell, that ought to be enough for her. But I want, even while I don't want, to tell her something.

I tell her about Hollin Road.

Our house was one of the ordinary semis, built after the war in a curved street that ran round the side of a hill. Between the houses across the road there were glimpses of a view across the valley to a place where there were no houses, only trees and moor, and in the valley between lay the campsite and the village where Nana and Grampy live.

Ordinary people lived on our road, a few old couples whose children had grown up and left, one or two younger couples who had no children, and a preponderance of families with children. There were children of all ages and some we were friendly with and some we were enemies of, but we did not get *too* friendly with any of them. Why? Well, we had each other. We had our cousins. Mostly though, the reason we were a little reserved was that we did not want to be in a position where we had to ask anyone into our house.

No one except family came into our house. Because we were odd, and we knew it, and we knew that however we could pretend outside, in our house everyone would see how odd we were and we could not pretend it away.

The oddness was not us, not really, it was Her, but it stuck to us like a smell of smoke. She looked funny. She never dressed like other women in jeans and t-shirts, or in smart suits, or in summer dresses. She never even dressed like Elaine – even looking like Elaine the pinafore-dress lady would have been an improvement. We tried not to be seen with her, which was not difficult as she never wanted to go anywhere with us. Midge seemed to believe that she kept to her room and her bed all the time but we knew that was not the case.

The signs were in the house when we came home from school. Her cloak would be hanging on the stairs and we would know she had been out, snuffling around charity shops, or buying chocolate, or dyes, or wool. Or there would be a strange vegetable smell because she had been round the garden picking leaves and boiling them up to see what sort of dye they made. Dyeing was her thing. And wool. If she could buy a nice piece of knitwear and undo it and dye the wool some new and nasty colour and knit it up again into something hideously useless it made her happy.

We, Beth and I, knew when she was happy, though how we did I do not understand. Her moods and her feelings crept out from under her bedroom door and we were attuned to them. We hated her, we tried to ignore her, but she mattered to us. We stayed there, in that absurd house, until we reached the age of eighteen. We studied for our A levels with the sole aim of getting away, and not having to go back. But living in a different place doesn't do away with her. She is still with us.

Her room was full of wool, in various forms and stages of being made and unmade, and downstairs there was quite a lot too. Our three piece suite in the front room, which was green moquette and had been old when I was born, was covered in patchwork blankets, several on each chair, all made of crochet squares. Crumbs fell into them and were not brushed away. When we had mice Midge would wait for a weekend or a holiday from school and take off all the covers and bung them in the washing machine and while they dried the chairs would be green and threadbare and uninviting, and the mice would go back to the kitchen.

For the year that Beth was at secondary school and I was still in the Juniors, I would walk up to meet her so that we could go home together. I would not go into the house on my own. This was the reason Beth and I were close – because I would not let her get away from me.

Sometimes when we got in our mother would be downstairs watching TV and we would go straight to the kitchen and get ourselves biscuits and squash and take them to our room, rather than sit with her. When we heard her radio go on again in the room next to ours we would go back downstairs and watch the programmes we wanted.

Even the outside of our house was not like others in the street. One time Midge decided that he had to do something about the front garden because it was a slum of weeds and litter. He persuaded Beth and me to clear it, and we did our best – I think he was paying us – but some of the weeds, the docks and the dandelions, defeated us and we just hacked them off and left the roots in, knowing that he wouldn't notice.

Then he got a lorry load of sand from somewhere and was just about to spread it over the garden when someone, some neighbour from down the road, told him to put a layer of plastic under it to stop the weeds coming back, and there we were, Beth and me, racing down to Nana, and round to Elaine, and searching under the sink and in the cupboard under the stairs, for any scrap of plastic. And we laid down all the bin bags and Co-op plastic bags and bits of old packaging and bubble wrap, and Midge shovelled sand all weekend until we had a desert for a front garden.

'Pot plants,' he said. 'That will brighten it up.' But of course we never got any. Then all the local cats came and used it as a de luxe toilet, and the next year all the big weeds came back and grew up, and we all just stopped caring.

Our back garden was a jungle. There were things like peonies that came up through the long grass and roses that sent long whippy branches up every year, a meagre bloom on the very end of each. When we were young Midge made an effort with the back garden – he cut the grass and sometimes pulled up some weeds, which would sit in a bucket for weeks while the bucket filled up with rain and the weeds gave off a vile smell. Whenever NanaDot came round she remonstrated with Midge and gave him advice on how to manage.

But as we got older and he got busier at work, he abandoned any efforts. If you stood at the bottom of our garden and looked up at the back bedroom window, you could sometimes see our mother peering out, her pale face and her vivid hair, with a foreground of briars and brambles, like something out of a fairy story.

And this, or some of it, is what I told Annie that night.

Midge: Lies

The plans for the party were pretty much in place. It was to be an afternoon occasion, so that Dot wouldn't get too tired. There was to be a marquee – a small one – on the camping field. There was to be a cold buffet, but also a table and chairs so that we could sit down to eat without balancing three things in two hands like circus animals. There would be music from the decades from the twenties to the middle of the sixties, by which time, Sid told me, no one could sing any more and it was all just noise. The music was to be quiet, though, so that people could talk in ordinary voices.

'It's not that we're deaf,' Sid said to me, 'but it don't get any easier to make out what people are saying when you've got some racket going on in your other ear.'

A photographer was booked – this was Elaine's present to them – so that everyone would appear in the pictures.

There were to be no other presents. 'We don't need any more things,' said Sid. 'My Dot will only get upset if there's a load of stuff she don't want.'

'What about some flowers though?' Beth said when I spoke to her, and it was agreed that flowers for Dot would be acceptable.

'Do you remember,' said Elaine to me one evening, 'that video the kids made of their Nana and Grampy?'

We were sitting in her garden in the last of the sunshine. When I'd arrived she'd been tidying a border. I love to see Elaine in the garden. She bends into the same shape her mother used to do when weeding and snipping and tidying.

'Let me just finish this,' she said from the back of the border where she was staking and tying some flowers which I knew would be tall and blue even if I didn't know their name. 'Go and put the kettle on.'

The grass was dry enough to sit on; tulips – I knew tulips – blazed near us as we drank our tea.

'I do now you mention it,' I said. 'I must admit I'd forgotten all about it.'

'It was a long time ago,' she said.

Now I remembered it happening, though I don't think I ever watched it. Jenny was in the middle of her A levels – this was some kind of history project. Patrick should have just finished his GCSEs, but as he was thrown out of school before the previous Christmas he didn't take them. However, he was handy with a video camera, which I borrowed from school for them to use, and Sid and Dot agreed, under some pressure, to be filmed talking about their life together.

'It's on video though,' I said. 'Who has a video player nowadays?'

'Take it to your technicians at school,' said Elaine. 'They can transfer it to DVD. Do you know where it is?'

'Not a clue,' I said. 'My best bet is to phone Jenny. Do you remember, when they did that I said to you that I thought there was some hope for Patrick. He really took something seriously, for the first time in years. We'd been so worried about him.'

'He was a little beast,' she agreed. 'But I didn't know you'd ever given up on him. I didn't.'

'Not given up on *him*. That's not what I mean. But I couldn't see where his salvation was going to come from. No qualifications, bad attitude, bad school record – even I couldn't fiddle his school record enough to be acceptable to an employer. We had no idea what he might do with his life did we.'

'He was lucky,' she said.

'Lucky how?' I was hoping she would say he was lucky to have had me, giving him advice and support.

'Lucky he never got caught by the police for some petty crime or other. Lucky that he had a talent, in the end. Lucky that his Nana took an interest in him. Without her I think he would have gone right off the rails, instead of only partially.'

'He's coming for the party?'

'Says he's looking forward to it.'

'And he knows that Troy might be there?'

'They are grown ups,' she said. 'Whatever happened, happened. They know more about it than we do. They'll just have to cope.'

'The more I think about it,' I said, 'the less I trust what I'm supposed to know. Maybe everything we did to try and help them get over it was wrong.'

'Did you never think of the possibility that they might lie?'

'Of course I did. I'm a school teacher. But they all agreed. They all told the same story.'

'Except Troy.'

'Well yes. At first. But you would expect that. He would naturally try to shift the blame. Or at least implicate the others to take a share. But eventually he did admit it.'

'Yes he did.'

She swallowed her tea and flung the dregs into the flowerbed. 'I don't see that it changes anything. Children remain damaged. A marriage remains broken. We may not be as sure as we thought we were of what set all that in motion but so what? We can't revisit it now.'

'What about the party?' I said. 'If one of them mentions it, if someone asks him to explain, if it gets opened up – what will happen then?'

'Anything could happen,' said Elaine. 'We can't predict so we have to wait and see.'

'And pick up the pieces again.'

'And pick up what pieces we can,' she said. 'Drink your tea. As you're here you can come and hammer some stakes in round the delphiniums.' That's what the blue flowers are, I thought. Delphiniums.

When I phoned Jenny to ask about the video she told me to look under her bed at home; she told me precisely which box to look in. I thought she sounded tired and dispirited.

'Work not going well?' I said.

'It's about the only thing that is,' she said. I suppose I should have asked about how she was getting on with Russell but I thought that if she wanted to talk about it she knew that she could.

'Not long now,' I said. Teachers know that always refers to the number of weeks until the next holiday.

'Three weeks,' she said.

I was about to hang up when she said, 'Midge. There's something I wanted to tell you.'

'What's that then?'

'You know the Fire?'

Of course I did.

'I was there,' she said. 'I saw it. I saw everything. You all thought I wasn't there but I was. I said I wasn't but I was. I lied.'

'Well, why did you?' I thought that was a reasonable question.

'I don't know. I suppose it was just the easiest thing to say. You know none of us ever talk about it, I don't even know the words I'm supposed to say.' It was as if she'd been listening to Elaine and me in the garden.

As soon as I could I phoned Elaine to tell her. 'So the issue is –?' she said.

'It changes things,' I said. 'If it's true that Jenny was there, it means that every one of them was lying. They all said she wasn't.'

'And the difference that makes is –?'

'I don't know. Unless she wants to tell us what she saw.'

'She didn't tell you?'

'I think she was sorry she'd said anything. She hung up on me.'

10

Jen: Knickers

I am nearly asleep when my phone receives a message.

'Miss you,' it says. 'Why not come and join me.' It's from Russell.

I get up out of bed and go downstairs to make myself a cup of tea. We have run out of milk, but never mind. I sit in the front room, on my own, with the gas fire on and the light off and think that it is Sunday tomorrow and I don't have to wake up early.

I think about Russell, down there, in the daylight of half a world away. I consider how much I miss him and I wonder how much he really truly misses me. I notice that his message did not contain the word love.

Then I start to think about Troy. So many years and then two small glimpses in a few weeks. And the prospect of a proper meeting soon. I will have to look into his face and wonder what he is thinking, how much does he remember, how much does he know, and how much does it matter to him. Not just the one thing, but the other as well.

I think about what happened between Troy and me when I was about nine – no, not 'about nine.' I was nine.

Beth went off that morning even though she knew I was unhappy without her in the house. It was in the Easter holidays, cold and windy as Easter invariably is in Yorkshire, mountainous clouds racing across the sky and piling up to blitz us with rain or hail if we ventured out to play. Beth went to call for James, leaving me in front of the TV with instructions to get stuck into the washing up. We were supposed to do it together but she had a new rule – if I hadn't finished my breakfast by the time she was ready to go out, then she was entitled to go out without me, and there was no obligation on her to wash the pots before she went, since I would be still using a cereal bowl. It would have worked the other way round, but she was always better at getting out of bed than I was and I think she was getting up earlier and earlier, just to spite me. Anyway, she had gone, and after a bit, I went too, leaving my cereal bowl all slimy with crunchy nut cornflakes down by the side of my chair. It would still be there when I came back, whatever time that was.

I did not go to call for the boys. I figured that by now they would probably be down at the Forest, so I struck out for the village and the campsite. I waved at NanaDot through her window but did not stop, and I did not call at the Clough, in case I got lumbered with playing with Ashley. The branches were heaving around in the wind, but there were plenty of leaves – not on the trees but at ground level, bluebells and wild garlic and wood anemones all pushing through the litter of last year's dead brown leaves. I couldn't hear any voices in the Forest but all the same, I couldn't think of anywhere else they might be so I kicked through the dead leaves to the Little Den. No one there. I threw a couple of stones into the stream, just for something to do and pushed the rope of the Tarzan a few times, but didn't have a swing on it because I was afraid of falling off and there being no one to help me back up the cliff.

Then I went to the Holly Den. At first I thought it was empty but then I saw that Troy was in there, on his own, drawing something in a little notebook.

'Hi,' I said.

He did not appear either pleased or cross to see me. He was just his normal self.

'What you doing?' I said.

'Nothing,' he said. He continued drawing but I think I stopped him concentrating because he suddenly scribbled on it and put the book in the pocket of his coat. He had a new Carbrini coat – black trimmed with orange and green. I wished I had one. He stood up.

'Where you going?' I said.

'Home,' he said.

'I'll come with you,' I said, and he didn't say no.

There was only one caravan on the campsite and the wind was making it creak slightly. The people had gone out. In the house Mandy was in the kitchen and Nev was fixing something on the dining room table. It was some kind of lock which had got stuck and he was taking it to pieces. Ashley was on the floor playing with a Brio train set which used to belong to Tricky.

Troy whispered to me, 'Keep quiet. Come upstairs.'

I went as quietly as I knew how past the door and up the stairs. Ashley was all right at times but he would be a pain if he saw us and he'd make us play with him till long after we were tired of his baby games.

Troy's room was up in the attic. He was all on his own up there and that was another thing I wished I could have, a room of my own, and preferably a whole floor of the house to be on my own in. Sharing with Beth was sometimes cosy and nice but she was very bossy, and very particular about my stuff getting into her half of our room. It was quite tiresome.

I had never been in Troy's room before. Only James had. I was pleased to be there before Beth or Tricky. There were drawings on the walls, of footballers and a boxer. The footballers were not bad but the boxer had a big head and a fat body and little legs. I said this and Troy said, 'I know, but I like his gloves.'

I had to admit that the gloves were pretty good.

Also on the wall there was a poster for West Ham football club. I was a Wednesday supporter myself but I was interested anyway.

'Do you want to see my programmes?' he said, and took a pile out of a drawer and gave them to me. We sat down on the floor side by side and he told me things about West Ham, like that their ground was Upton Park and they had more players in the 1966 World Cup squad than any other team and that you shouldn't say White Hart Lane, it was called Shite Hart Lane, which made me laugh.

I was still looking at the programmes when he said, 'Have you ever seen a willy?'

Well, I had, because James and Tricky were always peeing into the stream, or onto spiders' webs to break them so I just said, Mmm, or something like that.

'I've never seen a –' he stopped and said, 'What do you call your – you know?'

I knew we were having a rude conversation, but Beth and I often had them so it didn't seem that bad. I said, 'Beth and me say fanny, but my friend Joanne calls hers a tulip, I don't know why. A lot of people just say, Down there.'

He nodded and said again, 'I've never seen one.'

I suppose I kind of knew what he was going to say but I pretended I didn't. I thought maybe I should get up and go home for my lunch.

He said, 'If I give you this –' it was a programme for Sheffield Wednesday v Tottenham Hotspur – 'would you take your knickers down?'

I decided immediately that it was worth it. I liked football programmes though I didn't understand much about it, but more than that – it was Troy giving something to me and that added value. Beth had nothing that he had given her even though she was older than me.

'OK,' I said.

I took off my trainers and socks and my jeans. Before I went for the knickers though, I got hold of his Carbrini coat from the bed where he had dropped it and draped it over me, back to front, with the hood over my face. Then I took my pants off and sat on the edge of the bed. I seemed to sit there for a long time. I thought I could hear him breathing and I wondered if I could feel the heat of his breath, but I don't think I could. Then he said, 'OK. Thank you.' It was somehow very formal, as if we had stopped being friends. He turned towards his wardrobe while I got dressed, and then I stood in the middle of the room, not knowing whether to sit back down on the floor or whether to do what I had thought of, and go home for something to eat.

At last he turned round. 'Don't tell,' he said.

'Shall I go?' I said.

'OK,' he said and handed me the football programme. In the corner of the front he had recorded the score – Wednesday had lost 2-0. We went downstairs together and he went in and started playing with Ashley and I wandered on home. I don't think anyone knew I'd even been there.

I never told Beth, or anyone else, about the knicker incident. He said I shouldn't tell and I didn't. I didn't even want to and I think I'm right in saying I wasn't upset by it, though now I can believe the line that everyone would trot out that it was abusive. It didn't feel abusive. Weird, but respectfully weird, not abusive. I went away happy and I don't know that I ever thought much more about it, as an incident, though I always had a tiny private feeling that it made me special to Troy, and him special to me.

I would be happy to forget it now, of course, and even happier if I believed that he had forgotten. Even if he remembered, I hoped very much that he did not think, and had never thought, that it was because of that that the other thing happened.

Midge: Tired

At the beginning we were frantic, infatuated, Elaine and I. Frantically trying to meet, incoherent when we were apart, delirious when we were together. Not daring to see each other in company because we were sure it would be obvious what we were up to.

Sexually, Elaine was direct. Directive. ('There. There. Not that. That.') She appreciated, and told me she appreciated, what I did, unlike Glenys, who seemed to crouch, shrinking, waiting for me to stop and go away. Elaine was energetic and mobile; orthodox, which was fine by me, and cheerfully sensual. It was a relief to me to find that uncontrolled sobbing was not an essential part of making love.

At that time nothing else was important to us, or at least not to me. It wasn't long – Jennifer was only a new baby – before we found out that Elaine was pregnant. It was early on in our affair, she was still having occasional sex with Keith – 'And just as well,' she said. Glenys was wretched with motherhood. It was a turbulent time.

If – I have thought this over and over for so many years – if we had just trusted ourselves, if we had broken with Keith and Glenys back then, when we were young, then by now it would be an old story, nobody would care any more and we could have had years of happiness. But we were scared. Maybe it wouldn't last. Maybe it would damage the children. Maybe Sid and Dot would disown us. Maybe we had no right to that happiness.

Looking back on that time I wondered how I survived it. We were both in effect single parents of two small children; we were tired. I have known myself fall asleep at my desk in the small minutes between one class and the next, and be woken by a bunch of kids piling through the door, pointing and laughing. I bet they still laugh at me. 'Do you remember old Midge?' they'll say when they meet in the pub. 'Used to sleep all through a lesson, didn't care what we got up to.'

Elaine had even more reason to be wrecked by tiredness because for a lot of the time she looked after my girls as well as her boys. I would pick them up after school and take them home to Glenys who would be lying down with something icy on her forehead, completely unable to cook or talk to the children or even put them to bed.

But after they were asleep – sometimes even before – I would tell Glenys that I had to go back to school to pick up some books, or that I had left one of Beth's soft toys at Elaine's, and I would hurry through the couple of streets that separated us and stand for long minutes, just holding her. We dared not sit down, never mind lie down, for fear of falling asleep. Then I would peep in at the boys asleep and stagger home.

As soon as I saw him I knew Patrick was my son. I couldn't say so, not even, at that moment, to Elaine. I obviously wasn't allowed to enter into discussions about his name. At first I often thought that I was secretly claiming him as mine only because I wanted him to be, but as he grew it became absolutely transparent. Much smaller than James, much rounder in the face, curlier in the hair, softer in body and spirit. And as he grew older – and I see it to this day – secretive, devious even, fearful, unhappy. My son.

When we weren't making love we talked, of course, about our situation. We talked about Glenys, interminably, and Elaine told me about Keith.

'I should never have married him,' she said.

'Why did you?'

She never answered that directly. Maybe she didn't even know. But it was understandable. He must have been a good catch. Good-looking, with the fair skin and high colour of some sorts of Scotsmen – and indeed his father's family had moved south from somewhere remote, Ullapool I think, after the first world war. Intelligent, well-educated, with a well-paid and socially useful job. What was, as they say now, not to like? And totally honest. There has never been the tiniest suggestion that Keith Fairlie was anything other than completely trustworthy.

But Keith, so she gave me to understand, turned out to have a fault. A shortcoming.

'He doesn't like sex?' I had never met a bloke my age who admitted to not liking sex.

'I just thought it was the Christian thing. That didn't bother me,' she said. 'I just assumed it would be all right on the night.'

'And was it?'

'Frank,' she said. 'I loved him. We had just got married. He was a virgin and I wasn't exactly experienced. We muddled along like everyone does at first. But after James was conceived he seemed to go right off it. It was as if he'd done his duty and could give up.'

'What's the matter with him though? How could he not like making love with you?'

'It may have been beaten out of him. His father was quite a violent man, very religious, very fanatical. Almost everything he found ungodly or sacrilegious. Keith was beaten for listening to the radio because it was playing the Rolling Stones. What he watched on TV was monitored until he left home.'

I had nothing to say. Knowledge of child abuse, in those days, had not filtered down to ordinary people like me. The only people who really knew about it were the ones who did it, or were on the receiving end, and even they did not know what it was called. I assumed that Keith was exaggerating, to make his wife feel sorry for him, or excuse his poor performance.

As the children grew older somehow things settled down. They all eventually were at school and Elaine went back to work, term time only, for the School Library service. Nev and Mandy came to Yorkshire and Sid and Dot moved to the bungalow. Elaine and I saw each other whenever we could. We had our regular times and were also alert for any opportunities that might present.

For example, there was the time when it was my job to take the First Years to the Central Public Library, and Elaine and I kissed down in the basement, next to the great bound copies of the Sheffield Star. Nothing more than kissed – she was at work, after all, and I had twenty eleven-year-olds and a female colleague waiting in the junior library. Things like that – they were the pleasure and excitement in my life. They were the fun; they were almost innocent.

Then came what I always think of as 'that summer.'

11

Jen: Browny

That morning – bang in the middle of the summer holidays – Beth and I got up and had our breakfast in front of the cartoons on TV. Midge was cleaning the kitchen, the Bitch was still in bed. The day would proceed as it most often did. We were going to get together with James and Tricky and probably Troy and play in the Forest.

The Forest sloped away from the campsite towards the river, gently at first, then more steeply and came to an end at a small cliff, ten feet or so above the water. It had bluebells in spring, and brambles in summer, and tangles of branches, and fallen trees with great meaty fungi growing out of them in autumn, and stinging nettles. The campers were allowed to go into the wood but they did not often choose to, probably because there were no proper paths, no signs telling them which way to go, no board showing them a picture of a treecreeper or a wood anemone. They arrived, emptied their cars, pitched their tents and then drove all the way to Holmfirth or Chatsworth to look at something they had heard of. The Forest was all ours.

Tricky suddenly appeared in the room. Without speaking he moved Beth's cereal bowl and sat down. He pretended to be watching Inspector Gadget but we could tell he had been crying.

'Whatsa matter Trix?' I said, but he didn't answer. We knew that most likely James had run off and left him, dumped him in favour of Troy.

In the hall the phone rang. We heard Midge say, 'Don't worry, he's here.' And then, 'Not so bad. Coping.' We knew he must be talking about our mother.

When 'Why Don't You?' came on Beth and I went to get dressed while Tricky stayed, apparently interested in making potato prints or something.

'Come on,' I said to him. 'Let's go out.'

Midge said as we went past him, 'Have you made your beds?' He was looking in cupboards and making a shopping list. One of the best things about the holidays was that we didn't run out of things so much, and that he did the shopping instead of us having to do it after school.

'Get more cereal,' said Beth. 'Not Weetabix.'

We went out into the day. It was overcast but quite warmish and still. The birds had stopped singing now. We walked slowly through our normal boring streets to where the fields started and then along the footpath to the village. It was the longest way but the one we liked best. I kicked some dog poo at Beth and Tricky got stung by a nettle, but nothing else happened. In the village we stopped at Nana and Grampy's. Only Grampy was in and to our surprise – shock really – he was lying on the living room floor, listening to the radio and waving his arms to music.

'Whatsa matter Gramps?' I said.

'Bad back,' he said. 'Doc says, lie flat.'

'Doesn't he mean, in bed?' said Beth. You could see even then that studying law might be her thing.

'Bed's no good,' said Grampy. 'Too soft. I'm all right here, only I can't move. Your Nana's down at the Clough, helping Mandy with the children.'

Mandy and Nev had a new baby, Honey. She had been born in May, just when the campsite was getting busy, and caused all sorts of problems to everyone in the family. Midge and Uncle Keith and Auntie Elaine had helped out between their jobs, and Grampy Sid and NanaDot had of course been there every day, more or less taking charge as the baby yelled, and Mandy snapped, and Ashley snivelled, and Troy stayed in his room, and Nev rushed about holding his head and forgetting things.

We wandered on down the hill and into the house. NanaDot was standing in the kitchen holding Honey upright over her shoulder. There was a milky stream of baby puke down the back of her blouse. Mandy was peeling potatoes. She said, 'Looking for the boys? They won't be far away.' We liked Mandy well enough, but we were never really certain whether she liked us. She never said she was happy to see us, or asked us anything, but talked to us as if she was a teacher, or someone serving in a shop.

NanaDot said, 'Could you two girls be a really big help to us? Could you take Honey for a walk in the pram?'

'In the buggy?' said Beth. I knew she was playing for time. We definitely did not want to do this. We were sure Troy and James hadn't been asked to do it, so why should we?

'Not the buggy,' said Mandy from the sink. 'I want her to have a proper sleep. She's been up half the night.'

'The big pram?' said Beth. 'Oh Nana, I not sure we're strong enough to push it up the hill.' It was a huge heavy Silver Cross job that had been retrieved from Elaine's attic.

'There's two of you,' said Nana.

'And then coming down again,' said Beth. 'It's that steep, the pram might run away from us.'

'Don't if you don't want to,' said Mandy briskly. 'I can manage.'

'I've got to get back,' said Nana. 'Sid can't do a thing for himself.'

'It's all right,' said Mandy. 'Nev will be in soon.'

Tricky had been sitting on the floor, playing cars with Ashley, and now, seeing Beth and I were going, he got up to come with us.

'Can I come? I want to come with you. Mum, let me go too.' Ashley started on a high note and swiftly moved to a scream. He had learnt from Honey these past weeks that there was no point in reason or politeness.

'If they want you,' said Mandy.

'You'll look after him,' said Nana. We were outflanked and stoppered into a corner, so we had to let him come with us. Nana gave us a packet of crisps each, and one each for Troy and James as well. On our way out of the house we stopped in the shed to look at Browny and her puppies. Browny was a bitser of a dog, bit of retriever, bit of greyhound, rather a lot of something unidentifiable. The puppies seemed to have some sheepdog in them, Nev said. They were on their feet now, nipping and scrambling over each other, fenced in with pallets to stop them wandering. They didn't have names yet. We each chose our favourite though Beth and I knew for a fact that we would never be allowed to have one. There would be some sort of allergy or aversion that would make it unthinkable.

Midge: Purgatory

That summer was a hard time for all of us. Glenys and I were catatonic with hatred for each other. Whether she knew about my long-standing affair with Elaine I did not, and do not, know. At that time it was all rather beside the point. Elaine and I had called it off. No longer together. Something had shifted in her the previous spring, I never knew what set it going, and though I asked many times, she always claimed not to know. Some remark of Keith's I thought, or some idea that the boys were getting old enough to suspect. Since the Spring Bank holiday she had imposed a ban on meeting. But having to take the children places, having to help out at the campsite when Honey was born, using the same shops and school – and by now James and Beth were pupils at my school – these things meant that we could not avoid seeing each other. I had had to sit behind a desk at Parents' evening watching Elaine move round the room, each of us supposed to be concentrating on the progress of children, not on the grief and longing that filled us – filled both of us, I was convinced – and without the comforting prospect of talking together about it later.

That summer holiday was purgatory. Other years there had been visits to Elaine, whenever I could get away. Other years there had even been outings with the four children, where she and I could – each privately and unspoken – indulge in the pretence that we were a proper couple and they were all ours. This year there was none of that. I cleaned the house and fixed the things that needed fixing. I threw out rubbish and cleaned out cupboards. I reduced the garden to inch-high weedy stubble. When I was permitted to leave Glenys I went down to the campsite to help Nev. The more tired I could be by the end of the day the better.

The children would be there of course, mostly unseen as they pottered about in the trees, sometimes erupting into the field shrieking, chasing each other, then diving back into the undergrowth. My two girls, hair catching in the brambles as they ran, James, single-mindedly chasing like the sportsman he was, Troy, lurking back in the wood, rarely breaking cover, Ashley – only recently allowed to play in the wood with the others – laughing too much to run, and Patrick, smaller than he should be for his age, jaw clenched with the effort of being as good as the others.

12

Jen: Gang

Before that afternoon things had been going on for months between the three boys that Beth and I were not included in. I was eleven by this time and Beth was twelve, and we were becoming too old to spend all our time playing chase in the Forest. We went to other girls' houses sometimes, or into town on the bus to hang round the shops, and if we could get money off Midge we would go to the pictures or the ice rink. James and Troy, though they were older, didn't seem to want to do these things. They had a project of their own, which we only knew about from Tricky.

'They've got a gang. They say I can be in their gang. I just have to pass the test.'

Around the time that Honey was born, when all was confusion, Tricky and I were watching TV one wet afternoon and he told me some of his trials.

'Had to make a Tarzan.' (This was a rope over a branch.) 'And swing on it and jump off the other side of the River.' (It was only a stream with no name, but we called it the River.)

'Did you do it?' I knew he was scared of jumping.

'Sure I did. So I got to the next level.'

The next level had been to jump off the Cliff. This was a rocky edge next to the river and the landing was awkward because of all the stones and debris down there.

'Did you hurt yourself?'

He looked pleased with himself. 'Remember when I hurt my ankle. That was how.'

I thought that had been the end of it, but more recently, this summer, he told me some more.

'Last week, had to teef something off the campers.'

'You didn't.' I was shocked but admiring too. None of us had ever so much as had a fleeting impulse to do such a thing, the tents, cars, equipment, even the rubbish, of the campers was off-limits for every one of us. Though obviously not any more.

'And put it back,' he said.

'What did you take?'

'Saucepan.' He showed me how he crept up to the rear of the tent – luckily for him an old one with no built-in groundsheet – and reached in.

'Where were they?'

'Who?'

'The campers.'

'In the front, drinking beer.'

'They would have thumped you if they caught you. So would Nev.'

He managed to convey an arrogant strut without changing his position in the armchair.

'So what's next?'

'Hang on. I haven't told you about the tyre yet.'

'You did the tyre?'

'Yup.'

I was envious now. I had always wanted to roll down the hill in a tyre but either Beth would stop me, or the boys would refuse to help me. 'I tell you what,' I said, 'I could join this gang of yours. It's not difficult.'

'They won't let you,' he said. 'It's only for boys. If I don't get in I'll have to hang round with you and Beth for ever.'

'We won't let you,' I said. 'You'll have to play with Ashley for ever.'

'They won't ever let him join,' said Beth when I told her. 'He's just a game to them. We should tell him.' But we never did.

So after we said goodbye to Browny and the puppies we divided the crisps meant for James and Troy between us and ate them and went on into the Forest.

'I hope they don't peg me down again,' said Tricky.

'What's that?'

'Tying you down. Tent pegs and string. Then they ran away and left me.'

'How did you get out?'

'James came back and got me,' he said, ashamed. 'They said the ants would eat me alive.'

'Did they?'

'No,' he said.

'We won't let them do it again,' said Beth. We had been brought up with the idea that we should protect Tricky, though we never did a very good job of it.

Our usual way into the Forest – there were others – was through the Arch. This was a way under a branch of a tree, right on the edge of the field. Troy and James now had to duck to get under. Once you were under that branch you were properly In The Forest. You were surrounded by tree. The light changed and the air changed and the sound changed. It would have made a good den, under this tree where the branches hung to the ground, but it was too close to the camping field and our dens were further in. We could hear the boys shouting down by the river, playing on the Tarzan.

'Let's creep up on them,' I said.

So we did, very quietly, even Ashley, and we made them jump when we suddenly leapt out of the bushes and yelled at them. Troy was just about to push off from the Cliff and he swung off with only one hand holding on, and had to drop off at the bottom and climb back up. This made him annoyed, I could see, but he didn't say anything.

'Shall we go back,' said James. 'I'm hungry.'

As we wandered back through Tricky nipped off out of sight, and then returned to us. He had picked up the bits of rope and tent pegs from their stash. We understood, Beth and me, what he was going to do, and that we had to help him. It took till we were at the edge of the field before there was space to jump on Troy, all three of us, plus Ashley who had no idea what he was doing it for, and bring him down. James, looking round at the noise, came back and joyously joined in on our side.

Troy fought as if it was serious. He said nothing, saving his breath for kicking and punching. We got one leg pegged down but even then he twisted it free and gave James an almighty kick in the chest that winded him. Without our strongest man, and with Beth and me helpless with giggling, we gave up. Troy got to his feet and we all stood, suspended in time, until he shook himself like a dog and turned his back on us. We took Ashley back to the house.

'Come to ours,' said Beth to James. 'Midge has been shopping.'

Midge was in the garden when we got home, cutting all the flowers off a rose bush. 'More will grow,' he said when Beth asked him why he was doing it. We just looked at each other.

We ate a whole loaf of Mother's Pride and a jar of sandwich spread, and then, as Midge wasn't looking, James reached up into the top cupboard to see what was there and found a packet of Tunnocks caramel wafers. Then we watched Neighbours and then, when Beth and I were bored with the cricket we made our way, as if nothing had happened, slowly back to Hollin Clough. We didn't speak about Troy. It was all rather embarrassing. If we had succeeded, if he had been tied down like Gulliver, we would have won, we would have laughed and maybe he would have had to laugh as well. We would have untied him – James and Beth and Ashley and I would have untied him – and it would have been just a bit of play. But it hadn't been play.

As we passed NanaDot's garden we saw her talking at the gate to her neighbour Doreen so we just waved and went on down the hill. Troy was in his room,

Mandy said, so James went up to see him and we three went on into the Forest. The sky had cleared by now and the sun was flickering through the leaves. We wandered through the scrubby undergrowth to the Holly Den. This was a group of hollies that you could, if you didn't mind a bit of scratching, get into the middle of. In the centre of the ring it was almost dark, the leaves were so thick and impenetrable. I could see that Troy and James had been cutting branches, there was quite a large pile in the middle, and a pair of loppers too.

Beth screwed up her face. 'This is like a boys' den now,' she said. 'Where's all our stuff gone?' Because we had bits of carpet and garden chairs and other homely things, and they had disappeared.

'In the Little Den,' said Tricky. 'Troy didn't want them in here.'

'He should have asked,' she said.

The Little Den was three pallets propped up against each other, covered over with a bit of tarpaulin. It was only big enough for two and we used it when we wanted to sit somewhere and see out. You could see the Cliff from here and along the River a bit, upstream. Occasionally we had seen a kingfisher. We went to look and there were our chairs and stuff, not even put under the shelter but just dumped in a heap.

'Bastards,' said Beth. And we set to putting things to rights. Tricky wandered off.

It was quite difficult to get it all organised. I would have left it, and I said so, but Beth would have it that it was ours and we had to take care of it. 'The way things are going,' she said, 'we might need a den of our own.'

'What do you mean?'

'Boys' gang, no girls. Boys' den. Moving our stuff. Troy, what's he to us?'

'Ah,' I said, 'but you fancy him.'

'Nothing to do with it,' she said. She was pulling at the biggest bit of carpet, trying to turn it so that we could get it inside. 'Tell you what,' she said. 'Loads of carpet here, we could put some on the roof, make it warmer.'

'It will get wet,' I said.

'No, look. Get the tarp off, carpet on, tarp over the top. Easy.'

Well, I had nothing else to do so we more or less dismantled the whole den and started to build it again. We weren't big girls and we made a complete hash of balancing the pallets so they didn't collapse, but then Beth had the idea of using the trunk of a young sapling to support an end of one of them. This was all right but it changed the direction the den faced.

'Can't be helped,' said Beth. 'It won't matter.' The opening faced into the wood now. As we dragged the floor carpet in we saw, through the scrub, James and Troy coming into the wood. 'Stay still,' she said. 'They won't see us.' We realised that if we were careful we had a place from which we could spy on the boys.

They went into the Holly Den, and for a long time nothing happened at all, so that we began to get bored. 'Let's get the roof on,' I said, and we began to shake out the remaining bits of carpet to get rid of the ants and slugs. Getting the carpet to stay on the roof was something we had thought would be easy but the pieces kept sliding off and we were not quite tall enough to hold them on while we covered them over with the tarpaulin.

'Shall I get Troy?' I said.

'Absolutely not,' said Beth. 'We do this ourselves or not at all. I'll go back to the house and get a hammer and some nails.' She set off, taking a longer way out of the wood that would keep her out of the line of sight from the Holly Den.

'I'll come with you,' I said.

'Stay here,' she said. 'I don't trust that lot.'

So I sat down inside the den with nothing to do but to continue trying to learn to whistle. Then I saw the boys dragging out the branches they had cut. They were going to make a fire.

We were allowed, if Troy was with us, to make small fires. We put potatoes under the twigs but we were never patient enough to let them cook and though we ate them, they were still raw and no nicer than raw potatoes usually are. On a very rare occasion we would get hold of a packet of marshmallows, but usually then there was an adult with us who took charge of the whole business. On firework night, Nev let the village have a bonfire on the camping field and there was a massive fire that smouldered all night and some of the next day, unless it rained. The smell of smoke hung about for days, and we went through the Forest picking up the remains of rockets and piling them up like trophies.

What the boys were building now was smaller than Nev's fires but bigger than our usual little efforts. They would know of course, as we all did, that holly burns fiercely and will burn even when green. Not that we were country children. We might have grown up pretty much in the country but all our parents were town people, there was no one to tell us what the trees were called, or the birds and butterflies. Sometimes we made up our own names for things. But we did know that about holly.

I watched as they put a match to their structure, and I was beginning to think that spying was not such a brilliant thing to do, and I would have more fun if I went over and joined them, when Tricky came wandering back through the wood.

'Go away,' shouted Troy. 'We don't want you here.'

'Can't stop me,' said Tricky. Maybe his rebellion of the morning had given him some courage.

James said something that we couldn't hear. I saw Troy whisper something to him. Then James went to Tricky and spoke. Beth says that years later James told her that they offered him a last chance to join their gang. The test was this: he had to throw something in the fire, and it had to be something he was not allowed to burn. I saw him looking around vaguely.

The flames were leaping and crackling, turning the afternoon somehow dark. Then I saw Ashley coming through the brambles. He was carrying something and when he came nearer I could see it was one of Browny's puppies. He was holding it tight round its middle but it was squirming, probably alarmed by the fire, and he failed to keep hold of it. When he dropped it Tricky picked it up. The puppy must have nipped him because he dropped it again and though he picked it straight up I could see that he was annoyed and gave it a little shake.

'Don't do that,' shouted Troy, across the fire to him. 'Let me have it.'

'I'm not,' shouted Tricky. 'Why should you have it?'

'It's not yours,' said Troy. 'Browny's our dog, isn't she, so they're our puppies aren't they. Give it here.' He moved round the fire to where Tricky was standing, really struggling now with a puppy that must have been terrified what with the flames and the noise and the shouting.

'You won't get it,' screamed Tricky.

Then everything happened and I could never be sure what happened first. Browny came running into the wood. She must have counted her babies and come to look for the one that Ashley had taken. At the same time Tricky threw the puppy. Did he mean to throw it at Troy? Or into the fire? Or just down on the ground? Or had it just nipped him again?

It went into the fire. I screamed. I think we all screamed. Troy made a move towards the fire, where I could see – I could not take my eyes away – the puppy – the white one with brown ears – moving like someone having a nightmare, screaming too I think, unless that was me. And at the same time the big holly caught. A column of flame shot up higher than a house. Browny – she had been running round the fire, looking for a way to get at her baby – Browny came running, yelping, yipping, on fire along her back. Nev found her later, still alive, down at the stream. She had run down there and put her flames out, but been too weak to get back up the cliff. That was later.

Suddenly Beth was in the den beside me. 'Browny,' she was saying, gasping out the word. 'Browny. Did you see her? She's on fire. Jen, she's on fire.' I think she wanted me to come with her and find Browny, but I held her back. I clung to her and stopped her leaving because I did not want ever to move again, and I did not want her ever to leave me alone again.

The thing that happened next was that people came running into the wood. Two men who were just driving in with caravans, and some of their children, the ones that had not been caught and restrained by their mothers, and Nev, last because he had been furthest away, at the house, when the big tree went up.

Beth and me stayed where we were. Later we crept out, through the nettles, along the River as far as the bridleway and home that way. When we got home, crying all the way, we went to our bedroom and lay down together on my bed, heads on the same pillow, and then, though we did not mean to, we fell asleep.

Midge: Hurt

I started with Ashley. That was always my practice, to begin with the youngest, or weakest, or least intelligent, or most likely to forget, or be influenced. Mandy phoned me just as it was getting dark. Nev was out looking for Browny, she said, and Elaine had taken her two boys home, but could she ask me, as one whose children had not been involved, could she ask me to talk to each of the boys and find out what happened. 'If Nev gets hold of Troy,' she said, 'someone will get hurt.' She wanted me to talk to Troy, but I said I would start with Ashley. 'Before he forgets,' I said.

Ashley was five. He had been in school for one term and he was a bright enough little boy. Mandy sat in the corner of the room while I spoke to him.

'Did you take the puppy out of the shed?' 'No,' he said.

'Tell me how you came to have the puppy.' It had escaped, he said, he found it still in the shed but outside the fence.

'Who was with you?' No one, he said, he was just playing on his own in the yard.

'Where were the other boys?' Tricky was there, he said, but then he went away.

'Did Tricky get the puppy out?' No, he didn't think so, he thought it climbed out by itself, or maybe Browny carried it out in her teeth.

'But you didn't see it until it was outside the fence?'

'Then I saw it,' he said.

'And you picked it up and took it to the Forest?' Yes. 'Why did you do that?' To show Troy, he said. It was my best puppy, he said. He started to cry. It was in the fire, he said.

'I know,' I said. 'But how did it get in the fire?' It flew, he said.

I paused. I reminded myself that he was five, not fifteen like the children I normally asked questions of at school. 'Who made it fly?' He said he didn't know. He was still crying, not convulsively but quietly as if it had become a habit.

'Who was there?' Troy. 'Who else?' Tricky. 'Who else?' He didn't know. 'James?' Don't know. 'Was Beth there? Was Jenny there?' I was sure I would have known if they were, from what I had been told. Ashley said he didn't know.

'Tell me about Browny.' But he just looked bewildered, and the crying began to come in sobs.

'Come here love,' said Mandy and he ran to her and hid his face.

'That'll do,' I said, and she took him away to be put to bed.

I decided, while I was at the Clough, to talk to Troy next. James and Patrick, I suspected, would by now have synchronised their stories and could wait till tomorrow.

13

Jen: Sleep

I woke up first, before Beth. I was hungry. Then I remembered all the screaming and the smells of different things burning, and the shouting when the men came, and I stopped being hungry. I shifted a bit to try and wake my sister but she did not move. I listened. I could not hear the TV, or the radio that usually played in our mother's room. Our curtains were open and I could see it was very nearly dark. The day was gone. Where? Gone where?

I felt hungry again but I couldn't wriggle out without disturbing Beth. What was stopping me? I wouldn't normally care at all about waking her up. It was like I had to protect her, as she would have to protect me. It was like something had happened that was worse than falling down stairs, worse than coming bottom in a test, worse than being called names because your mother was a crazy lady. I closed my eyes and saw the spitting, sizzling puppy again, and thought, What if it was Honey instead? And that made me think I must never say that out loud, and it made me want to protect Honey, even though she was a nuisance and I didn't really care for her.

Then the strangest thing happened. Our bedroom door opened quietly and our mother's face looked in. I sat up. I didn't mean to, it just happened. I sat up – to say, Hello? or to say, Go away? or to say, Mum it was awful? – and Beth woke up a bit and punched me in the back.

Our mother came into the room and sat on the edge of the bed. She was wearing a long blue old-fashioned dress and pumps, and her hair was outlined against the faint light of the window, sticking out at quite regular angles like the rays of the sun in a little kid's drawing.

'I have to tell you something,' she said. 'It's not very nice.'

Beth still had her eyes shut as if she could get back to sleep by willpower but she reached and pinched hard the nearest bit of me she could find. It was my thigh and I had a bruise there next day.

'Something happened,' said the Witch, 'down at Hollin Clough. Midge has gone down there to help.'

'What?' I said. Beth said nothing.

'There was an accident,' she said. 'Browny was killed.' I could hear from her voice, though I couldn't properly see her face, that she was upset and trying not to cry. 'I loved Browny,' she said.

'Was she run over?' said Beth, eyes still squeezed shut.

There was a bit of silence. A couple of cars went past outside.

'No, not run over. There was an accident with a fire. She got burnt.'

'And it killed her?' I said. Beth pinched harder but I hadn't said anything wrong. Last we saw of Browny she was yelping, on fire, running like a demon through the undergrowth.

I think I tried to lean against my mother, because she pulled away sharply from me.

'Well,' said the Witch, 'as I understand it, the vet's been, and he had to put her to sleep.'

'Sleep,' I said, and Beth said angrily, 'Why do they say that? It's not sleep is it? He put her to death didn't he?'

'She would have died anyway,' said our mother. She really did seem upset. I didn't know that she even knew of the existence of Browny. She stood up. 'Did you get any tea?' I shook my head. 'Well, get yourselves something to eat, otherwise you won't be able to sleep.'

I felt as if I would sleep for ever, like Browny, if they would let me.

Midge: Expert

Troy was in his room. It was a small room, up under the eaves, and it looked like you would expect a boy's room to look. Discarded clothes piled on the floor, football posters on the wall (West Ham, he had never changed his loyalty to them), some drawings on the wall too, of cars and guns and football emblems, neat, competent drawings. A school bag shoved into a corner, untouched since school broke up. He would be in fourth year when they went back, Year 10 as we were going to have to learn to call it.

He was lying on his bed and when I opened the door – without knocking – he turned towards the wall.

'Troy,' I said. 'It's Midge. Your mum asked me to come and speak to you. Is that all right?'

He said nothing, did not so much as shrug, and that was the story of the next ten minutes. He was not asleep, I could tell by his breathing, which changed – faster when he was waiting for a question, slower when I asked one and he was deliberately holding himself back. I told him I only wanted to find out what had happened, I told him Browny had been found and the vet had been. I told him he was not being blamed but that it was important for all of us – especially Nev, his stepdad, who was surely someone he liked and respected, didn't he – to understand. We just wanted to understand, could he help us to make sense of what had happened, I knew he was upset, of course he was, everyone was, but it might help to talk about it.

He did not move and he did not make a sound.

'I'll come back tomorrow,' I said. 'Sooner or later, we have to get to the bottom of it.' And I left the room.

It was some weeks since I had been to Elaine's house and my heart was beating busily. Keith answered the door. A tall, distinguished, kind-faced man who might or might not know that I had been making love to his wife for the past decade or so, and who might or might not know that I wasn't any more. The fact that he was at home was an indication of how much upset there was in the family.

'Patrick's asleep,' he said. 'Dosed up with Calpol. You can talk to James if you like. If he agrees.'

We went into the living room. Of course I had been to the house many times before when Keith was at home. Birthdays, picking the girls up, taking the boys back, of course it had happened before. So many family events where we all had to be present, and I never knew what he knew. It was always hard for me. I felt he had taken my woman and at the same time knew that I had taken his. Remorse and anger and shame and jealousy, and all the time not knowing what he knew and what he felt. This time should have been hard too, but in fact it was easier. I had a job to do. I was in some way proud that Mandy had asked me to do it, and that the rest of the family had acquiesced. They trusted me and they trusted my experience and capability. This time, I was the expert here.

I looked around for signs of change but as far as I could tell, except for the vase of roses on the mantelpiece, everything was as I had last seen it, back in the spring. James was sitting on the sofa with his mother and the TV was on with the sound turned right down. I sat down at the other end of it, turning towards the boy. Keith sat in the armchair which I knew was his and which I had never presumed to sit in.

James – Captain Jim was Dot's name for him – was a good boy. He was a sportsman, a leader, a good student, the sort of boy you send out of class with an urgent message knowing it will reach the right person. A boy who will grow into a competent and conscientious man. He looked quite composed, but the fact that he was sitting so close to Elaine made me think there had been tears at bedtime.

His story was congruent with Ashley's. Yes they built a fire, yes, it got a bit out of hand. Ashley turned up with the puppy and couldn't hold on to it. Then Browny came running up.

'So who had hold of the puppy?'

He hesitated. 'Tricky had it. But it bit him and he dropped it. Then I didn't see who picked it up.'

'Someone picked it up?'

'I think so.'

'It didn't crawl into the fire by itself?'

'Surely,' said Keith, 'no animal would do that?'

'What do you think James?'

'I couldn't see,' he said. 'I was stood at the other side. The flames were in the way. I don't know what happened.' He began to cry, trying to gulp the tears away, sniffing and rubbing his eyes. He really didn't want to cry, he was not putting this on.

'Is it all right,' I said, to Elaine, 'if I come back tomorrow and talk to Patrick? Obviously you'll be there too.'

'So will I,' said Keith. He said it pleasantly, but even so I wondered if it was a warning.

14

Jen: Painkillers

'We always had a dog,' said NanaDot. 'Ever since we came here. First we had Bessie but she was daft dog and she got run over. Then we had Bonnie, she was Browny's mum, do you remember her?'

We said we did. Nana was sitting on a kitchen chair with one of the puppies in her lap, trying to get it to take milk from a bottle. It was the brownest of the puppies, a girl, the one that looked most like Browny.

'What about the others?' said Beth.

'We can't keep them all,' said Nana. 'Six is too many to deal with.'

We knew there were only five now but no one ever, ever told us about the one that was burnt to death.

'Mandy has got enough on her plate as it is and there's no point us asking your mum to take one is there? So one here, if we can manage to get her to feed, and your Aunty Elaine has one. I don't know how she'll manage, what with going to work, and your Uncle Keith so busy, but James and Tricky can look after him till they go back to school, and then he should be old enough to survive.'

'They're lucky,' I said.

'Not really,' said Nana. 'Their mum and dad hope that having a new puppy will help them get over a very nasty experience. And you two will have to be extra nice to them for a while, especially Tricky.'

Beth and I looked at each other to remind ourselves not to let on that we had also had that nasty experience.

'What about the other three then?' said Beth.

'The vet took them. He said he would try to find homes, but it don't seem very likely to me. They're only mongrels after all, and a lot of people are away on holiday. They'll have to be put down, I'm sorry to say.'

'I wish –' said Beth and Nana looked sharply at her and I said, 'No point.' And she stopped.

'This one hasn't got a name yet,' said Nana. 'You'll have to find out what your cousins' one is called. So, what are you going to do today?'

We didn't know. That's why we were there. We had woken up early, ravenous, and made our way through a whole box of Cocopops before Midge came down. We ignored him when he spoke to us and soon after, we heard him go out. We had, all of a sudden, only each other and we had drifted into Nana's like autumn leaves, without thinking.

'Go and see if Mandy needs any help with the baby,' said Nana, and Beth improvised. 'Actually we're just going to the shops for Midge. We wondered if you needed anything.'

She knew Beth was lying but she only said, 'No thanks,' and then I remembered to ask about Grampy.

'Is he better?'

'A bit. He's got some painkillers. But he won't be doing any heavy work for a while. You'll find him down at the Clough, he's up and about today.'

We wandered out, but not down to the campsite. We ambled back uphill, through the village – pub, phone box, bus stop, litter bin; it didn't even have a post office any more – and like a fairy godmother appearing, there was a bus standing at the bus stop, chugging as if it was getting ready to go. We ran and just caught it and sailed into town feeling as if we had escaped from prison.

Midge: Mercy

I went down to Hollin Clough first, thinking I should speak to Troy but Mandy said he was still asleep. Nev was digging a hole in the garden, beside the hedge, to bury Browny in. The day was already close and warm and his pale skin was pink and sweating.

'I'd better tell you,' he said. 'Ashley says it was Tricky threw the puppy on the fire.'

I wished he hadn't said anything. As far as I could see it was between Troy and Patrick now, as to who was the actual murderer. Ashley would not have had the height or strength to throw a solid, squirming animal that far, and I trusted James to be telling the truth when he said that he was at the other side of the fire. But Ashley could have been got at by now, by Troy; he could have been threatened, cajoled, bribed, or just confused. I decided I would see Patrick first.

Before that, I stayed to help Nev put Browny, mercifully wrapped in sacking, into the hole. He shed some tears and I put my hand on his shoulder, feeling awkward, as men do, but meaning well. Mandy called from the door to ask if we wanted coffee and he said no.

'Sorry mate,' he said to me. 'You go if you want one. I can't stand to be inside at the moment. It's that miserable you'd think someone had died.' He stopped, listening to what he had just said, and then we both laughed.

'I'm going into the wood,' I said. I was thinking that I might as well inspect the crime scene. Something revelatory might happen, as it does in crime dramas.

He came with me. The smell of burnt green wood hung in the air. No birds moved or sang. The remains of the boys' bonfire was puny beside the destruction of the stand of hollies. Three of the five looked to be completely destroyed, cut to the ground. One was only scorched on one side and the last was half a tree exactly, showing off its inner architecture, the leafless mesh of branches that must always exist inside the skin of leaves. On the ground we found a pair of loppers with their rubber handles melted, and some metal tent pegs.

'We've been looking for those loppers,' said Nev. 'Bloody kids.'

We did not stay long in the wood, there being nothing we could do except stand around mournfully, and before eleven I took myself to Elaine's, to see Patrick.

This time I did not sit on the sofa. I sat on a dining chair and asked Patrick to stand in front of me. He was looking sulky and heavy-eyed and – I didn't want to think this but I did – shifty. I felt sorry for him. He was only ten and he was on his own. His parents were withholding their judgement and until we had established something – sometimes known as 'the truth' – they would not commit to being on his side. James was in the other room, with the puppy, to be called in if necessary.

'Tell me what happened Patrick,' I said.

He looked me in the eye and went straight to the point. 'I had the puppy,' he said. 'Troy said it was his. He came round the fire. He grabbed it. He said, It's mine I can do what I like with it, and he threw it in the fire. Then –'

He stopped and began to cry. Elaine put out a hand and he went to her. I had not believed what he said.

I could not say that. Patrick was entitled to the support of his mother and the man who called himself his father. They had seen and heard as I had, the patently made up story, the pitiful acting job, the easy tears. He had behaved exactly as I would have done, at his age and at other ages, and I could not call him on it. I shrugged in Elaine's direction and Keith showed me out. 'You'll be going to see Troy now?' he suggested and I agreed but in fact I went home – the girls had gone out – and I phoned Mandy and told her that if Troy ever decided he wanted to talk to me I was available, but if not, then I couldn't see that there was anything to be gained by forcing him. It may be that it was cowardly. It may be that it was the worst thing I could have done.

15

Jen: Survival

The last two weeks of that summer holiday passed in a slow, heavy, dragging sort of way. James and Tricky went on holiday with their parents. The dog that they had did not survive. Midge said Elaine had chosen the smallest and weakest because she felt sorry for it, but it was too small and weak, and it died. The one NanaDot looked after grew up and became Bobbie, later the mother of Bowling – Bowling Green, get it? Sid's joke – who was later the mother of Bogey, an only pup and last of his line.

Midge took us to Filey for a day, but we had to go and see our other grandmother in an old people's home, which spoilt the occasion for us. Except for that day we hung around in pyjamas, draped over chairs watching TV, helping ourselves to any money we could find and dawdling to the shops to buy sweets.

Of course I had told Beth everything I saw. She was very cross with Tricky.

'I always knew he was a sneaky one,' she said. 'I never trusted him. He lies. He should own up.'

'Well, you tell on him then,' I said, 'if it's so important to you.' Tricky was always more especially mine and I felt sorry for him, though I could not explain why.

'Then they'll know that we lied,' she said. I realised that she and I were in it together, no matter whether we told or not.

'And James might not back us up,' I said, 'because then they'll know that he lied.'

'Suppose we tell Troy that we know it wasn't him,' she said. 'But then, what would he do? He might beat Tricky up.'

'Or us,' I said, 'for keeping quiet for so long.'

'We should just forget all about it,' she said, and that is what we thought we were doing, though in my dreams I still saw Troy, all lit with green light, and Tricky, sometimes red, sometimes black, and sometimes I had the puppy, and sometimes they threw Ashley into the flames, and always I had to stay awake afterwards to stop the dream from coming back.

I don't think any of us ever went in the wood again. Beth and I cultivated our friends and went to their houses and sat in their bedrooms and read magazines and listened to cassette tapes. We spent less time together. We sometimes went to Nana's and we would take the dog for a walk but we stayed on the footpaths and stayed away from the camping field. We didn't see so much of the boys either. James was getting involved in all sorts of sport. Not only football but ice hockey and swimming, and the following summer he went away for two weeks to a tennis camp. Tricky was suddenly busy as well. He was in every after-school activity going – chess and art, and the school play – and then he took up the guitar and had lessons, and by the time he caught us up at secondary school he was someone who was noticed for being talented and confident. He outshone me and Beth, easily, even before he acquired his bad reputation.

We didn't see Troy before the start of school. It was said later that he never came out of his bedroom although Mandy pleaded and threatened and told him nobody blamed him, and sent Ashley in to try to cheer him up. But apparently, from what we overheard, Nev had not been near him. Nev had heard, naturally, of Tricky's account and said that until Troy convinced him otherwise he had to believe the littler boy. Troy was still saying nothing.

Going back to school was a big relief.

When Troy went missing we were not as bothered as the adults were. Kids in the upper school seemed to run away quite often. But they were usually discovered at a friend's house, or at their nannan's, or in a certain caravan that a certain family kept in their garden. Beth reminded Midge that the police should be told to check out the caravan and he said they already had. As the days went on and Troy did not come back, I said to Beth that maybe we should tell what we knew.

'Absolutely not,' she said. 'We'd get properly done, and anyway, he still might not come back.'

We thought of him as being on the run and actually it rather thrilled us. It seemed to be a state of affairs that proved he was some sort of criminal type, and probably, even if he hadn't really killed the puppy, he would have been capable of it. And this made me remember the time I took my knickers off for him and I began for the first time to see that he had been very wrong to ask me to do that. I had never told anyone, not even Beth, and I realised now that I had been feeling guilty all along. Now I was able to see that it was all Troy's fault. But I still did not tell anyone.

So Troy had gone. We no longer had even the little fame that came from being related – 'sort of' – to him.

Midge: Fault

On the first day of term I was feeling pretty good. The evening before I had seen Elaine, returned from her trip to Scotland, and there had been definite signs that things might be back to normal with me. The boys were with her so there was nothing overt, but there were smiles, wide-eyed glances full of meaning, and as the boys went out of our front door she hesitated and I am sure would have kissed me if Patrick hadn't turned round at the gate to wait for her. I was feeling hopeful.

I was in my office looking at the detailed breakdown of the exam results, well before most of the staff or pupils were on the premises, and I was surprised when someone knocked on the door. It was Troy. I had not seen him for the past three weeks, unless I counted the view of his back as he lay mute on his bed. I was somehow surprised that he did not look more different, but then again, why should he? None of the rest of us looked any different, to normal eyes. Even Nev had recovered his pleasant calmness, even Mandy seemed to have no more than her usual level of anxiety.

I was not sure whether to be teacher or uncle. The boundary between school and home was usually clear, and I always reminded the kids at the end of each holiday that when we met again it would be on different terms, but not having seen Troy for so long, and under such circumstances, I felt it necessary to be less formal. It came out as a bit too jovial.

'Well, good to see you, what can I do for you?'

He did not sit down, or put down his bag, which, I recollected later, looked quite heavy. 'I've come to say something,' he said. He did not look directly at me, but over my shoulder, out of the window. 'It was my fault,' he said. Then he turned and went out.

I was surprised. I wanted to believe him because it would let Tricky off, but I did not. I wanted to ask him exactly what he meant – that he killed the dog, or that it was his idea to light the fire, or what? What exactly? But he had gone. I decided I would catch him later, after school. I would find out what his last class was and wait in the corridor for him. He would have settled back in by then, he would be feeling more like himself, back with other kids. His mum, I thought, must be relieved that he had got up and come into school.

Then a hundred other tasks filled my day: new staff, new pupils – Jenny among them – assembly for year 11, timetable glitches, a new photocopier that could only be operated by a trained technician which we did not have, a colleague who needed to go to a funeral on Thursday, the fact that the decorators had not put the numbers back on the classroom doors, and an outraged deputation of staff saying that their belongings had been moved from the staffroom. I taught a lesson too but that was the easy part of the job.

I was a little late to the maths corridor at the end of the day and Troy's class had already gone. Never mind, I thought, it would be better dealt with outside school, it was not a school matter at all. I would tidy my desk, go home at a reasonable time, feed the girls and ask them about their day like a proper parent, and then stroll down – it was going to be a beautiful evening – to the Clough.

So I did, and I had left school before the phone call came from Mandy asking if Troy had attended that day. This was before the days of computerised registers, but Dawn in the office checked the relevant register and informed Mandy that he had been marked present in the morning but not in the afternoon. Beth and Jenny and I were sitting at the table – I don't think they had eaten at a table for months – and talking cheerfully about school, and who was sitting next to who, and what the new PE teacher was like, and so on. Certainly, it was the most cheerful any of us had been since the thing happened.

Then Mandy rang.

'Did you see Troy today?' I asked the girls. No, they hadn't. They looked shocked at themselves for not even noticing that they hadn't seen him.

I went back to the phone. 'Have you asked James?'

'James never saw him,' said Mandy.

'Have you checked his room? Is anything missing?'

'Some clothes I think. It's hard to tell with a quick glance. And it's so long since I've properly seen him.' She sounded as if she was close to crying, but was managing to hold on to herself. I could hear Ashley in the background, so she would be trying to suppress her

123

panic so as not to upset him. I suggested some boys who were in his year who might have seen him, with whom he might even be with now, having wagged an afternoon's school, but I knew, really, that he had gone. A few minutes later, after I had replayed in my mind the way he was in my office, I rang her back to tell her to let the police know.

The thing about the police – they make you feel at fault straight away. Another thing – they never let you know what someone else has said to them. We had no time, as a family, to get our story straight, and even the idea of 'getting your story straight' makes you feel guilty. Naturally, they went to Mandy and Nev first, as the parents who reported him missing, and then came to me, as the last person known to have seen him. I did not know whether to mention the fire incident, but decided not to. It was three weeks ago, they would not find it relevant. Myself, I believed it was relevant.

When they had gone, I spoke to Beth and Jenny. 'Have you two seen Troy lately?' They said they hadn't.

'So when was the last time?' They looked at each other and shrugged their shoulders; synchronised shrugging, as if they had been practising.

'Since the fire?' I thought it was probably the first time the word fire had been said in our house since the day it happened.

They shrugged again. Their faces remained blank. I knew those looks. This is what they mean: It wasn't me. Whatever anyone says, I had nothing to do with it. I don't even know what happened. I wasn't there. And neither, by the way, was she. We were both somewhere else. Together. I don't know where, but it wasn't there. So forget it.

Next day I asked a boy who I knew to be his friend whether Troy had been in school the day before, and the boy admitted that he himself had answered to Troy's name when the register was called. 'She's a new teacher sir,' he said. 'It weren't her fault.' So Troy had laid his plans.

It took nearly a week before the police in London picked him up. Mandy of course was frantic by this time, gaunt and unwashed, the backs of her hands bleeding as she scratched the one with the other. She left Ashley in the care of Nev, took Honey and the car and drove down to Brixton, to the police station. I phoned Nev the next day to see how things had worked out.

'He won't come,' said Nev. 'She says there's nothing she can do to change his mind. He says he'd rather be on the streets down there than up here with us. She's just crying and crying on the phone, she's found a friend to put them up but she can't stay there for long, and he says, Troy does, that if she makes him come back he'll go away again and next time she won't find him. She's at the end of her rope, honestly, and I don't know what to do.'

That turned me against Troy. About the puppy, and Browny, I didn't blame him for that. I was fairly sure, though I didn't want to say it to anyone, that it was Tricky who'd done the deed. But this blackmailing of his mother, that, I thought, was out of order. He had no one else in the world, there was no other relative he could stay with while he got over whatever it was that rankled – the injustice I suppose, and the feeling of being a permanent outsider. Mandy had a life, and two children, with Nev and did not deserve to lose it. Nev did not deserve to lose her. Troy, apparently, made it clear that he would not consent to being any part of a family that included Nev. In effect, Mandy had to choose between her son and her husband, and she moved back to London, taking, naturally, Honey and Ashley with her.

What could Nev do? His livelihood was here. He visited when he could but it caused ructions with Troy and by the time the boy had left home Mandy, lonely I suppose, had taken up with some other man.

16

Jen: Message

It is one week and one and a half days until we break up for the Spring week, two weeks – and a day and a half – until NanaDot's party. The children are sticky and high after running about through lunchtime. The windows are open and air and diesel fumes visit us for the first time this year. My favourite classroom assistant, Seema, is working with me this afternoon and we have the art materials already waiting and organised.

A Year Six boy comes from the office with a note for me. 'Phone call' it has printed at the top of an A6 slip of paper, and tells me the time – 1.13, and the name of the person who took the call – Lauren – and then, in Lauren's round careful writing: 'Please phone home. You know the number?' I put it in my pocket to deal with at the end of the day. If it was urgent they would have said. It could not be Midge, he would be at work like me so it must have been Her, and she can wait. She only wants me to listen to some boring tale.

After school there is a staff meeting to finalise arrangements for the last half term of the year. Sports day, trips, next year's intake, reports for parents and secondary schools, SEN files, examples of work, information re summer schools and activities, Year Six disco. Routine, but there's a lot of it. I am planning to hand in my notice, actually, but no one knows this yet. I'm not sure I even know it myself.

Before I go home I check my staff room pigeonhole. Lauren has left another message. '2.37. Please phone home' and then my sister's mobile number. I collect some things together and then, at five thirty or thereabouts, while standing at the bus stop, I turn on my phone. It tells me instantly that people have been trying to reach me. I call Beth.

'Where are you?' she says. 'Why didn't you answer?'

'Meeting,' I say. 'I'm on my way home now.' The bus comes, full to bursting, I get on, I can hardly hear her for the noise of the engine. 'I'll call you when I get in. I can't hear you properly.'

My phone rings again as soon as I end the call, but I switch it off.

Annie is at home, and cross. She's been on a night shift. 'Your fucking family,' she says. Quaker or not, she swears like a builder. Maybe all doctors do. 'I've been trying to sleep all afternoon and the fucking phone has been going mental.'

'I was at work,' I say. 'What am I supposed to do?'

'For Christ's bleedin sake,' she says, 'ring them. I'm going back to bed. And do not –' she shouts this down the stairs '– fucking disturb.'

The sun is shining on the back step. I sit down and call Beth. And she tells me Sid and Dot are dead.

Midge: Crisis

Nev has always been a good son. Most days he has visited his parents in their bungalow, though the nature of the campsite business is such that he cannot commit to a regular time. This day – Thursday – he had to wait for a Dutch family to pay and leave, and for a delivery from Tesco of groceries for him and for Sid and Dot. Then he had a sandwich and a cup of coffee while he sorted the groceries into two piles, left a note for any customers to say he would be back in an hour – though his visits were often much shorter than that – and set off up the hill with the bag of shopping. Tea, biscuits, eggs, indigestion tablets for Sid, Sennacot for Dot, milk, bread, cheese and a week's worth of microwave meals. He let himself in and picked up a flyer for roof insulation off the doormat.

Sid was dead. He was in his armchair, not slumped, but elongated, as if he was just stretching his limbs before getting out of his chair and going to bed. Dot was on the floor, and still breathing, though Nev said it was not a sound that breathing usually made. There was an empty glass on the mantelpiece and a small neat pile of sick on the tiled hearth. Even in death Dot was careful not to make too much mess. He put her in the recovery position, he told me, and phoned for an ambulance. Everything, he told me, seemed to be happening without his volition. While he was waiting he put the groceries away in the freezer and the fridge and the kitchen cupboard. He noted that the sink contained two cups for washing up, which he thought indicated that they had not had breakfast. The two cups, he thought, were their night time drink, hot milk for Dot and weak coffee for Sid. He thought of washing the cups, just for something to do, but the ambulance responder arrived before he could make up his mind. Then the ambulance, lights and siren going. Then the police.

Nev did not ring his sisters. He called me first. I was at school of course but I had no teaching that afternoon and once I had found someone else to deal with a readmission after exclusion, I spoke to the Head and left. Between school and the bungalow I did not think of Sid or Dot, or Glenys or even Elaine. I thought about Caroline, the Head of my school, how we went back a long way, since she was a brand new teacher, Maths, and I was second in department, Geography, and how I used to help her out by removing one or two boys from her room into mine and how I sat down with her in the empty classroom when she almost failed her probationary year, and how I gave up my free periods to go in and add some muscle to her excellent teaching. Because she was trying to actually teach, not just contain, and it was making the kids' brains hurt. How she knew all about the state of Glenys and when she rose through her department and then into Senior Team she always did what she could to make things easier for me. She has been Head for a few years now. 'Just go Midge,' she said. 'Do what you have to do. We'll cover all your lessons next week, come in if you want to, let me know how things are going.' She meant it, she's a mate. She will retire at the end of next year, and I think I will too.

When I got to the village the ambulances had gone but the police car was still there.

'As soon as they came,' Nev said to me later, 'as soon as there was someone else there, I just folded. I couldn't believe I had called them, I thought they just knew.' He looked at me, wondering. 'How did *you* know?'

'You phoned me at school.'

'Did I?'

'What about Elaine?'

'Can you tell her?' he said. 'It will be better from you. In fact –' he got to his feet '– can you handle it all. I need to get back down the hill.'

The policewoman intervened. I had not really noticed that she was in the room. 'If you could wait a little while,' she said, 'just until we're finished here. It won't be long now.' She smiled at me. 'Mr Midgeley,' she said. 'Remember me?'

I shook my head. Several thousand faces had passed in front of my eyes in the course of forty years in the same school, but I felt bad that I couldn't put a name to this one.

'Emma,' she said. 'I'm sorry for your trouble.'

I didn't know who she was. There were too many Emmas.

'Emma Clark,' she said, but I still didn't know.

Her colleague came out of the bathroom with the contents of the medicine cabinet in a clear plastic bag. He said the ambulance crew had taken the empty bottles with them to the hospital. Then Neville's mobile rang and it was the hospital letting him know that they had not been able, as they put it, to save Mrs Green.

'Thank God,' I thought.

I went with Nev back to the campsite. A cold little breeze had started, as if, I thought whimsically, the elements were trying to blow some order into my head. We put up a notice telling people the site was closed for any new custom, and that for existing campers there would be no services like shower block cleaning for the time being. I made a cup of tea. When I took it to him he was watching the cricket on TV.

'Sorry,' he said. 'I don't know why, I just –' He turned off the set and began to cry, just a little. 'The thing is,' he said, 'the thing is, when they said my mother was dead, I was glad. It was like, it was like –'

'You're all right Nev,' I said. I didn't tell him that I had had the same feeling. Maybe I should have.

'We need to make some calls,' he said.

'Let me do it,' I said.

I called Jenny's school and left a message. I did not expect her to get in touch for a couple of hours. I knew Elaine was out walking with some friends, and I knew neither she nor Glenys should have the news delivered by phone. I phoned Beth.

'Hi Midge,' she said. Her voice was calm and happy, only a little surprised to hear from me at such an hour of the day.

I can't, I was thinking, I can't upset her when she's there on her own, with a baby to look after, she won't cope, she'll fall to pieces, what can I do? Then she said, to someone else, 'Over there, see?' and to me, 'Sorry, we're in the park, I was just telling Dan –'

'Dan's with you?'

'We're celebrating,' she said. 'He's finished, he's handed the damn thing in to his supervisor, we're celebrating with ice cream in the park. I'll send you a picture of Xander's first taste of ice cream, it's hilarious.'

'Beth.'

'What? Are you all right?'

'No we're not really. Beth, I'm glad Dan's with you. I have to tell you that Sid –'

'No,' she said, as if she knew what I was going to say. 'No, he hasn't died, you're not telling me, you're not are you –'

'And Dot.' I saw no reason to drag it out. I heard the deep breath she took. I almost heard her promising herself that she would hold it together until the baby had gone to sleep.

'Have you told Jen?' she asked.

'Not yet.'

'Want me to do it?'

I was relieved. 'Yes, you do it. Your mother doesn't know yet, I'm on my way there now. I'll call you this evening, OK?'

17

Jen: Real

I go home, of course I do. I'm not sure what the rules are about having time off when your grandparents have killed themselves just before their big party, so I leave a message on the school answerphone to say that I am vomiting. School doesn't like that, because the parents kick off if the children catch it off the teachers. I want very much to wake Annie and tell her, and have her feel sorry for me, and feel bad about shouting at me, but I don't quite dare. This is a woman who gave her boyfriend brain damage with one punch. I pack a bag and leave her a note. (Gone home. Death in family. If school rings I am unconscious with D and V.)

I am on the bus before I realise that I haven't shed a tear. That's because it hasn't really happened, I think, foolishly. I think about it, deliberately. My NanaDot has died, my Grampy Sid has died. They are dead. Still nothing.

I phone Midge to tell him I'm on my way. He sounds harassed. Keith is away, he says, he's just going round to make sure Elaine is OK. My mother has been upset, naturally, he says, but she's asleep now.

I call Beth. She sobs and snivels down the phone. She howls. Me – still no tears. After a bit she calms down.

'Isn't Russell with you?' she says.

So I have to tell her. 'We're not together any more. We split up.'

'What happened?'

'He left.'

'Just that?'

'More or less. I'll tell you another day, I promise.' Now that I've told Annie I guess it might be easier to say it all again.

'When though?' Beth was never one to let something lie.

'Ages ago. September.'

'And you never told us!' I'm sure the man next to me flinches at the power of her shout.

'I will. I will. Later. At the moment, Beth, I feel like I've got enough to think about. Did you talk to Mrs?'

'I did. I thought I should and all that. But she was quite calm. I thought she'd be hysterical, but no. Quite sensible, for her, not agitated at all.'

'Medication, do you think?'

'Possible. Midge sounded dreadful. I mean, all right, basically, on top of it, but worn down already. He says Elaine's gone to pieces and Keith's in Bristol, he's worried about Nev, he doesn't know when the Bitch will flip and he said he wishes he could put them all in one room and lock the door, with him on the outside.'

'Poor Midge. Are you coming over?'

'I can't leave the baby. I mean, Dan can manage for a day, and I'll come on Saturday, but he'd be clueless for any longer than that. And I can't come to stay while you're there, there wouldn't be room.'

'You could bring him. We could share, and Xander can come in with us.' (Neither of us has ever questioned the fact that our mother and father have a bedroom each; when we were young we did not know enough to find it strange and even now we think it is normal, because we always have.)

'I'd like to. I'll try. Maybe I'll bring Dan, he can sleep on the settee.'

'Bring a tent, there's room on the campsite.' And we laugh a bit, before she starts crying again.

There is nothing to do at home. Sid and Dot lie in the Medico-Legal Centre – morgue is a better name for it, in my opinion – awaiting autopsy and inquest. Midge and Nev and Elaine have rung everyone they can think of and are now, when I arrive by taxi, sitting at home with my mother drinking tea, all calm and spaced out as if they have been without sleep for three nights at some festival, and nothing is really real.

Midge: Responsibility

I have not now, and never have had, any way of knowing what Glenys is feeling. The lost, long-ago evenings when she cried on my unmade bed, the times she shouted at me for being stupid and crass, the times she threw my stuff – plimsolls and squash racquets and LPs – around my room, or when she clung on to me whimpering, they were all mysteries to me. Was this what women did? I had no sisters and my mother certainly had never behaved in any of those ways. I would sometimes see a small child lying in the doorway of the Co-op, kicking and bawling, and that seemed to me the nearest thing to what Glenys did. Was it, then, that she wanted something she couldn't have? And if so, what was it, and why couldn't she have it?

'The elbow,' said Rick, 'is what you need to give her.'

Pete agreed. 'Give her the elbow mate,' he said. 'There's plenty more out there.'

But if there were I didn't know them. Neither, come to that, did Rick and Pete. I wanted Glenys' body pressed against me, even if I had to go through some anguish beforehand. I liked to hold her and kiss her wet cheeks. When the weather got colder I suggested that we got under the blankets, and gradually I got some of her clothes off her, though actual full-on sex seemed still a remote ambition. But better a body in the hand, and in the bed, than one that was still on some dance floor, that I would have to go through all the delicate trouble of meeting and getting to know. Better a girl that wanted me for something and didn't reject me, myself, even if she rejected many of my advances.

I felt needed. I wanted to help. Elaine laughs at me and says I am the family Rescue Service, and that I rescued first Glenys, and then her, but I believe she is wrong. I did not rescue Glenys from whatever it was that tormented her, I made it worse. And when I needed rescuing it was Elaine who rescued me and I have always known that, and I know that it was me who got the best of that bargain, and that without it both Glenys and I, to say nothing of the girls, would have failed to construct even the poor family life that we have had. We would be blown away by the winds by now, dispersed and forgotten. I do not think I exaggerate.

She cried less, once the children had both been born, but then she did less of everything. Less talking, walking, observing, noticing, buying, eating. More lying down in the day and more prowling the house at night. This was when she and I stopped sleeping together and I took myself into the spare room which had been intended for the baby boy that turned out to be Jennifer.

Dot used to come to our house and try to persuade Glenys to get out of bed and take an interest in the children.

'They're your children,' she said. 'You had them. They're your responsibility.'

'And Midge's,' said Glenys.

'I know that,' said Dot. 'But he's at work all day, you have to pull your weight too.'

'It's just chores,' said Glenys, 'one after the other. Feed me, dress me, play with me. I can't bear it.'

'Of course it's chores,' said Dot. 'What did you think it was going to be? A house doesn't clean itself, children don't bring themselves up.'

Whatever she said made no difference to Glenys.

'She's right,' said Dot to me. 'It *is* all chores. Children *are* a chore, I agree with her.'

'Got to be done,' I said. 'I'm very grateful, you know, for the help we get from you.' It came out rather more formal and stilted than I wanted it to be.

'I like it,' she said. 'Children are a chore, but grandchildren are a gift.'

Yes, Glenys became much less intense and volatile – which was a relief for me and must have been less bad for the children – but she was no more reasonable. The demands and dislikes and impulses now hardened into imperatives and prohibitions that she stated calmly and proceeded with obdurately. She would *not* wash nappies. She would not shop. She *must* sleep as soon as I came home from work. She would not walk down the street with a pram or pushchair. She must finish crocheting this garment before she slept, even though she was not going anywhere to wear it. She would *not* eat meat or fish, and as she had never been fond of vegetables this meant that she, and the girls too for the most part, lived on sandwiches. She *must* dye this whole pile of garments a whole array of different colours, and she must do it *now*.

She was certainly not suited for any kind of outside work, and I don't believe anyway that she ever wanted any, but for sure she hated being a mother.

'Will you stop saying mummy,' she said – this was to me when I said something to one of the children, something like, Tell mummy tea is on the table.

'I don't want to be mummy,' she said. 'Mummies are dead things. Tell them to stop saying it. Find something else to call me.'

And gradually, when she stopped answering to it, they gave up calling her mummy.

Her parents and her sister, and Keith, wondered whether she was bi-polar – manic-depressive as we said then – but if she was, or is, we will never know because the doctors – and we saw some – could not identify anything that fitted well with their diagnostic tables.

Elaine and I could waste whole evenings supposing. Suppose it's a brain tumour? Suppose it's schizophrenia? Depression? Could she be anorexic? Post-natal psychosis? Agoraphobia? Keith, who knew people who knew about such things, thought it was a simple case of personality disorder, and though I didn't know what it meant, it sounded to me like a fair description. Sid kept to the belief that it was Malingering. The capital letter is one he insisted on.

Dot thought it might be hereditary. 'My mother was a bit like that,' she said. 'That's what sent my father into an early grave, having to run the shop and then go home and see to everything there.'

'Was she?' said Elaine. 'I don't remember her like that.'

'Before your time,' said Dot. 'After he died she pulled herself together. And of course by then there was no shop to run, me and your dad were doing it. But it taught me you had to work hard, no good slacking.'

In more recent times we have wondered about M.E. ('Ha,' said Jenny when I suggested it to her. 'That would be right. ME, ME, ME.' But she was always the more unforgiving of the two of them.)

Whatever anyone proposed as a diagnosis was never borne out by an expert investigation. Glenys was always triumphant after one of these fruitless forays into the world of waiting rooms and tests, just as she was always dismissive of our efforts to find solutions. Caroline thought yoga might help, Mandy once suggested Reiki, we offered the ideas of country walks, Tai Chi, swimming, but any sort of physical exercise was received by Glenys with a kind of tolerant dismissive smile. What could we possibly know of her condition, it said. Diets – allergy-free, gluten-free, dairy-free, high protein, high fibre – we've got the books but we've never had the cooperation of the patient. It's only in the past few years that my daughters have revealed to me their mother's chocolate habit. 'It was great,' they said. 'We knew she didn't want you to know, it was a big secret, so whenever she was in the bathroom we used to nip into her room and raid her supplies, and she could never say anything in front of you.'

Where did she get chocolate from, I wondered. They shrugged their shoulders and gave me that pitying look they are so good at. 'Must have gone to the shop while we were all at school.'

One time, Dot came up with the idea that she needed a holiday, and took her, one April, to Spain. 'She cried the whole time,' she reported when she came back. 'I think she must have been missing you and the girls. And the food didn't agree with her, nor the sun. And the flight was torture. I've never seen anyone in such a state.' There were no more holidays.

Now, when her parents have both died on the same day, she seems the most composed of any of us. Nev has the look of someone who emerges from a cinema, baffled and shocked by the difference between what was in front of him a few minutes ago and what is there now. Elaine is pink-eyed and puffy from weeping, the most unattractive I have ever seen her, and I love her at this time more than I ever have before. When Jenny arrives of course it all starts again. I myself am feeling more tired than at any time since our last Ofsted inspection, but it's my job to drag this evening to a close.

'I'll walk you home,' I say to Elaine, and Nev says that he will do it, it's not far out of his road, and I have to let it happen that way. Jenny looks exhausted and goes to bed without a fuss, and that leaves Glenys.

'Are you going to bed?'

'I thought I might stay up for a bit,' she says.

Any encouragement to get some sleep will be likely to increase her obstinacy, so I leave her and go to bed myself, where I lie awake, thinking that I could have been alone with Elaine this evening, while Keith is away, if had not been for her parents deciding it was a good day to die.

18

Midge: Divided

Elaine and I are greatly relieved when we find out that the inquest will be open and shut and that we can go ahead with the funeral on the same day as we were planning to have the party. There is much to do to organise a funeral, but not so much when you have spent the previous four months preparing for a major family party. Some people who would have come to the party are now not going to intrude – the girlfriends of James, Tricky and Ashley, the boyfriends of Honey and Jenny, have decided to leave us undisturbed as a family, either because they are wise and sensitive or because they do not wish to be introduced under such circumstances – which is also pretty wise.

But there are many more people to invite in their place – all Sid and Dot's friends from the village, from the lunch club, from the WI, the bowls club and the pub. Neighbours. People who have moved away but who still send Christmas cards. Elaine and I have gone through Dot's list, which she kept up to date with changes of address and – even more – crossings out of those who have died. When next Christmas comes Sid and Dot will be remembered again as wives say to their husbands, 'Oh no, they both died didn't they? Don't you remember?' Uncle Clifford has had a phone call, but has said that he is not well enough to come. Good, we think, because we don't know him and he would have had to stay the night.

We spend an enjoyable evening, with Nev and some bottles of beer, going through their photographs, choosing a couple for the order of service, and some to put up for everyone to see and remember them by. Sid and Dot on their wedding day, nervously smiling, Sid and Dot and the two little girls, photographed in front of the greengrocer's shop. A studio photo of them both with a baby Nev. On holiday. At some dinner-dance – Dot looking self-conscious in an elaborate hair-do. And so on. We put them in chronological order, ready to pin them round the marquee. (How? Jenny will know.)

We prepare the order of service and on the front – this is Keith's contribution, relayed to us by Elaine – we put 'they were lovely and pleasant in their lives and in their death they were not divided.' This, I suspect, is not something that will be able to be said about me and Glenys, nor yet me and Elaine.

Jen: Interview

In the middle of the night I am lying awake. I have emptied my mind of school. Once miles are put between me and Latisha and Domenika and Connor and James and Mrs Gammy and the three Mohammeds and Tyson and Seema and the lost pair of scissors and the fast diminishing stock of sugar paper and drawing paper – what do they do with it? – and the windows that won't close after I've opened them and the caretaker who blames me, and the pile of memos and instructions in the side pocket of my school bag that I mean to go through – tomorrow, when I'm up to it . . . as I say, once there are miles between me and all that I can think about other things. I wish I didn't. What I find myself thinking about in the midsummer dawn, which is, if you've never seen it, about four o'clock, is Russell.

Russell, in New Zealand. I imagine Russell cavorting with some Antipodean bikini girl on a beach, and sharply say to myself that it's winter over there, he's not in Sidney you know, and all the girls are likely to be taller than him anyway. He's not even taller than me. Stocky, like Midge before he was pudgy. Probably

Russell will end up rather pudgy too. Does this thought make me glad he's out of my life? No, not really.

We were good together. We laughed a lot. I liked him, I liked his family. I imagined having children with him, little square-shouldered children with expressive eyebrows and crooked teeth. Not that I would allow my children to go on having crooked teeth, but that was how I saw them in my dreams. I liked making love with Russell, I liked sleeping with him and waking up with him and even listening to him tell me about cricket. We loved each other. We did.

I cannot sleep in this bed. I'm too hot, I kick the duvet off. I'm too cold, I pull it back over me. The pillow is made of concrete. I force myself to think of my grandparents instead. A few tears would send me to sleep, if I could. Sid and Dot, Sid and Dot. How they loved us. We were always welcome, always fed and talked to and sent home at a proper time. Sid always took things more lightly than she did; he was more likely to laugh at us, Dot to admonish us when we were cheeky. She always worried more, she tried to make things go the way she thought they should go. She said she did not like being made to worry about things, she had gone through life believing that if you looked life in the eye and did what needed to be done that was enough. But she had us to worry about, and our mother who did nothing, and our father who did too much.

And Tricky, she worried about him too. He was an awful teenager. Coming from a 'good home' only seemed to encourage him to be more badly behaved.

He was in the year below me at school, always outside some classroom, having been put out for being loud, insolent, disrupting the lesson with his personal remarks and smartarse answers. Then you'd see him outside Mr Kavanagh's room, waiting to be seen, kicking the wall and frowning. Sometimes you'd look out of a classroom window and see him walking away, either because he'd been sent home to cool off and think about his behaviour, or because he'd decided for himself that school was crap, life was crap and he felt like going home. Beth and I had no sympathy for him, but once I went into my Nana's kitchen and found him there, crying at the table, while she sat beside him with her arm round his shoulder. He wouldn't let anyone else touch him like that.

Dot and Sid. Sid and Dot. Sid's jokes, which were never even funny once we got past seven years old. Nana's hugs. None of us will ever feel one again. Tomorrow we are going to see them again, digitally brought to life.

I remember doing it, Tricky and I, some sort of school project, done at another wretched time of my life. Between the planning of it and actually doing it, I had lost interest. It was a time – the first time in my life – when I had just lost a boyfriend. My first proper serious boyfriend, Julian, had dumped me, after some stupid row that was all my fault. The night before I had hung around with Tricky and his mates on the playing field, drinking vodka and allowing one of the boys to get his hand inside my knickers before I decided against it and went off into the bushes to be sick.

So I didn't want to get up next morning and face anyone, but I knew we couldn't back out after we'd spent time persuading them. Nana, I knew, was not keen to be interviewed. She liked talking about her life, she said, but she didn't see why it had to be filmed. So she only agreed, we knew, because she thought it might give Tricky something positive to focus on. She would do anything if she thought it might help him. They would be expecting us, a little nervous, a little pleased that we would take an interest.

We met at the bungalow.

'Where did you get to last night?' said Tricky, and I pretended I hadn't heard him.

We moved the furniture in their sitting room, so that they would not have their backs to the light. The slightest effort was giving me a blinding headache and I begged some aspirin off Nana. Then we sat them down and Tricky set up his tripod and nudged the two of them into position and I took out my list of questions.

So when tomorrow comes we gather in front of Midge's laptop, solemnly, me, Midge, Mrs and Elaine. Midge hands the DVD to me so that he doesn't have to work a machine, and I put it in and press the button.

And suddenly – without all that preamble you get with proper DVDs – there they are. Barely seventy, so young, so full of life that I think we might all, except me, start synchronised crying – and there am I, with my hair short and wearing a vest top that reveals a very chunky midriff and makes me blush.

Jenny: This is Jennifer Midgeley interviewing Mr and Mrs Green about their life and times. Mr Green, tell me something about your childhood.

Well, I've met Dot the first time when we was children. She lived in the next street to us and went to the same school and she was friendly with my little sister – my little sister Renee. So sometimes they would be in the street, playing and I would go past and see all these little girls with a skipping rope or playing five stones or in a circle singing, and one of them was my Dot, though I didn't know it then. I was older and I was one of the boys you know and I wasn't going to take notice of any little girls.

We was poor in those days, all of us were, not as poor as some, but poor enough. There was no money for extras, you understand. They was different times. No one had a car, that I knew, and now look, everybody's got one. And we didn't have phones or televisions, or microwaves, or any of these gadgets. If you had a pair of shoes you could think yourself lucky because there was kids in my street never had any, and they couldn't go to school, or else they shared with one of their brothers, turn about you know. But my dad was always in work so we were all right, and Dot's family was what we called well off, because her family had this little greengrocer's shop. Her dad went to the veg market every morning – it wasn't far, he went with a barrow, not a car – and brought back all the spuds and what not, and they lived above the shop – well, the kitchen was downstairs, out the back of the shop and then there was two bedrooms upstairs.

And Mrs Green – is that what you remember?

Well, of course I remember playing in the street – that's what we did in those days – it was safe enough you see, not much traffic to be worried about. I don't remember knowing Sid in those days, but I remember his sister, of course I do – she's in Australia now and nobody would have dreamed then that we'd all be living in different places.

And could you tell me about school, and what exams you passed?

Sid: There wasn't exams in those days. You stayed at school till fourteen unless you went to the grammar school, but no one I knew went there. Couldn't afford the uniform most likely. Anyway, school was all right if you behaved yourself but work was better. I went to work starting at fourteen like I say, and I worked in the East End as a warehouseman, and it wasn't a career like you young people have now, it was a job, that paid money that I gave to my mother for my keep and she gave me a few coppers back for pocket money. And a few years later Dot left school, and the war was on by then and she went to work in one of the factories that made uniforms for the soldiers. I used to like to think she made the uniform I wore when I was out in the desert.

And we met again while I was on leave, and once again it was my sister Renee that brought us together, she said, Come on out with me Sid to the pictures, and meet some of my friends. Because I was a shy boy, though you wouldn't think it now, and I never had a girlfriend. And there was a group of us went to the pictures, I can't remember which picture house it was, or what we saw, and when we came out it was dark, the blackout was on of course, and we walked home in the dark and I thought, well, it's now or never – it wasn't really, but that's what I thought – and I said to her, Shall I see you home, and she laughed and said, it was all right, she knew her way home – always independent you know, but I said to her, I might as well come round your way as any other – my sister had other friends to go with, we were quite a crowd – so I went with her, and I said, I've got leave till Sunday, do you go dancing, and that was the beginning of it. I would not have been so brave in daylight I can tell you.

So did you get married in your uniform?

Now then, are you telling me you've never seen our wedding pictures? No, I was out of the army by then, been out a couple of years, and we was engaged but we had nowhere to live, see. Her mum and dad only had these two rooms and her brothers were still at home – or one of them anyway – and at my house, well, I was the oldest and I had a sister and three brothers so there wasn't any spare room there. And I didn't want to start life with Dot in a spare room in someone else's house, I wanted to carry her over the doorstep like you saw in films and have it be our own little place. So we saved up and we waited. And then as luck would have it – though we wouldn't have called it luck at the time – Dot's dad took ill and died, quite sudden, and there was no one to go every morning to the market, no one except Dot, and we carried on like that for a while and then her mum says, I'm too old for this lark, she says, and she took young Clifford – that's your Uncle Cliff, I don't know if you ever met him – and they took themselves off to Wrexham, I think it was, where I think she'd come from years before. And so Dot and me took over the lease and we became shopkeepers. And that's when we got married, and we did have our own little place. We got our start and worked up from there.

So tell me about your wedding.

Oh now, there's not much to tell there. People didn't have these dos then like they do now. We went down the Registry Office, and some family came, and we got on a train and went down to Hastings for the weekend and that was that.

What did Nana wear?

You'll have to ask her that, don't expect me to remember. She looked lovely anyhow, and when we got back from Hastings we went round to the back door of the shop and opened it and – I didn't tell her I was going to – I just swept her off her feet and carried her all the way upstairs. Damn nearly killed me.

Jenny (laughing) So Mrs Green, has he got it right?

Dot: Well, he did carry me upstairs, I was screaming all the way, I thought he would drop me. But as to what I wore to get married in, it was a dress, not a wedding dress but quite a dressy affair that my sister-in-law lent to me. Blue, with a big full skirt – they were just coming in to be fashionable, and I had a little hat with a bit of net at the front and I had some flowers – I got them from the market and we made up the bouquet ourselves – it was some pink roses and a bit of gyp, and we had buttonholes for the guests – they were pink rosebuds. Well, you've seen the photos, but they're black and white aren't they, you don't get a sense of what it was really like.

And then you had your children. Were they born in that house?

Sid: Both the girls was born over the shop. But we had bigger ideas. I never liked the fruit and veg trade anyway, I never wanted to spend my days weighing out carrots. I did like running a shop though, I liked talking to the customers and getting a laugh out of them, but your profit margins on veg, well, you have to squint to see em. And after the war, well at first there wasn't the money around, but gradually things picked up, and I thought we'd branch out a bit. I used to go up Petticoat Lane on a Sunday you know, just to look, and I could see people buying things that they didn't actually need. You know, not essentials and not exactly luxuries, but things they liked the look of, just things that might make your house a bit more homely, a bit more comfortable. So I goes round to the warehouse where I worked before and I bought a few bits and pieces off him and put them for sale in the shop, and you know, people stopped by to look at them though they wasn't much. People came into the shop just to see what there was, even though they didn't buy nothing, not many of them anyway.

What sort of stuff?

Now that's a good question. I can't hardly remember at this distance. But there was brass stuff, that I do recall, because it was an extra job, polishing it up to keep it shiny. And Dot said, What was I doing it for, making extra work and I said if it meant extra customers – because if someone comes in just to look they might still buy a couple of apples more out of politeness than anything.

Dot: I can remember some of what we sold. We had little ornaments and glass dishes, that sort of thing. Brass toasting forks I remember, bits of embroidery. I didn't think it would last, Sid was a bit prone to getting bright ideas but they didn't always come to anything. But this one just seemed to take off.

Sid: Well, I liked it better than the fruit and veg and I asked the bloke at the warehouse – Ern, his name was – where he got it from and he said he went down the docks and got it off the ships what come in. So that's what I did, and there was more profit on it that way because I wasn't paying Ern's mark-up. And I was pleased that I wasn't Mr Green the greengrocer any more because my brothers used to rib me about it something chronic. And it grew from there.

And you ended up going abroad yourself to buy things?

Sid: Later on I did, when we took on a warehouse ourselves. You couldn't have stocked that just out of bits and pieces a few sailors brought across to sell. I needed to find proper suppliers. Yes, by the 1960s we went into the wholesale market, and we did well I must say. There was a lot more money about by then, people wanted something a bit different in their house, not three flying ducks across the wall, something a bit more exotic. Morocco was a good place, Tangiers, Cairo, Beirut – oh in those days Beirut was something to see, beautiful city before they started blowing it to smithereens. I used to go probably twice a year and when the girls were a bit older Dot used to go as well, taking turns like.

You don't seem like someone who would go and haggle in a strange city, Mrs Green.

Sid: You don't know her like I do. She was a good businesswoman, you know, pleasant with people but firm. Not many could put anything over on her. You've never seen it because you've only seen her living here, semi-retired as it were, where she doesn't have to be sharp at business. But when we had the campsite, who do you think did all the books, and all the ordering, and the tax and the insurance, and the forms for the tourist board? We'd have been nowhere if it wasn't for her.

Jenny: And how did you come to move to Yorkshire? And what do you think of it?

Sid: It was Elaine that started that off. She went to York University, as you know, and of course we drove her up and had a look round, and we was impressed I can tell you. And we went and stayed in Whitby for the weekend and it felt very different from home, didn't it Dot?

Dot: Fresh wasn't it? Refreshing. Unspoilt. Countryside as far as you could see as you drove over the moors. I didn't say anything then because we had a home and a business in London, but I thought to myself, We could retire up here.

Sid: So naturally, over the years Elaine was at University, and then Glenys was in Sheffield at the teacher training college, we came up on many occasions and we always liked it. We liked the Yorkshire people too, found them very friendly, straight-talking kind of people. And then both our daughters got married and settled in Sheffield – your Uncle Keith got that really good job here and we could see they might stay here for ever, so –

Dot: And we knew they'd start having children, and I said to Sid, You know, we've made some money and we're not getting any younger, why don't we cash it in and move up North. We asked Neville and he said he didn't mind – he was about fourteen then. And Sid said he would need some sort of occupation to stop him from going barmy, if I was going to be looking after babies all the time –

Sid: And as luck would have it, we were up here visiting Elaine and we came across this old little farmhouse for sale, with a paddock, the land had already been sold, you see, and I said, That'll do and we bought it.

Dot: And I think we've had our happiest years here, seeing you all grow up.

Grampy Sid, you've had really interesting life, and I'm going to come back next week and ask you some more. Before we finish for today, can I just ask you what do you see as your major achievement in your whole life?

Well now, that's the easiest question of the lot. The best thing I ever did was to take your Nana dancing, and get her to marry me, and be good enough for her so that she stayed married to me. That's my big achievement, and what's more I wouldn't change a day of it.

And NanaDot (oh crap, I've forgotten to call you your proper names. Never mind.) Mrs Green, what would you say is the greatest achievement of your life?

Dot: Well, I was very proud of the business we built up. We worked hard, Sid and me, and we got on in the world and did better than our parents did. It's the reason all our children did well at school and got on in life, that's what it's all about.

Sid: And seeing our grandchildren grow up, that's been a pleasure, hasn't it? If there is any sadness you know, it's that Glenys has such bad health –

Dot: – and of course, that Neville's children have gone so far away and that we don't see them so much as we'd like. Such a bad business, and I feel for poor Nev, not being able to live with his children . . .

That's where Tricky stopped the tape. He said it was finished, though I found out afterwards that there was plenty more that could have been used. I suppose Tricky just got bored.

I never did go back and do any more to it, as I meant to, but it doesn't matter now, there's enough. It was never looked at again, as far as I can remember. I took it to school and got a mediocre mark for it, and then forgot about it. It was never edited or made to look professional, though I know Tricky assured me he would do all that, easily. It just stops, with Dot tailing off, so that it is uncertain what she would have said next.

We sit in silence, now, the four of us. Elaine is crying again and I see that Midge – they are sitting on the sofa together – is sort of patting the back of her hand to comfort her, almost holding her hand. Mrs is looking out of the window. I feel very alone.

19

Midge: Black

A few more turns of the earth and we arrive at the day of the funeral. It is what would have been Dot's birthday. It is the day of what would have been the party that Sid so longed for.

We know now that Sid died of heart failure. The autopsy revealed a heart that must have been barely ticking. No wonder the indigestion tablets never worked. Dot, we prefer to believe, distraught at the idea of living on her own without him, swallowed all the pills she could find. This is a better thing to believe than that Dot swallowed the pills and Sid had a heart attack out of anguish, and the effort of trying to stop her. We take comfort in the fact that neither of them had a long, or hardly even a short, widowhood.

Glenys will not wear black. 'They wouldn't have wanted me to,' she said, 'and anyway, I don't have anything black.'

'I can lend you something,' said Elaine, but there was no moving her.

'Who will care? Who will even know who I am?'

'The children,' I said, meaning all of them. 'They might be upset.'

'If I was going to upset the children,' said Glenys, 'I would have done it long ago.' Which I could not even begin to deconstruct in order to argue the point.

It was however Beth, with her mediator's head on, who found an acceptable way out that did not involve either violence, or Glenys missing the funeral altogether.

'Look Midge,' she said to me on the phone, 'when did you ever get her to do what you want? She'll do it her own way won't she, whether you like it or not.'

'I think it shows a lack of respect,' I said.

'Not these days so much,' said Beth. 'Look at it this way. It's summer. It might be hot. Who has got black summer dresses anyway? We'll all be sweltering. Why not ask people to come in pastel colours. That way *She* won't stand out so much. We can say they were Dot's favourite colours.'

'What counts as pastel?' I asked.

'No, look, don't worry about what She wears. Whatever you say, she'll do something to annoy you. Just tell everyone else. I've heard of funerals where everyone has to wear red, or pink. Tell everyone nice colours, as it's to celebrate their lives, and the birthday, and everything.' I could tell she was about to start crying again so I said I would talk to Elaine about it. And Nev of course, I added.

And so it is that as we arrive at the campsite, where the marquee has been put up as it would have been for the party, we resemble a wedding more than a funeral. Glenys, confusingly, has opted for something quite subdued, a dark grey skirt and a pale green, rather see-through blouse, with a couple of clashing scarves round her shoulders and her hair tucked into a pink straw hat. Her purple stockings might be a little startling if you don't know her. Some of the friends and neighbours seem to have been rather put about by the dress code and have compromised by being overwhelmingly beige. I suspect they have all been on the phone to each other over the preceding week, and come up with this as unlikely to offend anyone.

Elaine is wearing dark blue, as she often is. I sat near her at the crematorium, with only Glenys between us, but she did not look at me, maybe because Keith was there on the other side of her. She will have been very near to tears, I know, as she has been ever since it happened, and many of them have soaked into my shirts when we have had the opportunity, but today she has to behave as if properly married and lean on Keith, and borrow his handkerchief. Why don't women ever have their own handkerchiefs?

Nev and Mandy and their children, including Troy, are across the aisle. My girls, and Elaine's boys behind us. Dan has stayed outside with the baby, in the sunshine. I can imagine him – Xander that is – enjoying looking at the piles of flowers that have been delivered for Sid and Dot and are now heaped against the wall outside.

I am the last person away from the crematorium, the last person to park my car at the top of the hill and walk down to Hollin Clough where I can hear the beginnings of louder voices, and even laughter, beginning to emerge from the previous polite hush.

I have been awake since dawn, I have been worrying so much about organisational details of seating and order of service, and Glenys, and how to cope with Xander, and cars and parking, and overnight guests, and vegetarian options, that it is only now, after the drive to the crematorium, after the service and the final rolling away of the two coffins, and the drive back, it is only now that the thought comes to me properly, in its reality, that two people I knew, and loved, who were good to me, and good to everyone they knew, they are gone, and gone for ever. They are not, now, anywhere. They will not answer their phone, or open their door, or look up when someone goes into their room. They are not, and do not, and will not.

I sit down on the garden seat and put my head in my hands. I will just have five minutes to myself, I think, and I sit in amongst the smell of lavender and roses – at least that is what I believe I am smelling – until Nev's old dog Bogey comes trundling up to me and makes me jump by licking my ear.

Jen: Funeral

It was a beautiful day for a funeral, or indeed for anything.

Beth and Dan had arrived the evening before, in time to put Xander to bed. I was relieved to see that her hair had grown to something normal and it was smooth and chic, and though having short hair made her look different, she was restored to what she used to be. Dan resigned himself to the front room sofa and Beth and I shared our old room, and Xander slept with us in his travel cot, and did not seem in the least disturbed by the way we talked for much of the night. It was early June. The sky was clear and it hardly got dark at all. In the almost-dark of the closed curtains I told Beth about Russell and his getaway. I told her, even, that I had avoided her out of a sort of shame that I had been abandoned, and a sort of jealousy that she had the things – husband, house, baby – that I wanted to have too.

'It's not always so wonderful,' she said.

'I suppose.'

'This,' she said, 'is going to sound really cheesy but I mean it. I missed you. That day you came to see me and took over for an afternoon, that was so nice, to know that you could do that for me. It was the beginning of recovery from whatever I had.'

'I didn't do anything,' I said. 'It was Midge and Elaine who sorted things out.'

'No,' she said, 'it was seeing you and the look on your face – you looking so shocked at the state I was in – that's what made me realise I have to let someone help me. So when Midge turned up I let them help. I wouldn't have otherwise. Dan had already tried, believe me.'

'I missed you too,' I said. I could not, even now, tell her that the image of her, sitting there, growing her baby, smug as a hen on a nest, had filled me with such anger and revulsion that I had thrown in the bin, unopened, the Christmas present she sent me and had never looked at the pictures of the newborn Xander that she posted.

We talked about Troy, we wondered if he would come and what we would think of him.

'Should we tell him?'

Beth did not have to ask what I was talking about. 'We probably *should* –'

'You mean morally speaking?'

'But it could do more harm than good. Why would we tell him? Would it benefit him? Or just make us feel better?'

'We could say sorry.'

'We could. We could explain the circumstances and he might accept it. He might forgive us. But what about all the other people involved? What about Mandy and Nev? Their marriage? What about Tricky?'

'He got away with it.'

'Oh, at the time, I grant you that. But do you think it did him good, having that on his conscience? I don't mean killing the dog, though that would be bad enough, but being the cause of breaking up Nev's family. And what about Elaine and Keith? Finding out now that it's been a lie all along.'

'And James,' I said.

'Oh he knows,' said Beth, so firmly that I believed her.

'How do you know?'

'I know,' she said.

I had still not told her, or anyone, that on the day before we broke for half-term I had gone to my head teacher and handed in my notice. Why did I do this? I thought I would move back to Yorkshire. I was confident that with my good references and good experience I could get a job by September. And I did not tell her – I never told anyone – about Russell's invitation to New Zealand. I'll tell her tomorrow, I thought.

'I suppose we should go to sleep,' I said, after a silence.

'I think so,' she said. 'Tomorrow will be a long day.'

There was something nice about it though. Something almost festive. Quite a few people came to Elaine's house beforehand and there were greetings and introductions, and cups of tea for those who had come a long way. There was even chatter, subdued chatter. No one called out or laughed, and even that quiet amount of conversation fell silent when the undertaker's cars arrived to take us to the crematorium. It was my first funeral. Sitting in the big black car with my mother and her brother and sister, and Beth, proceeding through streets I knew well, past ordinary people, I was detached from reality, as if it was me that had died and was looking down on an old life that no longer included me.

We were silent in the car. It felt forbidden to speak. Elaine put her hand over my mother's but I didn't think Mrs noticed. Beth stared ahead, Nev looked at his hands, I turned my head to look out of the darkened window. I believe that now, whenever I see a funeral car go past I will know that the people inside are inhabiting another place, and if I stare, they won't mind, or even notice.

At the crematorium even more people were waiting. As the cars set down their people, wives rejoined husbands. Yes I really noticed that. Beth went to Dan, who had Xander in his arms. Elaine went to Keith, Mrs went to Midge. The occasion seemed to demand that you held on to and took comfort from the obvious. I looked for someone I could hold on to. I did not expect Russell to have turned up – though I had, one evening when I was distraught, informed him by email of my loss. I looked for James and Tricky, and I found them, but they were standing with their parents, talking together and something held me back from interrupting them. I looked for Nev and he was talking to a woman who had her back to me. Then a voice spoke to me.

'Jenny?' It was Troy. Troy who I caught that glimpse of as he ran out of his front door, Troy who called me that day after the park as I sat on the back step. Troy who I had done wrong to. The very beginnings of tears came into my eyes but I did not know why.

'I'm sorry,' he said. 'I was very sorry to hear about –'

How many times had I heard that over the past two weeks? I smiled, I think.

'They were very good to me,' he said. 'They were the only grandparents I ever had and they were always good to me.' He was wearing a dark suit that he might have borrowed, or maybe he had lost weight since he wore it last. His face had hardened over the years, the jaw becoming heavier and the mouth thinner. His hair – no cap today of course – could be seen to be thinning on top. His eyes were as I remember them.

'It was good of you to come,' I said. 'NanaDot would be really pleased.'

'She was lovely to me,' he said again. He made as if to move away but I stopped him.

'Would you mind,' I said, 'if I kind of stand next to you. Everyone seems to be with someone and I need –' I couldn't say what I needed, but he nodded, and gave me a small smile, and we stood together, without talking, until we were called in to the service.

20

Midge: Besieged

Nev is already besieged by a muster of old ladies, like a cloud. Their white heads bob and they wave the hands that are not holding them up on sticks. A much smaller group of old men have found chairs and are gratefully, if painfully, getting settled. These are Nev's neighbours, his parents' friends and contemporaries, and they all want to tell him how wonderful Sid and Dot were, and how sorry they are, and is there anything they can do, just as they have been telling him for the previous two weeks. I have never had a great deal to do with any of the people of the village, and this subset of old ones, not usually seen around outside the hours of daylight, will leave me alone I believe. But one of the ladies – tall and gaunt but self-supporting – detaches herself from the crowd and comes over to me.

'Oh Mr –'

'Is it Doreen?' I say. This stops her talking while she thinks about it. 'Very good of you to come,' I say. 'Can I get you a cup of tea?'

'That would be lovely,' she agrees, and I set off to the place where Elaine is marshalling a couple of Year Twelve girls we have drafted in to help. Keith is nearby. I acquire a cup of tea and a piece of cake and take them for Doreen, who proves difficult to find. I spy her at last talking to Glenys, Glenys looking animated and engaged in a way she never is with me. I put the tea down next to the old lady and prepare to slope away but she grabs me with a skinny hand.

'You are an angel in disguise,' she confides. 'This lady – 'waving an arm at Glenys and striking her lightly on the nose '– has been telling me such interesting things about – about –'

'About Dot,' says Glenys firmly. 'She was my mother.'

'Well, I know *that*, of course,' says Doreen. 'I was a mother too, once.' She still has hold of my sleeve. 'But what I want to ask you,' she goes on, 'you being the father of course, you'll know, I wanted to ask you, when shall we see the happy couple?' I recall that Dot has been concerned lately for Doreen. If there was someone close by whose opinion I cared about I might try to answer her, but as it is I smile and nod in what might also be a demented way and leave her to Glenys.

Nev is still dealing with his deputation but I notice that Mandy has joined him. It was good of her to come, I think, all the way from South London, driving in her old bucket of a car round the North Circular (where I last went in 1975 and would never dare drive now) picking up her children on the way and toiling up the post-work M1 on a warm Friday afternoon. They stayed at Nev's last night and I am curious about how that went, although it is also true that they have not been strangers to each other. Nev went quite often – or as often as he could – to see his children when they were small, and they visited him here all through their teens. Just Troy, so I heard, would not see him, although he would see Sid and Dot when they visited. I know he's here, I would like to talk to him, but I wonder if he will be prepared to talk to me. I was, after all, the last person he spoke to in Sheffield. You could make a case for saying I was the one who finally drove him away.

Mandy sees me and leaves Nev to come over to me. She shakes my hand – she was never a kisser, as I recall. Her hand in mine is thin and dry and cool.

'How are you?' she says.

'Oh, you know –. How are *you*?'

'Not bad,' she says. 'It's strange to be back here, after so long.'

'Of course.' With an effort I say something about Honey and Ashley – good to see them, glad they could come, something like that. Then I can't think of anything to say and I wander off. I don't know if I did this properly or not.

I come upon my son-in-law Dan, a skinny, balding, intense young man, standing by the door of the marquee, mechanically rocking the pushchair in which they hope Xander will soon be asleep. A small wispy woman I have never seen before is doing her best to prevent sleep, waving her hands and jiggling the line-up of soft toys which no pram these days is without. 'What did you say his name is, again?' she says. Dan sighs.

Caroline appears at my elbow. 'Midge. How are you?'

'Not so bad now it's underway. Might be able to sleep tonight.'

She smiles her big new moon smile. Hers is not a face that can remain serious for long.

'It's not all on your shoulders,' she says. 'Although – wait a minute – I think I may have told you that before.' Impulsively – I think it must be impulsive – she reaches for me and hugs me. Her nose is level with the top of my head, her bosom is so big – and solid – that she can hardly get her arms round both it and me, but she fairly takes the breath out of me.

'Look after yourself, Midge,' she says, on my release. 'It's going to be a long day. I have to go now.' And with a last painful squeeze of the arm – my arm – she goes. Back to work, back to some unnecessary school improvement plan or set of targets, which, I think, I will never take seriously again, for look where it all ends. Death and forgetting.

Jen: Promise

When we arrived at the campsite the sun was high in the sky. Nev had cut the grass and it smelled sweet and fresh. The first person I wanted to see was Tricky, and there he was and he and I clung to each other for a moment or two and then drew back, both laughing, though he was crying as well, just a little.

He turned away to hug Beth, and then back to me. 'So good to see you,' he said.

'Oh Trix,' I said, 'isn't it awful.'

Then James came up and put an arm round my shoulder and kissed my cheek. His other arm was round Beth.

'Well here we are,' he said. 'All together again.'

Then Dan came along with Xander and the talk turned to babies and pregnancies. When it showed no signs of moving on I detached myself and wandered away.

I stopped to speak to Nev as he stood with a woman I did not recognise.

'You remember Mandy?' he said.

I had not recognised her, but as I looked she fell into place. Still tall and skinny, armoured with make-up and equipped with a hard stare.

'You Beth or Jenny?'

'Jenny,' I said.

Nev was looking at her as if I wasn't even there. I tried to think of something to say. Then I saw James waving at me. 'Oh,' I said, 'James wants me.'

'James?' said Mandy sharply and turned to look in his direction.

'My cousin,' I said. 'You remember James?'

'Yes I do,' she said, and I left her with Nev, feeling as if I was escaping from something.

I met Troy coming from the buffet with a plate of food.

'Have some,' he said, and I took a mushroom vol-au-vent. Dot always loved vol-au-vents.

Honey and Ashley joined us.

'Nice shoes,' said Honey to me. They were new. They were the first thing I had bought since Russell left and they were defiantly high, making me taller than he was. Just right though for standing next to Troy. We had a nice time talking about London, and work, and places to go, and where we lived. Ashley told us about his girlfriend, whose father was Pakistani and was making difficulties out of their idea of setting up home together before being actually married.

'Then get married, bro,' said Troy. 'Do what it takes.'

'Does she want to?' I said.

'We're thinking about it,' said Ashley. He was so much like Nev in so many ways. He looked like him, solid and ginger, and behaved like him, thoughtful and whatever is the opposite of impulsive.

The three of them seemed to me to be good together. Troy played elder brother, they both pretended to patronise Honey just the tiniest bit, and she pretended not to patronise them.

I asked Troy more questions about his work. He began to tell me about Young Offenders' Institutions. Ashley and Honey drifted off. I was dazzled by Troy, and by the interest he was taking in me and I really didn't take a lot of notice of whatever else that was going on. I knew that in a quiet corner of the marquee the DVD of Sid and Dot was playing and that people were stopping in front of it and commenting, but I didn't go over to hear what they were saying, and I didn't want to watch it again myself. I still had not shed tears, in spite of the magnitude of it all, and by now I was frightened of the very idea of crying. It had become a matter of honour, somehow, to remain in control, but I wasn't about to test myself too far.

I could see James and Tricky and Beth talking together and I kept thinking I must go and join them, but then Troy and I would start another topic of conversation and I would put it off. I knew that Mrs was trapped talking to Doreen and I thought Midge or Elaine might go and rescue her, but *I* wasn't going to do it, and as time went on it seemed, neither were they.

When I thought about it afterwards I realised that Sid and Dot had been dispatched. The little curtain had been drawn back and the coffins had rumbled through on this rather banal conveyor belt and then the curtain closed and that was that. We had finished with the sad part, we had done the hymns and prayers, we had stood with eyes streaming and experienced the loss of two people who were much loved. Then we were back in the sunshine and it was time to eat and drink and catch up with people and talk about ourselves. This must be how funerals are.

'Did you see me that day I knocked on your door?' I said. 'Did you know it was me?'

He looked bewildered.

'Back in February. Beth told me I had to go and find you and invite you to the party. And I schlepped all across London and knocked on your door and you came tearing out and hurtled down the street, and that was that. I went home again.'

'No memory of that at all,' he said.

'So I asked Honey to get hold of you.'

'You should have done that to begin with,' he said.

There was no one in the world more different from Russell than Troy. Russell was straightforward and his interests were technical. He wouldn't go to an art exhibition, or read a novel. His memory of school was that it was OK but blighted by poetry. He was short and quick in his movements, abrupt in his speech. He was polite though, genuinely considerate to anyone he was with, and I'd always loved him for it, but, talking to

Troy, watching him ignore people he didn't want to speak to (Uncle Keith, Tricky) I reclassified Russell's behaviour as creepy, ingratiating, inauthentic.

Troy was definitely cooler than Russell. His suit was awful but he wore it with an air that said, This isn't my suit, I'm only wearing it for this occasion to be respectful. It's just the best I can do.

He was easy to talk to. He looked into my eyes as he talked and appeared to listen closely to what I said. It felt as if there was no one else within earshot, although nothing was being said that they should not have heard. It felt to me as if I had made a new friend, with all the possible promise of something more.

He said, 'What nice brown eyes you have.' He said, 'Do you like to be called Jen, or Jenny?'

Troy seemed to me to be really rather perfect.

21

Midge: Tip

It is a party. I imagine that this sort of dressing – dark suits and pale dresses and neat jackets, are what would characterise a Buckingham Palace garden party, not that I would be interested, or know anyone who has ever been to one. There are flowers on the tables, as there would have been for Dot's birthday, and they seem more festive than funereal.

The day is so warm and still that people are taking chairs on to the field and sitting outside. Even Glenys is out in the sun. I can see that she is talking too much and too intensely, and that people are listening to her politely and then finding a reason to get away from her. I see her looking eagerly around for new people to talk to.

It is rather a reassuring thought, surprisingly, that nothing now stands between us and the old grim reaper. If things go according to plan, after mopping up old Doreen and the bowling club, he'll come for me and Keith and Elaine and Glenys, and some years later, Nev and Mandy. I feel comfortably sad at the neatness and inevitability of it all, and yearn, briefly, for the peace that would come with it.

I want to be close to Elaine. There is no reason why I should not, no one would find it odd if I went to stand beside her and spoke to her; they might even find it odd if I do not. But Elaine is behaving in a strange way. The little eye-meetings we usually manage to have, just to make contact and reassure each other, and remind the other that after this is over there will be time to meet and be alone, are missing. Today her eyes are avoiding mine. I know Keith is with her, but I have the idea that it is she who is sticking close to him, rather than the other way round. I know she has been extraordinarily stricken by the deaths of her parents, but then, if she doesn't come to me for some comfort today, what am I for?

She is on the far side of the field now, standing with Keith as he talks to the vicar. I myself have never spoken to the vicar, Madeline Manthorpe, and I can't imagine how such a conversation would go, but I know well that it is right up Keith's street. It might be about local good works, or food banks, or committees; it might be gossip about other vicars, or the bishop; it could well be about money – for the church roof, or whatever it is they are always moaning about, or for the setting up of some noble cause or other. Whatever it is, I would not be able to join in.

I walk up to where James and Patrick are standing and James turns his back and walks away. What has happened? Does he know? Patrick stays and talks to me, plausibly friendly as ever. Does *he* know?

'Uncle Midge.' What is this 'uncle'? No one else uses it; is it some code for what he knows but cannot say, or is it some ironic use whose meaning I don't understand?

'Patrick. How are you doing?'

'I think it went well,' he says.

'I meant, you. How are *you* doing?'

He chooses to misunderstand me again. 'Well, obviously, it's a shame isn't it. But we've given them a good send-off.'

As always, my heart dies inside me at his evasions and politeness. He is a better actor now than he was at the age of ten, but still an actor.

'When are we going to meet –?' I find I have forgotten her name, or maybe don't want to say it for fear of getting it wrong.

'Aoife? Well she would have come today, but Mum said probably better not. She's fine.'

'And the baby?'

'Fine too. All going well.'

'When –?' Though I know of course.

'August.'

'Not that long.'

'I suppose it's not.'

'Have you met Xander?'

'Certainly have. Fine baby. You must be very pleased. Doing well, I gather.'

I cannot stand any more of this. I walk away from him and look around for something else to attend to. I see Jenny walking towards Beth and the baby, I see Glenys sitting on a fold up chair with her eyes closed, I see James talking to his father, still in a group with Elaine and the vicar.

Suddenly Troy is in front of me. 'Mr Midgeley,' he says.

I look at him, bewildered.

'It's Troy,' he says.

'Yes, yes, I know. How are you?'

'Good,' he says. 'And yourself?'

'Fine,' I say.

I see the green of the hedge round the field, still fresh, not yet ready to tip into dusty midsummerness, the sky its proper heavenly blue, a couple of swallows swooping through the air. I want to shout and tell everyone to go home. The party's over, I want to say, without having the least idea why I feeling this way. I turn away from Troy and walk towards the gate. Everyone may or may not go home, everyone can do what they like. I can do what I like, and I do.

Jen: Kingfisher

Elaine came over to Troy and me.

'I'm glad you could come,' she said to Troy. 'My parents would have appreciated it. They always spoke well of you.'

Troy made his little speech about how good they had been to him.

Then she said, 'I must go and find my husband.' And Troy said, 'He's gone home, I spoke to him a short while ago, and then I saw him go out of the gate. He wasn't looking too great, as a matter of fact, as if the day had really got to him.'

Elaine looked puzzled, and so did I because I could see Uncle Keith in plain view. Then she said, 'Oh look, he's over there, with Nev, I'd better go and see if he's all right.' And she went off.

'What was all that about?' I said. 'There's Keith right in front of you, why tell her he'd gone home?'

He looked and then said, 'I must have got confused. I thought she was Mr Midgeley's wife.'

'But that would make her my mother,' I said, and he just shrugged and said, 'Why don't we go and take a look at the old Forest.'

Inside the wood, the day felt quite different. There was a loud noise of birds, the light broken by the movement of leaves, there was green and there was golden, and the black of the tree trunks against the light. Bramble stems from last year, beige and bristly, made our progress difficult and this year's brambles were stretching out too, full of vigour. Nobody came here any more, no children trampled down the undergrowth or broke branches of the trees, or bent them down to make dens.

'I loved it in here,' said Troy.

'So did I.'

'I used to come here at night sometimes,' he said. 'On my own. I bet you didn't know that did you.'

'But did you ever come here when it was filled with snow?'

'Of course I did.' We were quiet for a minute and then he said, 'Did you mind, you and the others, when I came here?'

'I don't think so.' I didn't want to shut him down but this conversation was going down a path that might end in a sheer drop. I had to be careful. 'We were used to sharing. One more shouldn't make a difference.'

'But did it?'

'What?'

'Make a difference?'

'Well. It was different of course. A new member always changes something. And it was different for each of us in a different way I suppose.'

'But for you?'

'It was – well – quite exciting. You were from the big city, weren't you. We'd never even been to London. James and Tricky had, but not me and Beth.'

'Your mum, I suppose,' he said, 'must have been a bit – limiting.'

'You could say that.'

'Must have made you quite angry.'

I'm telling myself, don't fall for it Jen, don't be led on, keep your dignity, no complaining, and with that thought still in mind here I go, offering him my whole blighted childhood on a plate.

'I don't know what would have become of us if NanaDot hadn't been there to pick up the pieces. If we were ill and off school we had to go there – she used to come in the car and take us, I remember sitting on the back seat wrapped in a duvet and being sick on it. *She* – I mean my mother – never even got out of bed.'

'She was ill?'

'She's not ill, she's never been ill. When she wants to she can get up and go out. Look at her today, there's nothing wrong with her. But I bet she's in bed all next week and someone – Elaine probably – will be running round bringing her cups of herb tea. She's lazy, that's all she is. No one else in our family has that attitude. Say what you like about us, we put in a shift, we are grafters every one of us from Grampy onwards, I bet even

172

Xander, before he can even sit up is working his mini socks off holding his toes or shaking that rattle. *She* is a different crate of goods altogether.'

'You're funny,' he said.

'It doesn't feel funny to me. Or to Beth, and it was worse for her because she was the oldest, she had the responsibility of me as well as looking after herself.'

'But your dad –'

'Oh I won't say a word against Midge. He's always done everything he can. He's a hero. But, you know, he was at work every day, he had to leave well before we did, he got us out of bed and then it was up to us to get our breakfast, and he used to tell us to take something up to Her, but we didn't, and after school we sometimes went down to play at the campsite, but sometimes we had to go straight home and then we had to wash up and hoover and put the washing in the machine.'

'Lots of children live lives like that,' he said.

'I know they do,' I said. 'I have them in my class. But most of them have mothers who care about them, as well as they can. *She* never was interested in us. Not the slightest little bit. And she said so, she couldn't even pretend to take an interest. So Midge had to come to all our school things, and Brownies, and things like that, and when we got home she didn't even want to know.'

'You never call him dad.'

'We never called them dad and mum. I don't know why. Everyone calls him Midge –'

'He doesn't like it.'

'How do you know?'

'Look at his face. Every time.'

'I didn't know. Do you mean *every* time, or only when Beth and I do it?'

'I think,' he said, 'every time. What *is* his name anyway?'

'Frank. I can't imagine him as a Frank. Though I have heard Elaine call him that.'

'Ah,' said Troy. 'Elaine. Anyway, go on, I've interrupted you. You call him Midge, what did you call your mother?'

'Her. We had different names for her. When we were little we started calling her the Worst Witch – that's a book you know – and then we thought we'd be really smart and call her Bitch, but we grew out of that. We wouldn't say it in front of Midge. Mostly, to her face, we call her Mrs. If we are talking about her to our grandparents, or a teacher, we will say my mother. What we never do is call her mum.'

'If I had had a dad,' he said, 'I would have liked to call him dad.'

'Sure.'

We were at the edge of the cliff by now, where the Tarzan swing used to be.

'Did you ever see a kingfisher here?' I said.

'I've never seen one in my life.'

'We did, Beth and me, I mean, a few times, but not so often that we got used to it. It was always special.'

'So,' he said. 'You had a crap childhood but you saw a kingfisher. I had a mother who gave up everything she had for me, but I've never seen a kingfisher. Swings and roundabouts.'

'Look,' I said. 'Don't move.' Downstream, on a branch the kingfisher sat, bright and still and always smaller than you think. We waited, and it shifted, and flew past us, unfeasibly luminous, russet and turquoise.

'There,' I said. 'Now you've seen one too.'

'Halcyon days,' he said.

As we came out of the Forest Beth came up to us, carrying the baby.

'I've been looking for you,' she said. 'Where have you been?'

'Just walking,' I said. I turned to Troy but he had wandered off.

'We're going back to the house,' said Beth. 'Then we're setting off home. I'm shattered, aren't you.'

'Yes,' I said, and I was, but it was overlaid by the frissons of mild flirting so I wasn't feeling it too much just yet. I took Xander out of her arms – he didn't seem to mind at all – and he grabbed a handful of hair and earring.

'Another good reason for having short hair,' said Beth. 'You'll find out one day, long hair and small babies are a bad combination.'

'I hear your words of wisdom, O bossy big sister,' I said, and we gave each other a hug, like old times and I let her take Xander back and said I would call her the next day. I watched her rounding up Dan, and the pram, and waving goodbye to people, and going out of the gate and up the hill, and I felt that we were all right again.

22

Midge: Sorry

It is all over. Glenys is back in bed. Beth and her little family have gone back to Leeds in time for Xander to go to bed as per the routine. Elaine and Keith are having another quiet evening at home with their sons and I should be pleased for them, but I'm not, I'm envious of them.

I sit in the darkening room and remember the day. I worry about Elaine and what her behaviour might have meant. I want very much to speak to her. Little scenes from the day replay across my brain.

Keith giving the eulogy. 'One of nature's gentlemen,' he said of Sid. I suppose I know what he meant. 'One of nature's Quakers,' he said of Dot. I thought he was wrong though I suppose he should know, being some sort of Quaker himself, the manufactured sort. But I should not cavil; he did a good job, a professional job, that sounded simple and sincere and produced a smile and some tears as it was intended to do.

James looking thinner than he used to be, his face and neck and hands red from the weather, putting his arm round Jenny and then, the same gesture towards Beth. Patrick giving them both big theatrical hugs, playing the part of a person who makes a living playing parts.

Elaine as she approached the buffet, Keith beside her, people getting out of her way as if she was special. I saw her meet Mandy coming the other way, carrying a plate of food and talking to Ashley. I saw Elaine stop, and say something; I could not see but I knew she would be smiling in a friendly sort of way. I saw Mandy cut her dead. I think that's the right expression. A sharp turn of the head, a sharp turn of the shoulder. Ashley glanced back at them – naturally he knew Elaine quite well, from his childhood visits – but followed his mother, still talking.

It took me a minute or two to work out who Mandy was when I saw her at the service. Her style has changed since I saw her last. She is a thin, worn out looking woman with frail wrinkled skin and very bright anxious eyes. She was civil enough to me, as far as I was able to take notice. I hope I was pleasant to her in return. I always had a lot of time, as they say, for Mandy.

Jenny comes into the house and switches on the light, startling me out of my thoughts.

'Sorry Midge,' she says, 'I didn't know you were here.'

'Where else would I be?'

'Sorry.'

'I'm sorry. I didn't mean to sound bad tempered. It's really nice to see you actually. I was feeling a bit – you know.'

'Sure,' she said.

'Do you want something to eat? Cup of tea?'

'Actually Midge, I'm not stopping. I'm going back to London tonight.'

'By bus?'

'No, actually, with Ashley. At least, Ashley's driving.'

'Didn't he come up in Mandy's car?'

'That's right he did, they all did, but Mandy's not going back today, didn't you know.'

'How would I know?' I know I sound peevish again.

'Someone could have said,' she says. 'I don't know who has said what to who, do I? Anyway, though, hasn't Mandy changed? I hardly recognised her. Nice haircut though, suits her, being blonde. Did you talk to –?'

'Why are you going?' I say. 'It's getting late, you've got a bus ticket for tomorrow, why go now?'

'I really do need to get some work done before Monday,' she says.

'And Russell will be missing you, I suppose,' I say.

'Probably,' she says.

I contemplate the evening in front of me. 'I suppose I could go and help Nev clear up.'

'I don't know if you'd be welcome,' she says, laughing. 'I think Nev and Mandy would like to be left alone.'

Yes, as Jenny comes down the stairs with her case, looking eager to get back to her boyfriend, and hugs me, and goes out of the door – left alone, that's what Nev and Mandy want to be, but they're not left alone are they, they're left together. The one that's left alone is me.

There are things I could do. A pile of policy documents to check and update. A pile of washing dumped in front of the machine. The girls' beds to strip, now that they're gone. The visible signs of Dan's overnight stay on the sofa to remove from the room. I could walk round the garden in the twilight and refresh my soul if not with leaves and flowers, at least with green weeds and an out of control lawn. I could read a book and play some music, and construct myself a nice salad to offset the buffet lunch that I ate too much of. Of course, and this will surprise nobody, I drink beer and eat peanuts, and spend the evening with the curtains closed against the sunset, sitting on Dan's sleeping bag, watching television. I wake at two twenty in the morning with the imprint of the zip in my face, go to bed and fail to go to sleep again until the moment just before the birds start up again and wake me up. Life is apparently back to normal.

Jen: Tired

Ashley drove us back to London, and at first Troy sat in the front passenger seat. We stopped at Leicester Forest East for petrol and bottles of water and he said to Honey, 'You go in the front. You were in the back on the way up.' He smiled at me as he slid in beside me and asked Honey to move her seat forward to accommodate his long legs. I smiled at him, possibly in a nervous way. It was five years since I started going out with Russell, nine months since he dumped me; I was not sure if I was ready for something happening, whatever it might be, and I was very not sure if I would know how to respond.

Honey fiddled with the radio and they complained about the age of their mother's car and its lack of an iPod socket. She scrabbled through the glove compartment and found a couple of CDs, which were not to anyone's taste, but we played them anyway. One was the Travelling Wilburys, the other I didn't recognise and couldn't remember afterwards.

'Did I tell you,' said Troy, leaning forwards to speak in Honey's ear, 'that we saw a kingfisher?'

'What?'

'We saw a kingfisher. Jen and me. In the Forest.'

'The Forest?'

Ashley turned the music up. 'If we're going to listen to this,' he shouted, 'it might as well be loud.'

Troy leaned back in his seat next to me. 'Guess I'll have to talk to you then. In sign language.'

But I was too tired to play any games. The motorway embankments flashed past, the blue signs kept appearing to tell us where we were going but never where we actually were, Honey kept her eyes on her phone, Ashley kept his on the road. I wanted very much to talk to Troy, to *be* with him, but I was too tired. Heat, and emotion, and loud music, and a lack of sleep the night before . . . something changed in the motion of the car and when I opened my eyes we seemed to be travelling sideways. But it was just that we had left the M1 and were going round a roundabout. My head was on Troy's shoulder, half of my hair was falling in my face, the music had gone. Honey was asleep and Ashley still drove, in silence, like a robot.

'All right?' said Troy to me. He had taken his shoes off and I could smell his socks. It seemed a long time since I had smelled a man's whiffy socks.

'Fine.' I loosened my hair completely and did it up again in a simple pony.

'I like it loose,' he said. Typical man, I thought.

They dropped me off at Annie's house. I offered them tea, but half-heartedly because really all I wanted was to go to bed. No, they wouldn't, thanks, they'd get off home, dropping Troy at some starting point for the trek back to Catford.

'You've got my number,' he said to me, as I got out of the car. 'And I've got yours.'

'Thank you,' I said, though I could not have said what I was thanking him for.

It was past midnight and Annie was just on her way to bed.

'I'm so sorry,' she said. 'I've been meaning to say sorry for shouting at you that time. I feel awful about it.'

'Forget it,' I said. Truly I had forgotten it myself.

23

Midge: Upset

'It was all quite calm,' says Elaine. 'I mean, no shouting, no unpleasantness. I don't mean I *was* calm. Inside.'

It is Monday evening. We have met at the campsite, to see Nev and remove some crockery that Elaine lent for the party. Funeral I should say. Mandy is still there with Nev. There is an air about them of something being resolved, though they have not said what the situation is or will be.

We are sitting now in Elaine's car, further along the road, looking out over the edge towards the Pennine hills, grey against a flaring sky, and she is telling me, or I believe she is, that we have a crisis.

'I didn't mean,' she says,' to provoke all this.' I still don't know what she is talking about. 'He just made some remark –'

'James did?' This had happened the evening before the funeral.

'At the dinner table. I can't even remember properly what it was but it implied something about us. I said that you and I had put in a lot of work getting everything organised and he said something like, It's not like you need an excuse to see him. Meaning you.'

'Doesn't sound –'

'It was the way he said it,' she says. 'As if he meant something. So I asked him.'

'Keith was there?'

'When he said it. But I waited till James and I were in the kitchen and Keith was on the phone to someone, and I just asked him. I said, What did you mean? and he knew straight away what I was talking about and he said, You and Midge, I know all about it.'

Thirty-something years, I think.

'Say something,' she says.

'Then what?' I don't look at her. I look to the west where the sky is red. There are probably words for the particular colours I can see but I don't know them.

She hesitates. 'It all went a bit wrong. I'm sorry, I don't know why I did this – to distract him I suppose from what he was talking about. I told him what Jenny said to you, that she saw what happened at the Fire.'

Why do that? I thought, but didn't say it.

She knew what I was thinking. 'I suppose I was pointing out something to him. Something like, I'm not the only one who has kept secrets. But it only seemed to make things worse.'

'What has he said? What is he going to say?'

'I don't know. I asked him not to say anything to Patrick. I sat up with him after Keith had gone to bed and we talked about it all.'

'You could do that?' It seems outrageous to me, outlandish, to talk to your children about your adultery. Does this mean that I will have to do it?

'He was upset,' she says. 'But he's known for a long time, so he says. Since he was a student.'

'How did he find out?'

'Just by observing, that's what he said. He observed me and Keith together and he observed you and me.'

'We've always been careful,' I say.

She thinks for a moment, then says, 'We've always been careful about what we *did*. I think James picked up something about what we felt. And maybe what Keith and I don't feel.' There are things she is not saying, I think.

'Will he say anything to Keith?'

'I hope he doesn't. But I did promise – sort of promise – that I would talk to Keith about it.'

Why, I think, spend all these years – thirty-five, more even – hiding the facts from Keith, constructing elaborate defences against being found out, and then tell him anyway. What would be the point of it?

'I was worried –' she gives a scrap of a laugh – 'all day – I mean the day of the – you know what I mean – I was bothered that he might say something. James I mean. That's why I stuck to Keith all day. I'm sorry –' she turns her head and looks at me, straight into me – 'I could see you looking all puzzled and lost, but I couldn't come near you either, in case I told you everything. I didn't want there to be any sort of scene. Not that day.'

The danger, as far as I can see, has receded. James has gone back to his island. At some point in the convenient future Elaine will communicate with her husband on the subject of their marriage. Yes, James knows, and has said so, but he is a mature man, a sensible, *nice* man, not an axe murderer, and he is far away.

'There's something else.'

I know now what she is going to say and I can't understand why I didn't jump to it straight away. Patrick.

'Patrick,' she says.

'He knows?'

'He left without saying goodbye.' I look at her again and her eyes are again shining with tears.

She has never been, to my knowledge of her, a weepy woman. Her big, very round blue eyes seem rather to challenge the world – Bring it on, they say, I can cope. She is not like her sister. I know she has cried for her parents – I would be shocked if she hadn't – but I knew she would cope.

But Patrick – if Patrick – if she should lose Patrick –

'And hasn't been in touch?'

'I texted him,' she says, 'just to ask if he got back safely, but he hasn't answered.'

She doesn't say but I know she is trying not to think of the possibility that her dear son, her black sheep, may

183

be a lost lamb and alienated from her, maybe for ever. And if she loses him, I lose him too.

'He didn't say anything to James?'

'I can't ask James. But he must have told him, that's how angry he is with me.'

'Why now, though, if he's known all this time?'

'I don't know. But what I think is that it's their age. Patrick is going to be a father. James has been with Shona for years now, they are thinking of starting a family. I think this is not so much about who you sleep with – who I sleep with – as about what sort of parent you are.'

Sleep with? I think. I wish.

'You've always been a good parent,' I say, which is true.

'I think so,' she says. 'But I think this is about you too.'

Jen: Ridiculous

James was Beth's special cousin and Tricky was mine. When we were very small we must have spent a lot of time at their house, while our own mother failed to look after us. I remember when their house had a long through-lounge, a big window at each end, and the four of us spreading toys the whole length of it.

We played with trains and cars and Lego, and we made tents over the chairs with tablecloths and old blankets, and Auntie Elaine read to us and did jigsaws with us, and sent us into the garden on fine days. She took us to the park, and to visit our grandparents and we watched TV in the afternoons until Midge came to collect us. Uncle Keith was a tall busy man, smart and grey in a suit and tie and if he ever came home while we were there he only put his head into the room and said hello and then went upstairs to his study, where he had an extra telephone.

James looked like Uncle Keith. He was tall too, always the oldest and tallest in his class at school, fair and blue-eyed, and when we did Norse gods at school it was him I thought of when it came to Baldur, the best beloved. Being the eldest of us four he was the one who divided a packet of fruit gums between us and the one who adjudicated when the dice rolled under a chair and someone would claim it was a six when it wasn't. He and Beth were the sensible ones, who were given responsibility for me and Tricky.

Tricky was cute. He had dimples and curls and people stopped in the street to ask his name. His birthday is in September, which put him in a school year below me, and put him in state of resentment too, whenever anyone reminded him. It was often my job to be on his side against the other two in a game (which was not fair, the two oldest against the two youngest) and we were especially good at hiding from the other two. He could stay quiet and still for much longer than I could; I could never resist jumping out and showing them where I was hiding, and then they would know the next time. Tricky stayed absolutely still, not even breathing I think, until they had gone and then he'd sneak away to somewhere else where they had already looked. The Forest was very good for that sort of game, and for playing Famous Five, and Indians, and after Elaine went back to work, when we were all old enough for school, that's when NanaDot took over the childcare and we had our very own private domain.

As we grew up I saw less of James and Tricky, but they were still there, holidays and Christmas, when we returned from where we were studying and we still were friends. And I'm still very fond of Tricky. And then, a week after the funeral, on Sunday when I was preparing for the week ahead, he turned up on my doorstep.

I opened the door feeling both cross (at being interrupted) and relieved (at being interrupted) and there he was, alone.

'Trix,' I said. 'What's the matter? Has something happened?' What sprang into my mind, for no good reason at all, was that my mother had died.

'No panic,' he said. 'I just wanted to talk to you.'

We sat in the kitchen. I made him coffee and toast. It seemed as if neither of us could think of any small talk to help the time along.

'What's up then?' I said once he was sat in front of a choice of Marmite and marmalade. And then he told me what James had told him.

And at first I laughed because it was ridiculous, and then I felt like crying because it seemed as if there was nothing left to hold on to, and then I wondered whether I had already known in some subterranean way. Then I started feeling sorry for Tricky, because the bit that affected him more than me was that it seemed most likely that his father was not Keith, but Midge.

'Are you sure though?' I was looking at him to see if there was some proof to be seen in his face. He didn't look like Keith or James, but wasn't that because he looked like Elaine? He had always looked a little like me and Beth, in the shape of his face and the brown of his eyes and the slightly rodent-y chin, but wasn't that because our mothers were sisters? Sure, his hair was – not quite curly – sort of wavy – a bit crinkly – and the only other person in the family with hair like that was Midge. Wasn't he? Or maybe Sid had once had curly hair, when he'd had any at all. Maybe Dot had. Genetics isn't as straightforward as one and one is two, I was thinking.

'I don't know,' he said. 'James didn't know. But it has to be a possibility, doesn't it.'

'But do you feel? I mean, is there any? You know what I mean. Has there ever been?'

He finished his toast and pushed the plate away. 'I can't really work it out. When I was a boy he was around a lot, and you know my dad was absent quite a lot, with his work. So I always liked to see Midge. And then at school he was there as well – that was a bit weird for all of us when you think about it – and that made him kind of omnipresent. But lately, the past few years, it feels as if he's disappointed in me in some way.'

'I think he ought to be quite proud of you,' I said. Tricky, having left school with nothing, became an actor, and nowadays makes a living, not from being a star, but from adverts and voiceovers and radio plays and occasional bit parts on TV. Patrick Fairlie. Probably not a name people would know, but they would recognise his face from being in the background of many a TV drama. 'He must think you've turned out all right in the end. I mean, being naughty at school can't be held against you for ever.'

'When I was rubbish,' said Tricky, 'you know, after the fire and all that, Midge was great. He did his best to help me. I might have been even worse without him. But the past few years, as things have got better with me, I don't feel like he wants to know. I just feel awkward with him now.'

I thought about the fire and wondered whether to say anything. I remembered what Beth had said, that for Tricky it might have been worse to be believed not guilty and live with the lie, than to be guilty and punished and allowed to get on and forget it. I had never thought of that before.

We sat in silence for a while and then I felt tears rising from somewhere into my head, and this was why. It was the thought of Midge cheating on my mother *just before I was born*. What did that make him? Did she

187

know? If she did had she been punishing him all these years? But I did not let the tears out, I pushed them down, with all the others, and wondered where they all gathered, and what they were waiting for.

Tricky and I walked around the streets for most of the day, sometimes talking about other things, and then coming back to some aspect we'd not thought of, or some part we needed to go over again. We sat in the park, though it was more overcast than it had been – great grey seas of cloud, and strings of little blue sky islands. We drank coffee and towards the end of the afternoon we sat in a bar and drank beer.

'Did you tell Aoife?'

'No. I'm not ready to yet. And I don't want to upset her. And anyway, she's a different part of my life.'

'You'll tell her one day.'

'I guess so. When I can. When the dust has settled.'

I couldn't foresee a time when the dust would settle. The list of people who didn't yet know – Beth, Sid and Dot (oh no, they were dead), Nev, maybe Keith, maybe my mother – the list of people who did know or might know but who were keeping the secret, the list of people who did not know which people were on the other list.

'I'll have to tell Beth,' I said.

'I want you to,' he said.

We drank more than was sensible and then I went with him across town to Victoria for him to get back to Peckham, and on the station we hugged and I clung to him, and then he said, 'That'll do Sis,' and we both laughed and then he went, and I went home, knowing I was not prepared for the next day and that I was going to wake up with a hangover that was due to alcohol and to so much more.

As I fell asleep a new idea came into my head. 'What if Tricky is his favourite?'

24

Midge: Miserable

I feel as if someone has removed the rope that held me – my little dinghy – to the bollard, removed it and thrown it into the water, to trail behind me as I drift and bob downstream. While Sid and Dot were alive I was confident that Elaine would not go abroad with Keith on whatever quixotic mission he had in mind. Now, there is nothing to keep her here. I do not flatter myself that I can keep her here.

It has happened before of course. There have been interruptions, sometimes only a few days, sometimes as much as several months, in our relationship. Always her, never me. She has said, We can't go on like this. She has said, This is no way to live. It has never been what a normal couple would call satisfactory.

But I never felt close to losing her for ever, or so I believe now. She was always going to be there, two streets away, and she would always be part of the same family and there would always be the opportunity to see her and get it started all over again. I do not know, if she goes to Africa, how I will ever see her again.

It has been too complicated. A brief affair, I have often thought, would be child's play compared to this. Imagine, all that lust and excitement overriding any guilt and shame; all that novelty helping you find ways to meet, ways to come up with excuses. If Elaine and I had had a giddy fling and then stopped, would we be happy now? If Keith had found out back then, would he have forgiven us by now? Would our affair have been just water flowing under some bridge, here and then gone? If I had made a new effort with Glenys, would she be normal by now, would we have a normal life, sleeping in the same room, going on holiday, discussing our children, buying plants for the garden and furniture for the house, having friends round? These are things that Elaine and Keith do, but we don't. Whose fault is all this?

She will go. I know she will go. She will email me photos of herself – tanned and thinner, in awful shorts – from Lesotho or Botswana. She will be teaching mothers about AIDS or breastfeeding, or reading to children or watching volunteers dig a well. I don't suppose she will actually be doing the digging, though Keith might. He will be tanned and fit too, and his little paunch and the worried lines around his eyes and mouth will have gone, and I will know that they are man and wife again, and I am forgotten. And they will decide to stay there for ever and Tricky will never come up to Yorkshire again and I will never see him or his child and there will never be a chance to make things right between us. And Glenys will never change and never improve and I might as well kill myself, except that I know I am too cowardly to do it, and anyway I have to stay alive to look after her, and protect Beth and Jenny from having to take the responsibility. And there will be no joy in my life.

So. I have not been a good parent. She said afterwards that she didn't mean it, or that was not what she meant, or something, but she couldn't unsay it, and I couldn't unhear it.

I have not been a good parent. To Patrick.

I'm sitting in my office at work, next year's draft timetable on the screen in front of me, and I cannot foresee any possible moment when it will matter to me whether or not the pupils' needs are met, whether the staff are happy with the spread of their free periods through the week, whether the rooms are big enough for the classes I'm putting in them, whether Modern Foreign Languages has enough IT provision. I know in fact that anything I try to do to this draft will turn out to be wrong and will result, in September, in some major collision of three class groups, one room and no teacher, and that I should close it down and ask Caroline to get someone else to do it. I should go home and have a nervous breakdown. Instead I highlight Food Technology and wonder what Patrick is doing now and what he is thinking of me.

I put my excuses in order.

I had Beth and Jenny to think of.

It was hard enough being any sort of parent to anyone when I had Glenys to look after as well.

Keith would not have let me be a father to Patrick.

It was never known for sure that I was his father – though I knew I was from the start. Before he was born even.

I had to be an uncle to him as I was to James, no more.

I did my best, as a teacher in his school, to look after him.

I had no business making him confused about where he stood in the family.

If I had been more parental, people would have noticed, Sid and Dot for instance.

You (obviously my remarks are addressed to Elaine, though she isn't here) always said not to give any money for him.

You always said, Let's see what happens in the future.

You always said, Leave things to sort themselves out.

I click on a box on the screen and it tells me that the set list for Option 6 Set 2 has so far not been finalised. I can't remember what I should do in such a circumstance.

I close down the programme. Have I saved my changes? I don't know. I send an email to Caroline headed 'Migraine' saying that I am going home to work. I leave it to her to decide whether it's my migraine or Glenys'. She is only in the next office but I know that if I go in and explain I will end up telling her everything and everything will be too much.

Jen: Histories

The week after Tricky's visit passed as if I was under water. Everything was blurred, strange creatures which were in fact Year Four children swam past me on manoeuvres I could not understand, sounds came to me distorted and thundery, and sometimes I couldn't breathe.

I wanted to talk to Beth and made a plan to go the following weekend to Leeds to tell her as I'd said to Tricky that I would, but she had already arranged to go to Dan's mother's for the weekend, would the one after do? It would have to, I said to her. I didn't want to talk to Annie about it, even if there had been time and availability in the week; I couldn't see myself talking to Honey – too young, too close; and it didn't seem right to call Tricky again just yet. He and I had reached some kind of balance and I didn't want to upset it.

On Friday afternoon, facing a weekend of fretful despondency, I gave in to an impulse that I thought I had sent away, and texted Troy.

We met on Saturday afternoon, outside the Serpentine gallery. It was a warm and stuffy afternoon and he was wearing shorts. I had put on a dress and was annoyed that I seemed both overdressed for a park and crumpled from the Underground journey.

'Something wrong?' he said.

'Sort of.'

'Is it too early for you to start drinking?'

I believed that if I started I would not be able to stop so I said, 'Let's leave it for a bit. Can I buy you an ice cream?' and we sat on the grass with our hugely overpriced tourist trap Magnums, in silence, and I wished I had not contacted him.

'Everyone all right?'

'Yes. No.' I could not look at his face, only at his brown bony legs and his big gaunt feet in their flip flops.

I thought of beginnings. If I tell you, you won't tell anyone else. I just need someone to talk to. I'm sorry to trouble you with my problems. This might seem trivial to you but –. Then I said, 'Oh sod it, I'll just tell you. Midge, my dad, has been screwing Elaine for years and Tricky is his son. And my brother.'

His feet did not give me any clue about how he took the news. I waited. I had to keep licking the Magnum because ice cream running down your arm is not a good look. He finished his before he spoke and flicked the stick away.

'Well,' he said, 'it's not entirely news to me.'

'You knew?' It was all I could think of to say, after a pause that seemed to go on long enough for the sun to shift its place in the sky.

'I won't say I knew,' he said. 'My mum told me years ago that she suspected, that's all.'

'That's all? Like, it's nothing?'

'Obviously,' he said, 'it's going to be something to you. But to me and Mum it was just a bit of gossip.'

'And she never said anything? And you never said anything? When was this?' I was making accusations which I knew to be unreasonable but I couldn't stop myself. All of a sudden, as far as I was concerned, it was all his fault.

'Hey, Jen,' he said, and put his hand on my arm, which distracted me a little from my ranting. 'I don't know who she's told. Probably Nev. Probably no one else. And it's not something she knows for sure, only something she observed when she lived up there with all of you – all of us – and it made her wonder.'

'What though? What did she observe?'

'I don't know. If she told me I don't remember. It wasn't anything of interest to me. I can't remember how the subject came up, but I didn't pursue it.'

'When though? Do you remember?'

'Not really. And I wasn't in touch with anyone involved, what would you want me to do? I was pretty grown up at the time. She wouldn't have told a teenager something like that, especially –'

'– one with a grudge.'

'It's not that dramatic. But I guess as a teenager I wouldn't have been trusted to keep my mouth shut. She said not to say anything to Ashley or Honey, because they still went up to Sheffield, visiting. She didn't want them to let something out by accident. I think maybe, ten, fifteen years ago, she told me.' He stopped.

I fished in my bag for a tissue to wipe my sticky fingers. I wanted to discuss the whole issue at great length and in great detail, as I had with Tricky. I wanted to pretend I had never raised the matter and remain dignified and calm. I wanted the day never to have turned out this way. I wanted to be at home. I wanted to be down at the bungalow with Nana and Sid. I wanted to be on my own in the Forest, crying. I wanted to be in bed with Troy.

'Come on,' he said. 'Let's go and look at ducks.' And I took his hand to be pulled up off the grass and he kept hold of it as we walked along.

'How did you find out?'

'Tricky came to see me. James told him.'

'How did James find out?'

'He says he's known for years. Observing. Again. You'd think Beth and I might have observed, wouldn't you.'

'They were probably careful.'

'Not careful enough.' I was thinking of Tricky when I said that and immediately felt disloyal at wishing him unborn. I said, 'I don't mean that like, I wish Tricky didn't exist.'

'I do,' he said.

'Do what?'

'Wish he never existed.'

I knew what he was getting at and did not know what to say. There was a risk, in today's situation that I might descend into telling him things I had kept quiet about. I regretted already that I had said to Midge that I'd been a witness to the Fire; I was afraid it might open the door to telling other people, even Troy, and he might never speak to me again. It was most important, this feeling that I must not alienate him, scare him, annoy him, give him an excuse to go away.

'Tell me,' I said, 'tell me all about your life in London. Tell me more about where you lived. What school did you go to? Were you happy?'

He smiled. He really did have a very sweet smile when he chose to use it.

'OK,' he said. 'End of dangerous conversation, is that it? You told me about your childhood, I'll tell you about mine.

'It was ordinary. We lived in Walthamstow, near where Honey lives now. I went to school. I didn't do very well. Mum got a job, Honey went to day nursery. After I left school it was better. I worked in B and Q, I played in a band, got busted a couple of times, only weed, that's all. Went to art school later, in my twenties, got a part-time job in this residential home – adult learning difficulties – found I couldn't be an artist.'

'Why not?'

'Not good enough,' he said. 'But I knew that really. I'd always thought I might be a teacher –'

'– like Midge?'

'Yes,' he said. 'I always thought Midge was a great bloke. He would listen to you. He would try to help you. He wasn't like that other one –'

'– Mr Kavanagh?'

'That's the one. Bastard.'

'Midge thinks so too. But you're not a teacher.'

'Not in a school. I told you about the lads I do art with. For now. Till they cut our funding.'

'Will they do that?'

'As sure as Christmas.'

'That's what NanaDot used to say.'

'So she did. I'd forgotten. Yeah, our funding is what you would call vulnerable. And who would care? This is a country that will stand by and let the government stop prisoners having books. If some scallies have to go without their art classes, well, so what? Serve them right.'

'I've handed in my notice.' This was the first time I'd told anyone. 'I thought I would go back home. Now, it doesn't seem like such a good idea.'

'Why not?'

'I think I will miss Sid and Dot more if I'm there. And I don't want to live at home, it's just too weird. And even more weird now, with the Midge and Elaine thing.'

'There's more than just two places on earth to choose from,' he said, and I nodded to agree with him, but what he said did not really make me think anything different.

The afternoon was fading and I thought it was OK to risk a drink. We sat outside and watched people going past, and the noise of the traffic made it unnecessary to talk. I wanted suddenly not to be there, not in London, not drinking at five o'clock on a Saturday, not with Troy. I glanced at him and was impressed by how composed he seemed. Composed, like a picture or a fashion shoot. Very London.

I thought of how out of place and uncomfortable he had seemed that weekend up in Yorkshire, and how with every mile back towards London he had become looser so that by the time I woke up in the back of the car his jacket was off and his tie was off and his shoes were off and his face was relaxed again. And here he was again, leaning back, appraising everyone who went past. It came to me that I knew nothing about him, his wives, his girlfriends, his children, his friends. I did not know who he was. I had let him see who I was and he was still hidden. I thought I might make my excuses and make my way back home but the idea of an evening alone stopped me. And I fancied him. I did not want to let him go.

'Would you like,' I said, 'to come and eat with me? I can stop on the way and buy something. I'll cook for you.'

'An evening in Leyton,' he said. 'OK.' Which was not a very enthusiastic response but it would do.

All through the journey from the West End to the outer East End I was regretting it. The tube was so hot and so slow and I felt as if he was a visitor who should be protected from it. The streets were so dirty and ugly and I forgot that he lived in Catford which was arguably uglier and began apologising for the surroundings, which were certainly not of my making. I was hoping Annie would not be at home because I wanted him to myself, and yet I was hoping she would be there because I thought the evening might go better with a third person. It would at least keep us off dangerous subjects. I was in a state of elated depression, or depressed elation, or something. I was a mess.

Annie was sitting on the back doorstep. I introduced them.

'I thought,' she said to me as I put the salad into the fridge, 'I might go out this evening.'

'Stay,' I said. 'Stay and eat with us. There's plenty.'

'Are you sure?'

'Sure,' I said. 'He's a sort of cousin.'

After we had eaten, we moved into the front room, which Annie and I used so rarely that it was tidy, and she put on some quiet music – not the sort that I like – and we decided we needed another bottle of wine. I went into the kitchen to get the corkscrew and nipped to the loo, and checked that my bedroom was presentable, just in case, and when I came back they were sitting directly opposite one another, leaning forward as if they were being pulled, eyes locked together. They were talking about being children. Annie would have started that off, I knew. She was just a devil for people's histories.

'I was never allowed to play out,' she was saying. 'My parents thought it wasn't respectable, not that it wasn't safe, but it was only rough children who played in the street and I might pick up a regrettable accent.'

Troy laughed gently, without taking his eyes off her.

'Tell me,' she said to him, 'where did you grow up?'

'Not far from here,' he said. 'Except for a few years in the north. I'm an East End boy, me.'

'Are you proud of it?'

'I suppose so,' he said. 'I don't think about it really. And I live south of the river now. Never thought I would do that.'

'Dudley,' she said. 'No one is ever proud to come from Dudley. Nothing to do, no history, no countryside.'

'The countryside,' he said, 'is overrated, if you ask me.'

'What are you talking about?' I said. I had to say something, to make them remember I was there. 'We had the Forest, remember. We could do what we liked there. We had dens and stuff.'

'You were really lucky,' said Annie. 'I mean, I was in the Girl Guides and we went to camp and made camp fires and all that, but it was very tame stuff, because there were always grownups watching you.'

'Oh they left us alone,' I said. 'We could do what we liked.'

Troy had stopped looking at her, he was looking at me, but saying nothing.

'So what did you do?'

'All sorts,' I said. 'Dens. Climbing trees. Tarzan swing. There was a stream running through it that we called the River. Hiding places.'

'Wildlife?'

'Well probably, but we never saw it. I think we made too much noise.' I could have mentioned the kingfisher but I didn't, and Troy said nothing.

'Fires?'

'Oh –' I was going to tell her, it was all there ready to spill out and I stopped myself. But Troy saw me stop myself. He knew what I had been going to say, and what I would have said if he hadn't been there. And I turned to him and said, 'I wasn't going to, you know, I didn't mean to, I promise I'll never tell anyone.' Which made it worse.

'Well,' he said, 'you don't really know anyway, do you? You only know what Tricky says. You don't know what happened.'

'Oh, I do,' I said. 'I do know.' Afterwards I could not remember whether I added, I was there, but it hardly mattered.

It was a few days before I saw Annie again. I arrived home from work shortly before she was going out.

'I liked your cousin,' she said. 'Nice man.'

'He's not really my cousin,' I said.

'I know,' she said. 'He explained all that after you went to bed. Anyway, got to dash. See you – whenever.'

I was still feeling ashamed about bolting off to bed that Saturday night, and the idea that they had sat there discussing me did not improve the way I felt. But I had been suddenly – when I was almost betrayed into talking about the Fire – suddenly a child again. Troy was – suddenly he was – someone, not an adult, not an acquaintance, he was someone whose space I should not share, because I had let him down all that time ago, and probably changed his life. And I knew too, that he must remember the knicker incident, he must be ashamed and embarrassed and trying not to think about it, and trying to believe that I had forgotten all about it, and wondering had I ever told anyone, and then he'll wonder, did I not stick up for him after the Fire on account of the knickers. And I can't tell him that's not true because then he'll think it is.

25

Midge: Guilt

What I gathered much later was that James and Patrick sat up after their parents had gone to bed, and drank some more. In the early hours – maybe around the time I was waking up on the sofa – they decided to have a walk around the streets to clear their heads. They were both due to drive home the next morning – Patrick to Southampton where he was filming something nautical, James back to South Uist to count kittiwakes, or something.

Once outside, I suppose the dark, the sound of their footsteps in the dark, together, the drink they had taken together, the time they had spent together that day, the loss of their grandparents, the thought of the next day when they would be at the far ends of the country – I suppose all these things led to a conversation where James told his brother about the relationship between Elaine and me.

I don't know how he knew. The affair was nearly as old as him and was the background to his life but we thought we had always been careful. Our meetings had always been limited – by Keith, by the constraints of our jobs, by the demands of Glenys and my duties towards the girls, and by the necessity to keep it secret. Once the children were no longer babies, or at least as soon as they could talk, we never, in their presence, went beyond a brief kiss and a touch of the hand, like something between a brother and sister. On the occasions when we took all four of them for a day out, we never held hands, though most of the time I was boiling with impatience to touch her and hold her. Certainly we looked at each other. Our whole lives since we met, it seems have been spent looking at each other, hoping for a little space, a little crevice in time and circumstances that we can use to be alone in. But I can't believe a look, or any number of looks would have given the game away. Surely not?

Did a teenage James come into the house one day – having forgotten his football boots, say – and hear something from the spare bedroom? Did he then wait outside to see who left the house? Or did he just keep his eyes open for weeks and months until he found out the truth? Or did it become clear to him when he was older, that his parents' marriage was an incomplete one – I won't call it a sham, because what do I know? only what Elaine will tell me. Did he begin to wonder, when he had girlfriends and started to look to his future, what is marriage? How do you do it? How do you know it's going to be all right? How do you be a husband? How do you be a father?

I always knew I should try to be a good parent and I did try. I kept my job, I brought in sufficient money. I did the shopping, I bought clothes for the girls, sometimes with Elaine's assistance, I put washing in the machine and took it out again and hung it up, and if I didn't iron it I don't suppose anyone noticed. Most things don't need ironing.

I suppose I knew the house was untidy, even dirty and I even knew the girls were ashamed of it, but I did not know how to put it right. I had never even lived in a normal house. My parents had employed a cleaner, who worked her way through the guest bedrooms every day, and another cleaner who came twice a week to do the bit we lived in. I never saw the process happening, or rather, it was a process divorced from me, it was part of the business. So how was I ever going to learn how a normal house is kept together?

I tried to hire cleaners but they never stayed. Maybe it was too dirty for them, or maybe Glenys sacked them. I never found out, and eventually I gave up and we muddled along, the girls and I. As they grew up of course they became better at maintaining some sort of order, or maybe just not as bad at making it disordered. Then when they hit the age of about fifteen they became aggressively clean and we were into a military regime of housework, with lists and rotas and punishments for non-compliance. Then they left home and I went back to my old ways.

But the real business of being a parent – taking them to Brownies, and swimming and the park, and noticing when their shoes had become too small, and brushing their hair and making them clean their teeth, and finding their PE kit on the right morning and reading them interminable stories and playing interminable games of Frustration and stopping their fights and changing their sheets in the night when they were sick – I did all that. I don't think I have too much to reproach myself with. They were much like normal children. They were never – hardly ever – left in the house alone, they always seemed fine, they looked after each other. If anything, having a mother like Glenys taught them self-reliance and resourcefulness. I can't think of any times except one when things went badly wrong. Beth still has the scar, though I think my scar must be deeper.

I went to the shops. It was a Saturday morning and I left the girls watching cartoons and went out into a cloudy chilly October day to the local Co-op to buy some things we needed. Cereal – they got through packet after packet of cereal – milk, bread, fish fingers, tomato sauce; all things I hardly buy these days. In the doorway of the shop I met Elaine coming out.

'Come home with me,' she said. 'Keith has taken the boys to his mother's.'

Keith's mother lived in Liverpool so this was pretty safe. I thought swiftly that in the afternoon I could find a pretext for taking the girls to be looked after by Sid and Dot, and Elaine and I could spend the whole afternoon together. Even longer if I could think of a good excuse.

'But come now,' she said. 'Just for a little while.' And I did. As soon as we were inside her house and the door was shut behind us I was holding her tight.

'Come upstairs,' she said.

'What about the girls?'

'Glenys is there,' she said. 'I need you now.'

I remember how lovely it was, throwing our clothes off and getting into the spare room bed, which was always our bed, and holding her and smelling her and crushing her. I wanted to stay there all day but I didn't; I remembered my responsibility and just as soon as we had made love – and talked a little, and made a plan for the afternoon – I got out of bed.

To be honest the phone ringing had broken into our conversation but we didn't hurry to answer it. 'I'm not here,' said Elaine, and I said, 'And I'm certainly not here.' And I got dressed and left the house – not much more than half an hour, I could swear – and ran, or at least jogged, back to the Co-op. There was a big queue at the till and for some reason I began to worry that I had been away from home for too long. Guilt, that's all it was. Beth was ten years old, and sensible. I knew I was worrying unnecessarily but standing in the queue there I had nothing else to do.

And then as I turned the corner into our road, there was an ambulance at the door, and Dot's car, and Elaine running down the road from the other direction towards our house. My first thought was that something had happened to Glenys. Let it be Glenys, let it not be one of the children. *Let it not be both of the children.*

As I went in through the front door, with Elaine just behind me, Jenny threw herself at me, and Dot came into the hall from the kitchen. Glenys was sitting on the stairs with her hands over her eyes and an acrid pool of vomit on the floor in front of her.

'Where on earth were you?' said Dot.

I put my shopping bags down. 'What's happened?'

In the kitchen, ambulance personnel were about to carry Beth to the ambulance. There was an awful lot of blood on the floor.

'She'll be grand,' said one of them. 'We're taking her t'Children's to have it stitched. Who's going to come with her?'

'You go Midge,' said Dot. 'She's been asking for you. I'll take Jenny down to the bungalow.'

'I'll clean up,' said Elaine. 'Shall I stay with Glenys till you get back?'

'If you don't mind.'

She gave me a smile that acknowledged her complicity.

Of course, that was all before the mixed blessing of mobile phones. The phone call at Elaine's had been Jenny. She knew, she said, that she mustn't leave her sister. She wasn't sure that she was allowed to call an ambulance but she risked it, because Beth had fainted. Jenny had been scared at first to rouse Glenys from sleep but when she gathered her courage and tried to get her to take charge Glenys fainted too.

'I can't remember now, 'said Jenny, 'what I did first. I'm all confused.'

She said this sitting beside me on the sofa, eating chocolate. Beth had been kept in overnight and I had had to come home, tell Elaine and Dot all about it, and then go back for visiting, taking Jenny with me to see her sister.

Beth was sitting up in bed. 'I won't ever do that again,' she said.

'Nor will I,' said Jenny.

They had decided to make a Hallowe'en lantern. You couldn't get pumpkins in those days, at least not in our end of Sheffield, but I had bought, earlier in the week, at their request, a large turnip. The night before they asked me to help them carve it but I was too tired. So when I went out on Saturday morning they decided to get on with it. Neither of them could adequately describe what had gone wrong, but it had proved hard to do and they had used the largest and sharpest knife they could find. So large and sharp that it was not kept in the cutlery drawer but at the back of the cupboard, in what I called my toolbox – a shoebox containing a hammer and a screwdriver and not much else, where I had hidden the knife so they didn't get hold of it. I was not a neglectful father. I did not know they knew.

For a long time after that I hardly left them, and it was not clear to any of us for whose benefit it was, that closer supervision.

Jen: Manipulated

'I'm away this weekend,' I said to Annie. 'I'm going to see my sister.'

'I wish I had a sister,' said Annie.

'Mm,' I said.

We were sitting in what I suppose is technically the front garden of the house, a space about sixty centimetres deep, home to one plastic pot containing one dead plant. We were perched on the wall, looking down the street, enjoying the shade on what was a very hot and airless evening, eating chocolate biscuits and watching our neighbours come and go.

'It must be nice,' she said, 'to have someone who has known you all your life, who you can talk to about anything.'

'Mm,' I said again.

'Don't you think?'

'Sometimes,' I said, 'those people are just the ones you don't want to tell everything to. I mean, I've told you things before I've said them to Beth. It's easier, I don't know why.'

'I tell anybody anything,' she said. 'I have no discretion and no discrimination. You seem to me to be more on the secretive end of the scale.'

'I suppose so.'

'So, when you were growing up, did you have friends as well as a sister? I mean friends you told your secrets to?'

'We both had friends,' I said, 'but we couldn't bring them to our house because of our mother.'

'Why, what would she do?'

'I don't know.' I had never wondered about that. 'I suppose she might have been a bit scary for them. She doesn't like children. And we wanted her to look like a proper mother. We would have hated people seeing her looking so bizarre. So we never encouraged anyone to come, not even to call for us.'

'Good thing you had your sister then,' said Annie.

'And we had our cousins too,' I said.

This of course leads me to think about Tricky, and Midge, and Elaine. I haven't yet said anything to Annie about all that, though I know she would love it if I did.

'I had a best friend,' she said. 'I sat next to her in school all through juniors. She's in Dubai now but we email all the time. Maria, she's called. We used to get up to all sorts – her parents were not as strict as mine but even so they wouldn't have knowingly let us roam all over town. Hers thought she was at my house and mine thought I was at hers.'

'We could have gone where we liked,' I said, 'and yet we never did. We played at the campsite. We were out of sight of the grownups I suppose, but it never felt as if they were far away.'

'You didn't take risks then?'

So I told Annie about the time when Beth had to be taken to hospital because she cut herself with a knife.

'Does she have a scar?'

'Oh, a big long one up the inside of her arm. Looks like a very enthusiastic suicide attempt.'

'And you were alone in the house?'

'No our mother was there, but I wouldn't go and get her out of bed, and Beth said I shouldn't phone for an ambulance. I think we'd had one of those talks at school – you know, when they tell you stuff like you mustn't waste the emergency services' time. She was always very law-abiding, Beth.'

'So then what happened?'

'Oh, after a bit she stopped arguing and I dialled 999. That bit was quite exciting. But all the blood was really scary. Certainly put any idea of being a nurse out of my head.'

'You get used to it,' said Annie. 'Same as vomit and faeces and people's insides. I don't like burns though. I've seen plenty but I never get used to them.'

'I still get nightmares about fire.' I couldn't remember if I'd already told her this. 'Not often, but if I have a nightmare, it's about the fire.'

'You told me. So what happened? It got out of control?'

Did she engineer that? I did not suspect it at the time if she did. I believed she was my friend and so I told her the whole story. And she said all the right things and I felt bad about Troy all over again, and she understood that I was only eleven then and didn't have any power to control what other people did, and then we moved on to talk about other things.

I made a decision and told her that I would be moving out and going back to Yorkshire.

'You're going to live at home?'

'Only for a few days until I find somewhere of my own. I can't stand being around my mother for more than a day or two, but if my dad's there it's not so bad. I probably should have some talks with him anyway.'

'What about?'

'Oh, this and that. Work mostly.' It was a bit late to start being discreet but I didn't know that.

'I'll miss you,' she said. ''But we'll stay in touch. Won't we.'

'Yes,' I said, and I meant it.

She went off to work soon after that, and I ate what I could find in the kitchen – crisps and grapes – and did a little work, and went early to bed. I never knew how exhausting grief could be. Many days now I did the minimum preparation I could get away with and crashed into bed by eight o'clock, plummeting into sleep like jumping off a cliff. Then I would be awake by four, worrying about the day ahead but too torpid to get up and do anything about it.

Just as I was going to sleep my phone pinged. I knew – I knew by the way I felt joy through my whole body – that it was a text from Russell, and it was. Then I was cross with him.

I had given up expecting a reply and had long been wishing that I had never sent one to him in the first place. Did he think I was trying to make him feel guilty – even more guilty – about leaving me? Did he even think I was lying, just to try and bring him back? I felt embarrassed at the thought.

Anyway. He said he was sorry he hadn't replied before, and he was sorry to hear of my trouble. There was an excuse about losing his phone charger, and a more credible reason that he had been trying to work out how to reply to me.

I was not going to reply to him straight away. If he was going to pretend there was no such thing as instant digital communication, then so was I. I lay in bed and thought of elegant and telling phrases that I could use to let him know that I was a) all right without him, b) still very fond of him, c) conscious of being badly treated by him, and d) –

I must have fallen asleep, and in the morning my best phrases had faded away and I could not remember them.

26

Midge: Visitors

I am not expecting a visitation. They have not warned me that they are coming. I am standing looking out of the front room window at a grey drizzle. I am wearing a pair of pyjama trousers and a very dirty T-shirt and holding a cup of coffee. I have only just got out of bed, and I have no plan for the day. I have things I must do but I am not planning to do them.

I see a car stop and park outside without recognising it as Beth's. I see two heads above the fence, I see them straighten up and one looks directly at me, and I realise slowly that it is Jenny, getting out of the passenger seat and I assume she has brought her boyfriend to meet us, and then I see with even more surprise, that the other person is in fact Beth. Then I wait for her to unpack the baby from the back of the car, but no, she locks it and they both approach the front door.

'Is everything all right?'

'No, it's not,' says Beth.

They have made themselves a pot of tea, they have complained that there is no bread, they have enquired where their mother is and appeared relieved when I say I have not seen her for days. From the way they are behaving I do not recognise that they are distraught; they are businesslike, brisk, dismissive. This is how it must feel when bailiffs arrive and dismantle your life.

'You know why we're here?' says Beth, and I think possibly I do, but I tell her, No, I don't.

They look at each other. 'You say it,' says Beth to Jenny, which is very unlike her.

'Dad,' says Jenny, and stops, apparently stunned at what she has said.

'Go on,' says Beth.

'Last week,' says Jenny, 'Tricky came to see me. He told me, Midge. He told me everything James told him.'

'How was he?' I say.

'In bits,' she says. 'Honestly, it's thrown him completely, he can't make sense of it, he keeps going round in circles, it's not something you can take in all at once, me and Beth are the same, it's just a bombshell.'

'He didn't suspect then?' Because I always hoped that he might.

'Neither did we,' says Beth. 'Look Midge, you've changed everything, you must see that. Nobody is who they think they are.'

'That's not true,' I say. 'You and Jenny, you are still sisters, and you haven't got any other sisters.' They look at each other again, and I realise that the idea of having more siblings somewhere is one they haven't considered until now. 'Honestly,' I say, pretending it's all light and easy, 'I haven't got a harem and a string of –'

'Good,' says Beth sternly. 'One is enough.'

'And your mother is still your mother, and James is still your cousin and Elaine –'

'Yes, what is Elaine?' says Jenny. 'Is there a word for what she is to us?'

Is there even a word for what she is to me?

'You see,' I say, not knowing what I will say next, 'you have to understand, I tried not to hurt anyone.' This sounds trite and self-justifying, I know, and for some of my life it has not even been true – I did not make any effort not to hurt people, beyond keeping quiet about what was going on. If they had found out and been hurt, as now they have and they are, well, I would apologise, but I would not go back and change anything, even if I could. 'I'm sorry,' I say, 'if it has upset you.'

'Does She know?' Jenny waves her hand towards upstairs.

'I don't know.' And at that moment Glenys comes into the room. She is looking dishevelled, but that is normal for her, as is the shawl and the glass of water.

'I thought I heard voices,' she says, and sits down.

'We came to talk to Midge,' says Jenny. There is a long silence and then the girls go into the kitchen to make more tea. Glenys and I sit. She is very thin and I notice she has cut her hair recently and not dyed it, so it is entirely grey. Her shawl was once shocking pink, about forty years ago it shocked the folks in the High Street, but dirt and washing have removed all capacity to shock. She looks like a refugee. In the three weeks or so since the funeral she has gone steeply downhill.

When Jenny and Beth come back into the room – I notice they have raided the top cupboard for biscuits as they used to do as teenagers – it's clear they have made a decision. 'We think she ought to know,' says Beth. 'Do you want to tell her or do you want us to?'

'It's not really your business,' I say. 'This is something between me and your mother.' I am trying hard for dignity here and I really don't want the words openly said in my house, with all of us here. They look at each other. They pass their mother a cup of tea. She looks at it suspiciously but starts to sip it anyway, even though I can see it has milk in it, and there'll obviously be caffeine as well.

'Do you know,' says Glenys, apparently lightly, 'whatever it is, I'm not sure that I want to know. And if I do, I'm sure your father will tell me, in his own good time.'

She puts her mug down. She gets to her feet. How stiff she is, how creaky, how old. She hobbles out of the room. The room deflates. Beth dabs her eyes. For now, it's over.

Jen: Loose

We had been sitting in this room looking at each other for too long. Beth and I no longer knew what to say, or even why we came.

It had taken us – me and Beth – all of Friday evening and most of Saturday to unpick and go over, and generally examine everything we knew, and everything we felt, and it seemed that there were still areas that would keep coming back to us as unfinished.

'How dare he,' said Beth. 'I was only a baby.'

'I wasn't even born,' I said.

When we were making salad in the kitchen she said, 'Does it make you feel sorry for Her?'

'If she knows,' I said. 'But if she knows, surely she would have thrown him out? But if she doesn't know – should we still feel sorry for her? For not knowing.'

When we were loading the dishwasher – me wishing I had a dishwasher – she said, 'It changes everything.'

'Yes,' I said.

'No,' she said, 'I mean, *everything*.'

When we were in the off-licence buying a bottle of wine I said, 'I hope Dot never suspected. It would have really upset her.'

'She would have put a stop to it,' said Beth.

'Do you think? Do you think anyone can put a stop to something like that?'

'Keith could have.'

'How?'

'Don't know.'

'Those times,' I said, 'when he left us alone, with Her, when he had to go to work in the holidays – do you think he really went to work?'

She stopped dead on her way to the checkout. 'Surely,' she said, 'he wouldn't. Would he?'

When we were pushing Xander round the park she said, 'Do you wish that he'd left Her? We could have all lived together.'

'You mean without Mrs?'

'Of course. Midge, Elaine, four children. Would you have liked that?'

I thought about it but however long I thought, I knew I could not reach a conclusion. 'Don't know,' I said.

'Nor do I.'

Propping Xander in front of a cushion she said, 'Tricky is Xander's uncle then, not a second cousin. Tricky's baby will be his cousin.' Xander took the news by flinging himself backwards and having to be propped up again, like a teddy bear.

After Dan had gone to bed I said, 'Beth, how do you actually feel about all this?'

She thought for a long time. 'I suppose a bit of me is glad that he had some pleasure in his life. I'm sorry for Tricky, it must be confusing for him.'

'But what do *you* feel like?'

'Angry,' she said at last. 'Outraged. What about you?'

'Betrayed,' I said. 'Wobbly. I'm scared to speak to him.'

'What we'll do,' she said, 'is, we'll leave Xander here with Dan tomorrow and we'll go and see him together.'

Afterwards Beth drove back to Leeds, dropping me off in Sheffield at the bus station where I got on the National Express to Golders Green. Nothing was resolved, nothing really felt any better. All I could feel really was guilt and shame at the state of our house. So scruffy, so dirty and uncared for. And Midge himself, wrecked, miserable, not because of our visit but because he and Elaine had fallen out. Well, I should know how he felt if anyone did, and if I could get up in the morning and have a shower and go to work and keep myself together then I didn't see why he couldn't. And he could do something about the house.

I reached into my bag and pulled out Midge's thesaurus. Soft old proper pages, better in every way than an app. I had taken it off his desk in front of his eyes, and he had said nothing to stop me, though his eyes followed it all the way into my bag. I didn't know why I'd done it. I suppose to show him that I didn't ever need to go back there again.

I looked up 'adulterer.' Rip, rake, roué, lecher, satyr. These all sounded quite jolly, quite fun in a wicked sort of way. None of them made me think of Midge. 'Loose fish' though – wet, floppy, useless – yes, that came the nearest.

But 'loose' – that kind of described how I felt. I looked it up. 'Free,' it said. 'untrammelled, unbound, unfettered, uncurbed.' None of these described the sort of free I was. Mine was unsupported, dismissed, discarded.

I had thought, when Russell left me, that I was alone, but I hadn't been. Then, I still had Midge, and Sid and Dot, and even Beth. Now Beth had Xander and Dan to put a long way in front of me. Sid and Dot were dead. And Midge had never even been there when I thought he had. I had become a teacher because he was a teacher. I had looked up to and admired him and loved him all my life, but all my life he had put someone before me, before Beth and before our mother.

And Elaine had been there all my life too, a lot more present than my proper mother. It was Elaine who took us shopping for clothes when we were younger, and Elaine who told us about periods, and told us stuff about boys, and condoms and how it was all right to say No and we never had to do anything we didn't want to. We called on Elaine when we made a mess of our cooking and when the washing machine door wouldn't open and when we needed our clothes altering or our hair curling. She was a good aunt to have and a reliable safety net. And all the time she was sleeping with our father and he was putting her first. Elaine, of all people. How lazy was that, to go for the nearest, easiest person.

I sat in the coach and watched the sky go gradually dark with clouds. Little spiteful raindrops scattered on the window and I hoped very much that Annie would be at home.

27

Midge: Hopeless

I am working late at school when Elaine comes to see me. It is a long time since she has been in my office – in fact the last time she came here I had a different office, a tiny cubicle tucked away at the top of the stairs, and we locked the door and made love on the desk. I remember picking up all the Geography exercise books from the floor and having to sort them back into the correct classes.

Now my office is next to Caroline's and has a large window looking out on to the main entrance. My predecessor here – Brian Kavanagh – used to conceal himself behind the venetian blinds and take note of who was coming into school late, or improperly dressed. Staff I mean. We would find a note in our pigeonhole telling us how many times we had hurried in at eight forty-five instead of the required eight forty, or reminding us that the dress code included a tie. In summer women teachers were reprimanded for showing their bare arms.

I don't do this sort of thing. I never have but nowadays I care even less what people do. I know I should retire.

I am still going through the timetable for next year, checking off class sizes against room capacity. It's tedious but demands just enough concentration to stop me thinking about Elaine, for several minutes at a time. Then I find I am looking blankly at 10Y/option 8 (RE) and wondering why some time last week I highlighted it as a query, to be dealt with this week.

Then I look out of the window, eat a biscuit, wander into the office to be cheered up by Jane or Greta, wander back and sit down in front of the same problem. Click on it to make it go away. Move on to 11X/option 8 (RE) and notice that they seem to be in the same room at the same time with the same teacher. Is this deliberate? The RE department, all one of it, has gone home. Maybe the Head of Humanities is around on the premises.

Before I can go and look for her, the door opens and Elaine comes in.

Something must happen in one's memory. Seeing her again after less than a fortnight should not make her look different but it does. She looks less herself, more like someone I don't know as well. Then I blink a bit and she becomes Elaine again.

I would like to jump up and hold her tightly to me, but something in her demeanour forbids it. She sits down with the desk between us and leans forward, resting her elbows on the surface.

'How are you?' I say.

'How are you?' she says.

We cannot answer these simple questions so we look at each other. Then she looks down and says, 'I need to talk to you.'

'Yes,' I say.

'I haven't got long,' she says. 'I told Keith I was going to get my hair cut. Before we go on holiday.'

'Where are you going?' As if it matters.

'Scotland,' she says. 'West coast.'

'That will be nice. I suppose.'

'Frank,' she says, 'I told him. Keith. I told him.'

I try to think of something sensible to say, or even something that will ask a question I want the answer to, but what I do say is, 'Was that a good idea?'

'I think it was a mistake,' she says.

'You think he'll send his friends round to beat me up with baseball bats?' This is an attempt to stop her telling me any more. I don't want to know.

She smiles a little. 'He's more likely to send his friends round to inflict a prayer of forgiveness on you,' she says. 'He's forgiven me. It's very uncomfortable.'

'He didn't suspect? Before I mean. Before you told him.'

'He says he didn't suspect you. He thought I might be getting satisfaction elsewhere. He believes it's his fault for not catering to my needs.'

'He didn't say that?'

'I'm paraphrasing. Frank, I handled it so badly. I shouldn't have mentioned your name. He didn't know and it could have stayed that way. I could have given him a made-up name. That was my biggest mistake.'

'Darling,' I say. I can only say words like that when I am sure no one is listening. 'I would hate it if he thought you had been unfaithful with anyone else but me. Aren't we in this together?' Though maybe not, I think.

'And then,' she says, 'he began to make assumptions. Like that I was sorry and repentant and wanted to start again, and I let him believe it. I let him think these things. He wanted to think them and I didn't want to tell him not to. So he's made all these plans – we're going on holiday, we're going to visit Keith's sister, and then we'll go to see James and show him that everything is all right between us, we're going to pray at the monastery in Iona – can you believe it?'

'Um,' I say. 'You're not really the praying sort are you?'

'I am now, apparently,' she says. 'I am a lost woman who is found. We're going to pray for you too, so he says, whether you like it or not.'

'I don't like it,' I say. 'I might need help from somewhere, but it isn't from Keith. Unless he'd like to – no, I'm sorry, I shouldn't wish him ill. It sounds as if he's been very – reasonable.'

'Not reasonable at all,' says Elaine. 'It is considered reasonable to shout and threaten and cry and blame, don't you think. He's enjoying himself far too much. I'd go as far as to say it turns him on.'

That is worse than the baseball bat. My only comfort, for all these years, when I haven't been with Elaine, is that she has been with a husband who preferred to sleep in a separate bed, who did not want or need to touch or kiss or hug or see her naked or lie beside her, or in her.

I think very hard and try to stop myself saying it, but I have to say it. 'So has he? Have you?'

'Not yet,' she says. 'We have to do the praying first.'

'You're not going to do that though, are you?'

'That's the thing,' she says. 'I said I would go to Scotland with him. I said I would try. I couldn't help it Frank, I couldn't think what else to do.'

'You could have told him you were leaving him.'

'To go where? To move in with you and Glenys? Why should it be me who has to burn my boats?'

The hopelessness is filling the room. Dimly, I hear noises outside the window. The cleaners are leaving the premises. Soon Dave the caretaker will be knocking on my door telling me he's about to lock up.

'I have to go,' says Elaine.

'Won't he notice that you haven't had your hair cut?'

'No,' she says, 'he won't notice.'

We walk together to the car park. She has parked next to mine, wing mirrors almost touching.

'What shall I do?' I said. 'What do you want me to do?'

'I want you to do what you want to do,' she said, and I could tell she was a little annoyed with me. 'I can't tell you what to do.'

Jen: Rucksack

'What shall I do?' he said to me.

There was less than one week to go before we broke up for the summer. Less than a week until I had no job. My earlier plan – to go home to Yorkshire – was abandoned. For the time being I was going to stay with Annie, and put my name down for supply teaching next term – a desperate measure if ever there was one, but it felt as if nothing could make my life much worse anyway.

I was walking home from the bus, still, in spite of the year's ending, hauling a bag full of paper and a school laptop that I had to work on tonight if the rest of the week was going to go according to plan. My phone rang and it was Midge. Their last day was already happening and I could hear in the background the sounds of laughter from the pub garden.

'What do you mean?' I said. I turned off the High Street so that I could hear him better.

'I've got no one to talk to,' he said. 'I phoned Beth but she would hardly speak to me.'

'She's probably busy,' I said.

'She's angry,' he said. 'She's livid. She doesn't even want to understand.'

'Midge,' I said, 'we *can't* understand. How can we?'

'All these years,' he said, 'you and your sister have been on at me to get a life. Get a life, Midge, why don't you get a life. And when you find out that I did, you behave as if I shouldn't have a life. What would you have done?'

'Other people,' I said, 'get a divorce and get married again. At least then everyone knows where they are.'

'Think about it,' he said. 'Do you think I didn't want to? What would have happened to your mother, do you think?'

I made a noise that dismissed my mother from needing to be taken into consideration. 'It's so messy,' I said. 'What about poor Tricky? Not knowing who he is. Not fair on the boy, is it.'

'What about me?' he said. 'Have you thought how it's been for me, believing Patrick is my son and not being able to act as if he is? And Elaine. Trust me, Jenny, this hasn't been easy for us all these years.'

'So,' I said, 'what's the big problem all of a sudden. If it's been going on all these years, and all that's changed is that some people know about it, what's to stop you just carrying on as usual.'

'Elaine,' he said. 'She says we have to finish. She's going to Africa with Keith. Scotland first, and then Africa.'

'Does Keith know all about it then?'

'He does now. She thought she ought to tell him, so she did. James may have had some influence on it. But I thought it was a bad idea.'

'You would, of course.'

'Don't be nasty Jenny. As I told you, I don't have anyone to talk to.'

'Caroline?' I said.

'It's the end of term. She's got a million things to do. To be honest, I've been a passenger since, you know, your grandparents died. I've been useless. I can't load any more on to her.'

'Oh Midge,' I said, and I felt my eyes fill with tears, there in the street.

'Jenny,' he said. 'Will you come home next week? Just for a few days. Bring Russell, I'd like to meet him again. I need some living creatures around me. Will you come?'

'I should have told you,' I said, 'Russell and me split up.'

'When? Why didn't you say?'

'Last year. Nearly a year ago. I haven't seen him.'

'And you never said. Does Beth know?'

'She does now. I didn't tell her for a while, because – well, I don't know really. It's all right, don't worry about me.'

'I'd like to worry about you,' he said. 'It would make a change from worrying about me. Come home, why don't you.'

'I might,' I said. 'I'm not promising.'

'All right,' he said. 'No promises, but I'll get the house cleaned up. I know it was a mess last time you came.'

I put my bag down on the doorstep to look in my bag for my key. I wanted to be at home – properly at home – so badly. I wanted to be able to walk down to the village and remember my Nana and Grampy. I wanted to help Midge clean up the house. I wanted there to be air around me instead of fumes. I wanted to go and spend time with Beth and see how the baby is growing.

I said goodbye to Midge before I gave in and made promises, and let myself in. In the hall, at the bottom of the stairs there was an unfamiliar rucksack, just a small one. I could see from the light that the back door was open. My first thought was that we were being burgled but my second was that Russell had come to find me.

I put my bags down. I took breaths. I could not stop myself from smiling. I went through into the kitchen, and true enough, there was someone there.

Sitting on the kitchen step, face turned to the sun, was Troy.

28

Midge: Company

The last day of the summer term is actually a bit like Christmas. There are rituals. The kids get to go home early, then there are leaving speeches, and emotion, and a sort of giddy exhaustion, exacerbated by alcohol. When we have drunk the staff room dry some of us go to the pub.

I tell myself this will be my last ever last day before the summer holiday. I tell myself I will leave before the next one. I wonder what life could be like without a job to go to every day. Without other people. With no incidents and dramas to take my mind away from myself.

I wander out of the pub garden and because I cannot bear to go home I wander down towards the campsite. Two cars, one with a trailer, are at the gate and Nev is seeing them in.

'Be with you in a minute,' he says. 'I'm closing after this one. We're full.'

He waves them to their pitches, puts the No Vacancies sign up and comes with me into the front garden. Mandy is sitting on the bench, a glass in her hand.

I haven't seen her since the funeral and hardly recognise her. She is wearing shorts and her long thin white legs are flushed with pink. Her long thin nose is a mixture of sunburn and face cream. She has on a white top, the sort with hardly any back to it, and her hair has been cut even shorter. All this must be what is making her look years younger.

I have been drinking beer since three thirty, although at a slower rate than some of my colleagues, but I still accept the offer of another one. Nev brings out a chair for me and Mandy makes room for him on the bench.

Swallows flit in front of us. 'They're not bats are they?' says Mandy. 'Because I hate bats. I hated them last time I lived here and I hate them now. But I'll put up with them this time.' As if it was bats that had driven her away.

'D H Lawrence hated them too,' says Nev. 'He says they are like bits of broken umbrellas.'

'Poetry,' says Mandy scornfully. She turns to me. 'Did you know that this man –' she smiles lovingly at Nev – 'did you know he was into poetry?'

Did I? Probably not. Nev has always seemed to me a man of few words, not a man who felt at ease with words, or made friends of them.

We sit for a while in silence.

'I've been drinking,' I say. 'You can tell me to go home if you like. I just needed some company.'

'Fine,' says Mandy, and Nev nods.

We sit for a while.

'Glenys all right?' says Nev. I imagine he's been thinking for sometime before coming out with this sentence.

'No different,' I say. I think a bit and then say, 'What do you think Nev? What do you think sent her the way she is?'

He shrugs as I knew he would. Mandy makes a small dismissive noise. She has no time for people who do not wrestle with their circumstances.

'It's just,' I say, 'she had a good start in life, you know, good parents, comfortably off, she's not stupid, she could have made something of her life, and now – it seems like a waste. It *is* a waste.'

Nev speaks, after thinking for a long time. 'The parents,' he says. 'They weren't that good really. There was quite a lot of neglect.'

'Really?'

'I should know,' he said. 'I was there.'

'What sort of neglect?' I can be forgiven, I think, for being sceptical.

'For a start,' says Mandy, 'they sent Nev to boarding school so that they could go swanning off to Africa or wherever any time they wanted.'

'Not really what you'd call –'

'I would,' she says.

'I don't mean,' says Nev, 'neglect in the sense of not being fed, or not having shoes on our feet, more in the sense of being ignored. They were busy, you know, building up the business, making money. There weren't after-school clubs, nothing like that in those days, and anyway, I don't think they would have wanted to pay out for someone else to look after us. We were just left to get on with looking after ourselves.'

'But if that was a cause of her – condition, then Elaine would surely have been affected too. And you.'

'Takes people different ways,' says Mandy. 'Elaine goes through life feeling responsible for everyone. She thinks it's always her got to pick up the pieces. They both want attention, but Elaine wants it for being good and Glenys wants it for being different.'

'Looking back,' says Nev, 'I can see she was abnormally competent. Elaine I mean. Bossy. Your Beth is a bit like her actually. It was only when she went off to Uni that I was sent to boarding school. I guess there was a bit more money by then.'

'Don't kid yourself,' said Mandy. 'There was always enough money if they'd wanted. It was just easier to let the three of you bring yourselves up, any way you could.'

'But,' I say.

'I know,' said Mandy. 'Things changed. They were great with the grandchildren weren't they. Completely rewrote the book.'

I can't take it in. I can't understand why Elaine has never told me any of this. I want to see her. I need her. Of course, the next best thing is to talk about her.

'Elaine – neither of them – has never told me any of this.'

'She wouldn't,' says Mandy, who apparently can speak for Nev with his approval. 'You can hardly get Elaine to admit there has ever been anything difficult in her life. You've got to know that.'

I had never thought about it. We had our own shared troubles – we talked about them all the time. I couldn't remember that she had ever told me much about her childhood; I assumed it had been ordinarily normal. 'I haven't seen Elaine lately,' I say. 'Have you?'

'Look,' says Mandy, 'you don't have to pretend. We know all about you and Elaine.' And Nev says, slowly, 'Known for years mate. Mandy here spotted it years ago.'

'You never said.'

'What was there to say?' he says. 'What difference would it make?'

'But what shall I do?' I say, just like, if I remember rightly, I said to Jenny. And I tell them that Elaine won't see me, and that she's going to Africa with Keith, and that my children are confused and angry and that I don't see any joy in any future I can envisage.

'Are you saying,' says Mandy, 'Elaine would stay with you if you left Glenys?'

'I don't know.' The last of the sun melts into the earth and now bats do begin to fly in front of us.

'Ever heard the term, commitment-phobic?'

'What?'

'It means,' she says, 'someone, usually a man, who won't commit himself, and he's always backing off, and putting things off, and saying Maybe, or Next year, until –'

'Yes,' I say,' I know what it means. Are you saying that's what I am? Because what about Glenys? I've looked after her all these years. Is that not commitment?'

'No,' she said.

'And actually,' says Nev, 'I would say it's not just you. What about Elaine? She hasn't ever made a proper commitment, to you or to Keith. Has she?'

'Cowardly,' says Mandy. 'I'm sorry, I know she's your sister Nev, but she doesn't face up to things. In that way she's as bad as Glenys.'

I shake my head to show I disagree, and it reminds me how much I have drunk. I stand up to go.

Mandy looks out at the darkening world, where squads of crows are flying to roost. 'And anyway,' she says, 'what does Glenys want? Has anyone ever asked her?'

Jen: Apologies

'How did you get in?' I said.

'Annie gave me a key,' said Troy. I was astonished. I didn't know things had gone that far, or indeed that they had gone anywhere. And he had, after all, held my hand that afternoon in the park.

'Oh,' I said. I had been aware that Annie had been missing some nights, but thought she was just doing extra shifts.

'I hope I didn't scare you,' he said.

'What? Oh. No. I thought you were –'

'Someone else?'

'Well,' I said, recovering and sounding a bit more brisk, 'I certainly wasn't expecting you.'

'Didn't you know Annie was seeing me?'

'No,' I said, and I filled the kettle and switched it on. 'Tea?'

'Too hot,' he said.

I could not leave the room and leave him there. I could not think of an excuse to do it. I did not want him to think I was angry with him, I did not want him to feel embarrassed. And yet I did not want to talk to him. As always it felt full of the possibility of exposure, and then anger, tears, something uncontrolled.

And I had the feeling that if I went out of the room and saw that rucksack in the hall, then I would have to come back in to make sure that it really wasn't Russell. That was unhinged, I knew it was, but the feeling was so strong, that he had come to find me, in spite of its complete lack of logic or probability, that I had to keep Troy in front of me as proof.

He sat there, on the step, occasionally drinking water from a bottle. I sat on a hard chair. Midge, Russell, Troy, Tricky, they swirled round my tired brain like children in a playground. I was not responsible for any of them, I believed, but they would not stop being present.

'Are you all right?' he said, after a long silence.

'*I* am,' I said.

'Who isn't then?'

I didn't answer.

'Midge, I bet,' he said. 'He's gone to pieces hasn't he?'

'What do you know about it?'

'I guessed, that's all.'

I thought that maybe his mother had said something to him. I said nothing.

'Do you remember,' he said, 'all those names that your Nana had for you? What were they now? I only recall Tricky, because everyone calls him that.'

'Not everyone,' I said. 'Elaine and Midge call him Patrick.' I thought for a bit. 'I don't know what Keith calls him.'

'And Honey was called Bee, wasn't she,' he said. 'She still likes to be called that, sometimes. But I can't remember the rest of you.'

'James was Captain Jim,' I said. 'He hates that now, but it was kind of appropriate for him. He was the oldest. Until you came along.' I hoped I didn't sound rude. I didn't want to be rude. 'Ashley she called Bud, or Buddy, do you remember? I don't know why. Beth was Busy Lizzy, or Biz, or sometimes Wizzy, or Izzy.'

'And yours? Something that began with a J?'

'Junie, she called me. Jennifer Juniper. It's a song.'

'That's right. I know it.' Thankfully he did not sing it, but even so I felt like I might cry.

He got up off the step and came into the room. 'You're not all right are you,' he said and handed me a piece of kitchen roll. 'What's wrong?'

That was a stupid question, I thought. Surely he knew what was wrong. 'I'm homesick,' I said.

'This is not about that boyfriend then?' So Annie had told him about Russell.

I blew my nose and passed my hands down my face, hoping I would come out from behind them smooth and placid. 'It's nothing,' I said. 'I'm just tired. Take no notice.'

He sat back on the step. 'Tell me about being homesick,' he said.

So I did. When I first came to London, when I was eighteen, it was great. I was a student, I was in the big city, I was far away from little old Sheffield, and my deviant family. I had got away from the safety of the North. Beth only got as far as Manchester.

As everyone does, I reinvented myself. I was not the person who stood just behind my big sister, waiting for instructions; I was not the person whose life was constricted by a crazy mother; I was not the person whose father was there, right there in the same school, so that even though I was never bullied, I was never trusted either.

I liked London. I liked finding my way around, getting lost and finding myself again. I liked my course, I liked teaching, I was good at teaching. I had friends, many of them – Helen, Becky, Em – all of them now far away, in one way or another. I had boyfriends, some more, some less serious. I felt normal, and I felt as if I was in the right place.

I graduated, I got a job, I moved on, I moved up. I went home only rarely; I did not need to go more often – I knew they would be there, unchanged and waiting for me. I expected that one day I would meet someone to be with permanently, and that we would probably move out of London to somewhere we could afford, and we would have a child, or two. I was confident that this would happen, just happen, whatever I did.

Then there was Russell and it seemed like it was happening, and then he was gone.

'But you said homesick,' said Troy.

'I was planning to go home. You know I gave my notice. I wanted to go back north. I feel like there's nothing for me there now.'

'So?'

'How can I? Now? Sid and Dot are dead, my father is – well, not dead, but different.'

'He's not different,' said Troy. 'He's just the same as he's always been. You know something about him that you didn't know before. Get over it.'

'The thing is,' I said, 'there is too much to get over. I don't know where to start.' We sat for what seemed a long time, in silence.

Troy's phone pinged and he looked at the text. 'Would you like me to go?' he said. 'Annie's going to be late. I can walk to the hospital and meet her if you want to be alone. Or I can stay.'

I was not going to ask him to stay, but I thought if he went I would cry until I had a reason to stop, and I did not know when that would be.

'Have a drink,' I said.

'Have you got beer?'

We had beer. I took my chair into the yard and sat closer to him. It was so hot that I went to the fridge and put ice cubes in my beer.

'You can't do that,' he said.

Long silences. The pulse of Friday evening traffic from the road, the beep of the pelican crossing, occasional voices from neighbouring houses, the smells of cooking through open back doors, music through open windows.

'Here's a place to start,' he said. We were on our third beer. 'Let's get some old debris out of the way shall we.'

I was muzzy with heat and alcohol, just alert enough for this to make me anxious, but not quick enough to head him off.

'I think,' he said, 'that probably two apologies are in order. I'll go first.' He took a long drink and did not look at me. 'I'm sorry,' he said, 'that I asked you to take your knickers off.'

I said nothing.

'It was wrong,' he said. 'I knew it was wrong at the time. I hope it has never caused you – a problem.'

'It's OK,' I said, after thinking for quite a while. 'I knew it was wrong too, though I didn't know why. But I wasn't ever upset about it.'

'Honestly?'

'Honestly. I've still got the football programme.' And we laughed, a little.

Then he said, 'Your turn.'

'What?'

'Your turn. To apologise.'

I waited. He waited. Then I said, 'For the Fire.'

'For what you didn't do,' he said.

'Yes,' I said. 'I knew it wasn't you. I was there, I saw it.'

'Where were you?'

'Down by the stream. Beth and me, we were rebuilding the Little Den. She didn't see, she'd gone back to the house for something, I was there on my own.'

'You knew it wasn't me?'

'I didn't want Tricky to get into trouble. He was miserable. You and James were being horrible to him.'

'Did he tell you to lie?'

'He didn't tell me to do anything. I didn't even lie, I just never let anyone know I was there. Nobody ever asked me. I didn't know what you were saying, or what James was saying, or Ashley.'

'Ashley told the truth,' said Troy, 'but they preferred to believe Tricky. And James lied as well.'

'And then you ran away,' I said. 'I didn't know we were never going to see you again.'

'You could still have spoken up.'

'Why did you go away? I mean, really, why wouldn't you come back? Was it so important?'

'Would you want to stay,' he said, 'where no one believed you? I stayed in my room for two weeks waiting for someone to step up and tell the truth. Waiting for James, and Tricky. No one came near me except my mum. Nev didn't speak to me. Would you want to carry on living with people like that?'

'I'm sorry,' I said. 'I didn't know it would matter, and then, when it did, it was too late. I've thought about it a lot. When I knew that we might meet again, I wondered whether I should say anything. Decided not to.'

'Well,' he said. 'Who knows what might have been different?' He patted my hand. 'When I saw you, at the funeral, I recognised you straight away. I thought you looked nice. Lovely. I fancied you. But there was this thing in the way, and it never quite happened, did it? Do you know what I mean?'

'I suppose so. You got Annie to find out, didn't you? She told you.'

'Annie's great,' he said. 'I should thank you for introducing us. I know it's early days but it's amazingly great. But I hope you didn't think anything else. Did you?'

Arrogant bastard, I thought, but I said, 'It's OK. I'm not actually looking for a relationship right now. I think Russell and I have things to sort out first.' Which I had never said, or even thought, before.

He patted my hand again. 'You'll do fine Jen. You'll be all right.'

29

Midge: Wife

For years I have never gone into Glenys' room without knocking. And again, this time, I've knocked, I've heard her call, Come in. I've opened the door.

She is sitting in her chair by the window. In her lap is what I recognise – I think – as the cover of one of the front room chairs, and she is unpicking it back into its individual squares.

'Either come in or go out,' she says testily. 'Don't just stand there.'

I go further into the room and close the door, but there is nowhere for me to sit unless I sit on the bed. The other chair is piled high with stuff – clothes mostly I think but also cushions, slippers, carrier bags of unidentifiable contents.

You never know what you will get from Glenys. It can be silence, chatter, questions, still, on occasions, tears. Today silence seems to be what I will get and I would like very much to offer her a cup of tea and then back out. I have spent many days now, wandering, apparently aimlessly, round the streets. It was not aimless, my wandering, though it turned out to be fruitless. I was hoping to bump into Elaine by accident, I was thinking about what I would like to say to Glenys, I was considering a number of different futures.

I never caught so much as a glimpse of Elaine though I passed her house a thousand times. Keith's car was gone, but hers was still there. She did not respond to any texts to her mobile and I could not risk leaving a message on the landline. The heavy weight in my chest had grown until I seriously wondered whether this was a heart attack coming on.

'How are you?' I say to Glenys, and she looks up sharply as if that innocent opening has made her suspicious. The bright light from the window makes her look grey and dull. Unusually for her, she is wearing something sober, a sort of dark poncho, if that is the word, over pyjamas.

'There's something I'd like to talk to you about.' I sound like a person behind a desk, working my way round to a reprimand for some minor matter. 'Is that all right?'

She makes no answer but continues snipping and pulling lengths of wool.

The phrases that I composed and polished have deserted me, and all I can think of to say is, 'Do you think, if I left, you would be OK?'

'Where are you going?' Has she misunderstood me? Does she think I'm going out, just for an hour, or a day? But I choose to answer as if she knows what I mean.

'I don't know where I will go. I would need to find somewhere to live. You can stay here, in the house.'

She continues with her work. 'Is this what Beth was talking about?' she says. 'Is this what she wanted you to tell me?'

'In a way, yes.'

'In a way.'

'Glenys,' I say, and this time some of my rehearsed speeches come back to me, 'this is not a marriage, what we have. We don't love each other. We could both make a fresh start.'

Snip. Snip. Pull. Drop piece of wool on to the little pile on the window sill. Outside the window, the dusty August garden blows restlessly in a hot unpleasant wind.

'No,' she says, and then nothing at all for a good while. I begin to think I might leave her to think about it.

'No,' she says again, and I notice that her scissors now are not snipping carefully through the seams, but slashing randomly so as to destroy the squares. Well, I think, it doesn't matter to me.

'I'll leave you to think about it,' I say. What a fatuous thing to say.

'I will *not* think about it,' she says – shouts rather. I wish I had packed my things already, and sorted out somewhere to go. 'You will *not* go,' she shouts.

I back out of the door. I hear the scissors – I suppose – hit the door as I close it. I hear what must be her fist hitting the window, and wait for the sound of glass crashing, but it doesn't come.

'Do you think I don't know?' she yells after me. 'I know all about it. I know everything.'

I have to leave the house. I am afraid of the force in her that I have set in motion. As I unlock the front door she is at the top of the stairs, unmoving, looking wild but speaking quietly. 'Don't ever come back,' she says, 'or I will kill you.'

Jen: Dust

'He's scared to go back into the house,' said Beth.

'For God's sake,' I said. 'What does he think she's going to do? Burn it down like Jane Eyre?'

'It wasn't Jane Eyre who burnt it down,' said Beth.

'For god's sake, I know that,' I said. 'I've seen the film.'

'Anyway,' said Beth, 'Mandy rang me and told me. She must be wondering what sort of madhouse she's moved back into, but I have to say she seems to be enjoying it, in a way. Midge is staying in the bungalow, only till it's sold though, he'll have to find somewhere else. Nev has been to see the Bitch, apparently she's all right, coping on her own.'

'We always knew she could.'

'Crazy as flies in a bottle, he told me, but she's got food and stuff. She's OK. Wouldn't talk about Midge or anything.'

'What about Elaine?'

'Don't know. Nev says no one has seen her. He thinks she must have gone with Keith up to Scotland, without telling anyone.'

'I have to get out of London,' I moaned. 'It's horrible here, I hate it. But if I go home, where could I stay? I'm not staying with Her, if she's gone completely mad.'

'Stay with Midge in the bungalow,' said Beth.

'No thank you,' I said. I was too uncomfortable with Midge now, and it would feel just too weird to stay in Sid and Dot's house anyway. And I couldn't intrude on Nev and Mandy while they were having some sort of second honeymoon.

'Well then,' said Beth, 'you'll just have to sleep in a tent.'

I picked a spot right at the edge of the Forest. Most of the birds don't sing this late in the summer, but I could still lie in bed early in the morning and hear some cheeps and squawks as they woke up.

Strange to say that I had never before slept in a tent. It was only a tiny one, that Nev hauled out of his shed for me. He made no comment on my decision. The thing that was most peculiar for me was arriving at the bus station and there being no Midge to meet me. I had to wait half an hour among the harsh lights and sudden draughts and solitary people of the Transport Interchange for a bus that would take me to walking distance of the village.

It was after nine when I got there, and Mandy had just gone to bed.

'Bit early, isn't it?' I said.

Nev was filling the kettle and I thought he had not heard but he must have done. 'Mandy's been talking to Troy,' he said.

'And?' Though at that moment I began to know. If I had thought of it before I would not have come home.

'She knows you saw what happened,' he said. 'She's not too pleased with you.'

That was all he said, and I could think of nothing to say to him. He gave me a cup of tea, and showed me how to put up the tent. He gave me a mattress and a sleeping bag and a pillow, and I crawled in and slid into sleep.

In the night I woke up and listened to all sorts of noises. People were talking quietly in other tents and awnings. A child was crying somewhere at the far end of the field. There were small rustlings in the grass around the tent, and a louder scuffling that I thought might be badgers in the Forest. I lay awake for a bit, and then went back to sleep, feeling unexpectedly peaceful.

The thing is about camping, I discovered, do what you will, you wake up early. Other people's children start playing outside your tent, dogs come sniffing round, you hear the scrape of saucepans on camping stoves, you smell bacon frying. Also, you need a pee and you know you have to walk across the wet grass to the toilet block.

I did not know what I had come home for. I figured Nev would tell Midge I was there and I hadn't asked him not to, but I was not going to seek him out, not yet. I had kind of hoped that Nev would invite me to eat with them, but he hadn't, so I would have to go shopping for some ready-to-eat provisions.

Beth was not at home. They had gone with Dan's parents to the seaside. Pictures of Xander on the beach seemed to arrive on my phone every minute. It appeared to me that coming here was a stupid idea, looked at objectively, but in myself I was strangely content. I walked into the Forest as far as the stream, to see if the kingfisher was visible, but I saw nothing except a few blue tits, and a squirrel lolloping up a tree trunk.

I walked up the road past the bungalow, standing for a minute in front of it, assuring myself that I did not have to go in. I ate a Snickers bar that I had thoughtfully packed. It was delicious. I thought how great it would be to have chocolate for breakfast every day instead of the sensible low fat options or, more often, nothing. Then I thought of my mother and her diet and decided I would buy some cereal bars for the following days.

I walked through the village, along the jennel, into the streets, past the same houses that had been there all my life. I went slowly round our bit of Sheffield, calling into shops for things as they came into my head. Buns mostly, and cans of drink. Apples, though I am not a fruit person. I walked past my old school and wondered if Midge was in there. I looked at the houses, as I walked past, of people I had been at school with, knowing that they would all have moved on by now.

I had a cup of tea and a bacon sandwich in a café – empty except for me, and at last, when I was bored with ambling and it must surely have been past midday, set off at the same slow pace towards our house, I was going home, partly because I had nowhere else to go and partly because I had thought of a job to do.

I let myself in. It smelled bad, of unemptied kitchen bin and unwashed clothes, and damp. In the kitchen, the kettle was slightly warm so I knew She had been down that morning, even if she was asleep again by now.

I had come to sort out my things. All the boxes under my bed needed clearing, in case someone else got to them before me – I had been made a bit anxious when Midge asked if he could look for that video. And now, if Midge suddenly decided to sell up, I might not get the chance to go through them before he chucked them in a skip.

First I needed to let Her know I was there. I made myself a cup of tea and went upstairs. It became less smelly as I went up. She was sitting up in bed, radio on, and she did not look surprised to see me. Nor pleased.

'Hi,' I said. 'I'm just here to tidy my room.' Looking round I wondered if she could attach any meaning to my words. But we were all used to the midden that she chose to live in. One of the panes of her window was cracked right across.

'Don't talk,' she said. 'I'm listening to this.'

How nice to see you dear, how are you? Sit down, tell me all about yourself. To be fair though, when she does behave like that it gives me the creeps.

I left her and pulled out the boxes from under my bed. I remembered buying these in the hardware shop, before I left home to go to Uni. I recalled sorting my stuff, throwing away some, putting some in the boxes for some unspecified time in the future, which had now arrived.

There were schoolbooks, and old exam papers and report cards and certificates. My Record of Achievement in a dark red folder that looked like a restaurant menu. More certificates. I probably never acquired as many as Beth but I must have come home at the end of every term loaded down with them.

Of course I never even bothered to try and get my mother to take an interest. She seemed to have something approaching a phobia about anything to do with schools. And Midge, as we grew up a bit, we realised that he did not take certificates seriously. He thought they were a sham, 'the opiate of the classes' he said feebly. Looking at the great pile that I have, in all colours of paper and card and ink, in this or that pompous font, signed by various teachers and countersigned – not manually – by Mrs Young, the head, Caroline, looking at this lot I had some sympathy with Midge's point of view. But kids like them. And so do their parents.

I put them in the pile to be thrown away. I added my small collection of football programmes.

I liked looking at some photos I'd kept. Me in the school play in Year eight. Tricky was supposed to be in it too. Our Day Out. Tricky was the youngest person in it, the only Year seven allowed, because he pleaded so hard. Then at rehearsals he was so good they gave him a speaking part, and then on the last night, just before the curtain went up, he swore at another kid backstage, and was told off – and walked, just walked off, home, and his lines had to be given to someone else at a minute's notice.

The next year they wouldn't have him in the play because of that, and so I wouldn't be in it either, even though it was Oliver, and I thought – probably over-optimistically – I had a chance of playing Nancy. That was the end of my theatrical career, though not, of course, Tricky's. I suppose – well, I hope – that by now he must have learned how to be a team player.

In another box I found all the usual tat that accumulates from a childhood. Soft toys, rubbish jewellery, ribbons and slides and scrunchies, diaries with the first three dates filled in and then nothing, badges, pens that were once, for some reason, too special to be used. Compilation tapes too embarrassing to be looked at closely.

A small pile of letters, bound with about a dozen rubber bands. I knew what these were. They were letters I wrote to Troy in the months after he ran away. They were letters of apology and self-abasement. I implored him to come back – it would be nice to believe that they were the product of true recognition of what I had failed to do, but really, I was just being melodramatic and believing that I was in love with him. I considered that eleven was a proper age to be in love.

I was thankful that I never sent them, and I never sent them because I didn't know his address. I could have asked Nev, I knew, but secrecy seemed to me to be important. I dropped hints to NanaDot but if she understood my hints then she also understood that telling me where to find Troy would be a dangerous thing. Too many people had run away to London already.

I was going through all the postcards that were ever sent to me – at least twenty – when I heard the front door being opened. I assumed it was Midge, coming back to fetch some things and I listened to his footsteps coming up the stairs, and to the opening of Her bedroom door. The voice I heard, however, was Elaine's.

'Hello Glen.'

I didn't hear an answer, and then the door closed and I could hear no more. Oh shit, I thought. My mother will tell Elaine I'm here and she'll come looking for me. And I really don't want to see her.

The only place to hide was under my bed, so I scrambled, as quietly as I could, into the space left by the boxes. I thought of all the skin particles and loose hairs that had dropped and been pushed by draughts to the still place under my bed, during the many years – let's say sixteen – that I slept in it. And then there was another eighteen years' worth of undisturbed dust, added since I left home, siftings of the house and my parents, accumulated from the air currents that moved unnoticed from one room to another, adding year by year to the great gritty rolls of fluff that I was now lying in.

Dust to dust. I hoped Elaine would go soon.

It was probably not a long time that I lay there, trying not to sneeze and needing a pee, before I heard my door open and Elaine's voice call back to Her, 'No, she's gone.' And then a further time, while Elaine brought my mother a cup of tea, and went into Midge's room, and came out again and, finally, went downstairs and out of the front door.

I emerged and looked out of the window. Elaine was walking away, not in the direction of her own house but down towards the village and the campsite, presumably to see Midge. So, I thought, it is possible, people do sometimes come back, and make up, and kiss.

I went back into my mother's room. You would not know Elaine had been there except for the steam that wisped up from the cup of tea.

'You still here?' said my mother.

'Are you all right?' I said. I had been assuming, I realised, that before he left Midge had told her about him and Elaine, but it was possible she still did not know.

'Where's Midge?' I said.

She looked at me sharply. She is not stupid. 'Why ask me?' she said.

'Well,' I said, 'he's not here, is he? I thought you might know where he's gone. And when he's coming back.'

'He can do what he likes,' she said. 'He always has done.'

How can you say that? I was going to say, but stopped myself, thinking that she was at least partly right. Instead I said, 'What did he tell you? Is he coming back?'

'Did he send you to see me?' she said.

'I haven't seen him' I said. 'I know where he is though.'

'Then why ask me?'

I was still standing, still by the door. I had hardly ever, in my whole life, been further into my mother's room than this. I thought that and it made me feel sad. Then irritable.

'I don't know why you married him,' I said. 'I don't know why you bothered to have children. You never loved any of us.'

'Nobody ever loved me,' she said, quite calmly.

Then we both stopped, on the edge of that cliff. Then she plunged over it. 'I could have had a life,' she said. 'I was stuck here at home, with you and your sister, wasn't I? I could have been doing what I wanted.'

'You always did exactly what you wanted,' I said. I may have shouted a bit at that point. 'When did you ever do anything for anyone else? Midge did it all.'

'Midge,' she said, as if he was dust, something you could blow, with nothing more than your breath, to make him disappear. 'You girls never saw through Midge like I did. All that Daddy, Daddy stuff, and climbing all over him. You were both just sickening, Daddy this and Daddy that.'

'Don't be stupid,' I said. 'For a start we never even called him Dad. He's always been Midge.'

'Only because I told you to,' she said. 'He was a useless father. And while I'm telling you things about your father, what about this one. He's having an affair. Did you know that?'

'How do you know? Who with?'

'I put two and two together,' she said. 'He's gone, hasn't he. So he must have gone to *her*.'

'Who though?' She didn't know who, did she?

She looked at me. 'You didn't know did you? Your precious Midge has got a lady friend and you didn't know about it. Ha.' She didn't know, I could tell.

I looked at her, sitting there on her bed, with her cup of tea that someone else had made for her and I thought that although she looked quite pathetic, thin and faded like rubbish, I didn't feel anything for her. I was not scared of her any more either.

She reached to her radio and turned up the volume. I waited for maybe half a minute, then I went back to my room. I looked at the scatter of minor possessions and felt nothing for them but disgust. I gave the nearest box a kick and then abandoned the task, and the room, and the house, and felt as if I was leaving for ever.

30

Midge: Surprise

It is a surprise to see Jenny standing outside the bungalow. It is about three weeks since she said she might come up, but she hasn't answered her phone for days, and I have had to believe that she's too angry with me, or maybe just too busy with her own life. Anyway, on a second glance the person is too hunched and scruffy to be her. She is standing there, not making any move to approach, and I conclude that it's just a customer from the campsite who happens to look a little like her.

Nowadays I often see people who aren't there. Elaine often. This makes me wonder if she is dead and haunting me. But surely someone would have informed me. Or maybe they did and I have forgotten.

Because I also see Sid and Dot, passing in front of a doorway, sitting by a window when I go into the room. I hear them too, muttering to each other as they get into bed at night, talking in their sleep, or chatting pleasantly as they wake in the morning.

I am supposed to be sorting out their belongings. Nev said this would be a help to him, at this busy time of year. We haven't heard yet what their will says, but we make the assumption that the bungalow will be sold, and their personal items distributed among the family. I am supposed to be making a list, and photographing the more valuable looking bits of furniture for the children to choose from.

It feels to me, at the end of every day, that I have spent more time than I strictly should just standing, just looking at something in my hand – a post card, a candle holder, a calendar made for them by James in 1986. I am supposed to identify such minor items and make the decision to throw them away. I have a black bin bag for the purpose. So far it contains some sewing patterns from the days when women wore dirndl skirts and little jackets and pillbox hats. Even those, I wonder whether they should be saved. Are they of historical value? Would someone want them?

Things go through my head. I wouldn't call it thinking.

I went with Nev back to my house and while he spoke with Glenys I hurriedly put some clothes in a few plastic supermarket bags, and picked up my work briefcase and my laptop and hurried out of there, shaking slightly. I think Nev must despise me for this behaviour.

I have left Glenys, just like that, that easy. Would I have stayed if she asked me to? If she had said she needed me, would I have felt I was bound to her? I don't know the answer to these questions and I don't need to. Clearly, she hates me more than I hate her and the thing that puzzles me is why she didn't throw me out years ago.

I have burnt my boats, I want to tell Elaine.

My children come into my head often. Beth and Jenny, those monsters of sense and control. And then I think of their goodness. There is goodness there, more than just prim morality. They are clever, serious young women, who want to do the right thing, and who *do* do the right thing. I would just like to see in them some of the softer virtues, some humour, frivolity, trustfulness, forgiveness. My favourite virtues. My virtues. Perhaps.

Patrick comes into my head. (I would never have named him Patrick, but it was a decision that was not thought to concern me.)

His sly, dissembling eyes, his professional sincerity. What people call his hidden charm. As a little boy he had real charm, something natural and freely offered. When he became a troubled child, and teenager, he could still pull out that charm and use it.

I have known him apologise to teachers at school after the most outrageous disruption of their lessons, and get away with it. 'Don't listen to him,' I would think – I never said it, how could I? And they would say what a nice boy he was really, underneath, and I would think, No, that's not it, the real boy is that swearing, peevish, toxic little nihilist, that charm is the sugar on the top. Do not believe in it.

But I couldn't say it. They all knew he was my nephew, he was the dubious apple on the shelf that also held the rosy wholesome James and Beth and Jenny. They could not – because teachers are not always subtle in their summing up of the hundreds of children who pass before them – comprehend that he was bad.

I could not comprehend it myself. Elaine and I could not comprehend it. He had been loved and nurtured the same as James. He had the same parental models of calmness and rectitude as James did. When he was ten he did something very wrong, and he got away with it. His family might have had strong suspicions that he had done it, but we treated him as if he was a good boy. We carried on as normal. What else was possible?

Most of all Elaine comes into my head. She never leaves it. My whole body aches with the feeling that she should be here and she is not. I see her in the distance, I start to hurry towards her, but it is always someone else. Does this mean that I have forgotten what she looks like? How can I miss someone if I don't remember what they look like?

Now, looking out of the window I see Jenny and I think it is the same phenomenon. Then the person walks away and I know it really can't have been her.

I go into the kitchen and look out on to the garden. It's all a bit of a tangle. If I had noticed before I would have offered to help Dot do something to tidy it up, I think. And yet, why would I think that? I never even managed to keep my own garden under control, it looks, front and back like the garden of the most deprived and hopeless family, long grass and old boxes and plastic bags caught on the bushes. Even Dot, approaching the age of ninety, used to manage better than me.

The sink is piled with dirty mugs and plates. I imagine Mandy coming in and looking scornfully at it. I imagine Dot made restless in her grave by it, if ashes can be restless. Turning in her urn – you never hear that said. The sun goes behind a cloud and the colours of the garden go dull and changed.

'Right,' I say out loud. No one else is talking to me so I might as well do it myself. 'I'm going to do one thing today. One thing at a time. First things first.'

I lift all the crockery out of the sink. I run hot water. I add washing up liquid. I put my hands into the comfort of it.

It is as I am putting the last item – frying pan – on the draining board that a shadow goes past the window. Jenny, I think and my heart softens and soars.

But not Jenny. My heart has no further to go, but it does even so. In through the back door, smiling a small smile, coming to claim me, I hope, Elaine. Elaine my own love.

Jen: Wet

I woke up listening to rain. I lay there for quite a while resisting the notion that I needed to get up and go for a pee. I thought of Russell. New Zealand – if that's where he still was – would be edging towards spring now, as we were edging towards autumn. I dozed a little and imagined myself as a grassy field with Russell nibbling me all over, like a flock of sheep. When I woke up again I cried a little.

When I got up I found that my clothes, in a pile on the end of my sleeping bag, were wet, and so was my rucksack with my spare clothes. The tent was leaking. I was hungry, and becoming, now that I was out of the sleeping bag, cold. I cried some more.

I unzipped the door and looked at the sliding grey of the rain. The trees dripped steadily. Across the field a family sat at a table under an awning and looked back at me, grinning smugly. They had a tent they could stand up in, chairs they could sit on, a big four-by-four they could drive away in.

I put my feet into my damp trainers, wished I had brought a coat with me, put a wholly inadequate jacket over my pyjamas and crawled on to the soaking field. Squelched over to the toilet block.

Mandy was in there, emptying the bins. She laughed when she saw me. 'Bad night?' she said.

'Everything's wet,' I said.

'Oh dear,' she said, mockingly. 'Where's your resourcefulness? Worse things happen at sea you know.' I did not feel resourceful. I did not think I would ever feel buoyant again. I went into a cubicle so that she would not see me crying, but when I came out she was still there.

'You might as well come up to the house' she said. Her voice was still unfriendly, grudging, but no longer mocking. 'You can dry out at least.'

'It's all right,' I said. 'I can go up to my mother's house. I know you don't like me. I know why too. I won't bother you.'

I put my damp jeans on over my pyjamas, took my rucksack and went up the hill. As I passed the bungalow I saw the curtains were closed and wondered if Midge was still there. I went to Hollin Road – home I suppose I should call it. I hoped I would find some clothes there, but there was only a dressing gown. Dust flew out of it when I shook it, but I had to put it on. I put all my clothes in the dryer and sat in the kitchen and waited. There was no sign of life from Her.

After a bit a key turned in the front door and Nev came in. He took off his wet cagoule and hung it over the banister post before he spoke to me. That's the way he is – one thing at a time, deliberate.

'Come back to ours,' he said.

'Mandy doesn't want me to,' I said.

'I don't *want* you to,' he said and it was the first reproach I had heard from him.

'I can't go anywhere till my clothes are dry,' I said. I hoped this would make him go away. I wanted to feel abandoned by everyone, to prove that it was acceptable to go on crying, since I didn't believe I could ever stop.

He didn't say anything then, just sat on the other chair and waited with me.

Just as I was getting my things out of the dryer, my mother appeared in the kitchen.

'Oh it's you,' she said, whether to me or Nev or both, I couldn't say.

She switched the kettle on, made a cup of tea and went out, without saying any more. It reminded me of living in a student flat where random people showed up, did something or nothing, and faded away again. I felt no more curiosity about her than I had about them.

'Come on,' said Nev. I was dressed again and beginning to weigh up the possibilities open to me.

'I suppose,' I said as we walked down the road, 'I could move in with Midge. Temporarily I mean, while I look for a job. Until the bungalow is sold.'

'Maybe,' he said. His tone of voice did not encourage me. 'Thing is,' he said, 'Elaine's back. I think she's there with him, at the bungalow.'

'I don't want to see Elaine,' I said. 'But I don't want to live at home with Her.' I meant with my mother, and he understood what I meant.

'No I wouldn't want to either,' he said. 'For all she's my sister and all that, she'd drive anyone out of their wits.'

'Will she be all right on her own, do you think?'

'Fine,' he said. 'She's not so crazy that she can't look after herself. She'll cope.'

'The only other place I've got to go to,' I said, 'is where I was living in Leyton. A lot of my stuff is still there, but I got my deposit back and Annie might have let the room by now.'

'Is this Annie who Troy seems to have hooked up with?'

'Yes. I didn't know you knew about her.'

'He talks to Mandy quite often,' said Nev. 'He tells her quite a lot. He told her he had a good conversation with you a few weeks back.'

'Yes,' I said. 'It was good. Sort of put some things to rest.'

'Don't cry any more,' said Nev. 'You're reminding me of your mother. And it will only irritate Mandy.'

Nev delivered me to Mandy like a naughty child. I sat in the kitchen and remembered NanaDot and could have cried again, but stopped myself. Mandy fed me on tomato soup and egg and chips, and I felt about eight years old. Bogey sat under the table in the hope of stray chips. Nev had a cup of tea and then took himself into the yard to do the sort of things he does.

'Well then,' said Mandy. 'What are your plans?'

I shrugged and she got cross again. 'I'm trying to help,' she said. 'But I won't bother if you won't help yourself.'

'I talked to Troy,' I said. 'I apologised to him for keeping quiet. I should have spoken out, I know. But we're OK now, me and Troy.'

She took my plate away and put it on the draining board. She filled the kettle for another cup of tea. When she turned to face me I could see the old Mandy. Her hair was blond and short instead of black and Goth, her make up was subdued, but even so, her eyes bulged slightly and her cheeks and nose were pink, and the old, cross Mandy faced me across the kitchen where we first met.

'Good,' she said. 'Good that you and Troy are OK. You've apologised, jolly good for you, what a heroine you are. I suppose that puts an end to it does it.'

'Troy's OK,' I said. 'He's fine with it.'

'Certainly,' she said. 'He got what he wanted in the end. I gave him some grief about what he did, believe me –'

'What do you mean?' I said. 'What did he do?'

'Running away, I mean,' she said. 'Refusing to come back here. Making me go back to London with him. He knew I couldn't leave him down there. I knew he'd run again if I tried to drag him back here. Oh, I know he was at fault. But I'm talking about you, little sneaky Miss Perfect. You knew. And you wait – how many years? And then you let it out to suit yourself. You little cow.'

'I was a child,' I said. 'I didn't know what to do. Beth said it would be best to keep quiet.'

'So it's Beth's fault now. When are you going to take some responsibility? When is anything ever going to be your fault?'

'I didn't know he would run away,' I said. 'I didn't know he wouldn't come back. No one told us stuff. Then it was too late.'

'Too late,' she said scornfully. 'Look at you, sitting there, being waited on. Look at you, running home to mummy and daddy as soon as it gets tough, letting Nev come looking for you. Grow up, will you.'

I did not feel grown up, though I had believed for years that I was. I looked at the table and I was helpless to stop one tear splashing down on it. I tried to brush it away without Mandy seeing it.

'Go on,' she said. 'Turn on the waterworks. It won't wash with me, love. You were the one who could have changed things, you and that James – oh yes, I blame him too, and his parents. And I'll tell you something while I'm at it – if that Elaine thinks she's going to set up home with your father in that bungalow she's got another think coming. You can tell her so if you want.'

'I don't think I'll be talking to her,' I said. It was the first thing I had said that was really not some sort of excuse.

'Fine,' she said. 'I can tell her myself, no problem.'

'Mandy,' I said, 'isn't it all in the past now? Could we – maybe – get over it.'

'You are a fine one to talk,' she said. 'Your sister – at least she's made a life for herself, she's not crawling back here whingeing, she's not crying because she's got a bit damp in a tent. Get over it. You try,' she said, 'you try being a mother to an out-of-control fourteen year old, when you've got a newborn baby and a five-year-old crying all the time for his dad. You try being homeless and having to be rehoused in a tower block with piss in the lifts and junkies on the stairs.'

'I didn't know,' I said.

'You didn't think,' she said. 'I don't mind you not knowing when you were a kid, but what about a couple of years later? Couldn't you have broken your precious silence when you realised what had happened? Did you have to wait twenty years – more than twenty years – before you face up to it? And I don't think you've faced up to it yet. Have you? That cousin, brother of yours, whatever he is, he killed the dogs – well, he's not going to own up is he? He's going to lie his way out of it. I don't blame your dad. I've got a lot of time for old Midge, he did his best and he was caught between the lot of them. But you –'

'What would you have done?' I said. 'You would have stuck up for your own son, wouldn't you?'

She stopped and I thought it might be all over. I had never in my life been told off in that way, although I had delivered a few tirades to kids in my class that came close. I thought that I would never do it again. After that brief thought Mandy's voice, Mandy's questions, Mandy's anger, came back at me, in my head, in waves. I wanted to run away, I wanted Nev to come back in and rescue me. I continued to sit at the table. At last I said, 'What do you want me to do?'

She sat down too. She seemed limp now, pale and defeated, though if there was a winner it was her.

'I don't care what you do,' she said. 'I'd like you to stay away from Troy, but I can't force you to, I know that.'

'Don't worry,' I said. 'I like Troy, but I'm not after him, honestly.'

'Make no promises,' she said, 'but thanks anyway.'

'I didn't know,' I said, 'that you had such a hard time. I suppose I didn't know much about how things worked. Later I thought Nev would have been paying maintenance.'

'So he was,' she said. 'but he never had much spare. Your Nana and Grampy helped too. After the first few months we got a better place. It wasn't so bad, we survived. But I missed Nev, and so did Ashley. That's what was the worst thing.'

'So why did it take so long to come back?' I said.

'Events,' she said. 'Other people. My job. Being pig-headed. I'm back now though.'

'I'm glad you're back,' I said. 'I really am.'

'What about Tricky?' she said 'What does he say about it all?'

'I don't know,' I said. 'I know this sounds weird, but I've never mentioned it to him, ever. It's not something we talk about.'

She nodded, as if she expected nothing else. 'Maybe you should, she said. 'It might be preying on his mind.'

'It might,' I agreed.

Nev came back in. 'What do you want doing with that tent?' he said. 'It wants hanging up in the shed to dry, really, and the mattress.'

'Whatever,' I said. 'Thanks for the loan of it but I won't be here tonight.'

'You off then?' he said.

'If I could ask you a favour,' I said. 'If I could just stay here to charge my phone, would that be all right? And then I'll get out of your way.'

'You're not in our way,' said Nev, but he looked relieved all the same to be seeing the back of me.

31

Midge: If

We have woken up together. We have looked at each other and laughed, disbelievingly, at the idea of being together.

We have sat together over breakfast and although I know that Elaine wants to get on with the job of sorting out the mess I have made of her parents' house, I want us to continue sitting here all day, until it is time, or we are moved, to go back to bed.

'We won't have much money,' I say.

'I'll get a job,' she says.

'Why do you want me?' I say, and she laughs and puts her hand over mine on the table.

It is what I have always wanted, if only it had been possible, if only we had been able to work it out. If only.

If only it wasn't a fantasy.

We have not woken up together. We sat on the sofa until three in the morning, arguing, and then I fell asleep in the middle of whatever she was saying, and she must have gone somewhere else to sleep because when I wake up I am cold and alone and rain is beating on the window.

It might have all been a dream, except that Elaine's coat is on the chair, and her shoes are on the floor where she kicked them off, and there are cups with the dregs of tea in them, and biscuit wrappers on the floor, and screwed up tissues everywhere.

I make myself a cup of tea, and after considering, make one for her as well. I stand outside the bedroom door with it for some time, listening to her silence, wondering if I will make things worse by going in and waking her.

'You think,' she said last night, 'that just because I have left Keith, that I want to tie myself to another inadequate man.'

'I would do my best to be adequate,' I said. It was at a stage in the evening when I still believed that a favourable outcome was possible.

She had cried when she arrived, she had told me that she couldn't tolerate another second of Keith's company, that she had made her way back from Mull in the clothes she stood up in, weeping on station platforms and in railway carriages for the death of her parents and the end of her marriage, and the estrangement from her children.

'I wanted to see you so much,' she said.

Why then, why did she change her tune?

'It wasn't how I thought it would be.' That was all she could say.

Then we each said an awful lot more, but none of it got us to any place where we could stop and be together. At one point I said that she should go and live with Glenys, as I was never going to be allowed back into the house, and she even nodded as if she was taking the idea seriously.

'But I love you,' I kept saying, as if that was all that mattered, and that if I said it often enough she would come to see that it mattered and was the only thing that mattered, and would love me too.

'Don't you love me then?' I asked her, and she said that she didn't know, and that maybe she never had loved me, she didn't know.

Who *is* this woman? I thought, and I said, 'What was it all about then?'

'I don't know,' she said.

At some point in the evening she said she hadn't eaten for hours and I foraged around in the kitchen and brought her biscuits and crisps and chocolate bars. She threw a large slab of fruit and nut across the room and said that I had no idea, but after a few minutes she relented and got through a packet of chocolate Hobnobs with only a little help from me. If there had been any drink in the house we would have got through that as well, and there is no knowing what might have happened. If we still smoked we would have filled an ashtray with stubs, each one wet with tears.

If.

In the end I take the cup of tea in to her. It seems a shame to waste it. She is in Sid and Dot's bed, no sheets, no pillowcases, no duvet cover, and the curtains have not been closed. She is showing me how temporary she is here.

'Cup of tea,' I say and she stirs and rolls over. I put the tea down and wonder if I could get into the bed with her. What have I got to lose? Dignity I suppose. She puts an arm out from under the cover and I realise she is fully clothed. I keep hold of my overrated dignity and leave her to drink her tea in peace.

It's quite a while before I hear her in the bathroom. In the meantime I have tidied the room and am looking for something to do which might impress her with the idea that I am not inadequate, and in fact I take out one of the kitchen drawers with the idea of making a start on sorting it out.

She comes into the kitchen. 'I'm sorry,' she says.

And I turn to her full of relief but she stops me. 'I don't mean that,' she says. 'But I'm sorry I made a scene. I don't know what came over me.'

'It was both of us,' I say.

'Probably.'

'Shall I make us some breakfast? I think there are two eggs. Toast?'

'Is there bread?'

'Some.'

So we do sit together over breakfast after all, and she tells me that she has decided. She is going to live on her own for a while. She is going to experience being separated from Keith before committing to anyone else.

'But then?'

She doesn't know. Not when but if.

'But do you love me?'

'I suppose so,' she says.

Her phone rings and she goes back into the bedroom to answer it. 'It might be Keith,' she says. While she is out of the room I worry. Am I confident that she will not go back to Keith? What might he be saying about me that will change her mind? She'll come back in and tell me she's going again.

I am looking out of the window, at the road that leads up the hill towards Hollin Road, where I will never live again. The rain has stopped though the trees are dripping on to the still wet pavement. There goes the woman from yesterday, up the road, on the other side, rucksack on her back, hoodie pulled up to keep the drops off her hair.

As she passes, she glances – so quickly, so briefly – towards me. She takes a hand out of her pocket, she moves it, raises it, slightly. Was that a wave? Was it intended for me? Do I know her?

Elaine comes back, still listening to whoever it is on the phone, smiling with tears in her eyes. 'Yes, yes,' she says. 'Lovely. I'll tell him. Yes, I'll tell him too. Yes, everyone. And yes, we'll come and see you soon. Very soon.'

'Patrick,' she says to me.

Jen: Clearing

They have put me into the sitting room on my own while I am waiting. It is very tidy. Mandy is not a woman who could tolerate random objects piled on chairs. I don't feel as if I'm allowed to touch anything. I stand for a bit and look out of the window at the lessening rain. Far to the west the clouds may be clearing a bit, though I know better than to expect a fine afternoon.

The strip of garden in front of the house, where Nana grew her flowers, is looking tidier too. Mandy has been busy. I wonder whether she will soon run out of things to do here and be up chivvying my mother and cleaning her house and knocking her garden into shape. I will never know, I say to myself.

Beyond the garden I can see campers emerging from their vans and awnings, looking up at the sky, calculating whether to pack up and move on. Go south for the day, or north.

Me too, that's what I'm calculating. I am sure that I cannot stay here. North, south, east, west.

South to get my stuff from Annie – and take it where? Or to see Tricky, and the unknown Aoife – but would I want to upset them, so close to the baby being born? West to see Julia? Maybe, maybe not.

North to see Beth, if she's back from the seaside? But she's going back to work any day now, she has to get Xander settled in a nursery, she won't have time for me. Further north? James in Scotland? I could go and see him. That would be an adventure. James on his island. (Skye is it? That's the only one I know the name of. It sounds lovely.) His girlfriend Shona, who I've never met. I've only seen a photo, on a hillside, wearing a woolly hat and a serious jacket. Binoculars round her neck.

There is James – as guilty as me. Troy was his friend and James, to protect his brother and the rest of his family, let us all believe that he had killed the dogs. There are things I should say to James.

There are things I should say as well to Nev, and Mandy. There is an apology to be made to Nev and Mandy – not because they need to know I'm sorry, but to let them know that after all this time I have noticed, even slightly, what it did to them. If Troy had been believed he might have come back. He would never have gone.

Certainly there would have been less damage. If Tricky had been blamed as he should have been, he would have been punished and then forgiven. There's a big difference between a ten year old and a fourteen year old in what can be forgiven. Tricky would not have had to run away. If I had known the consequences of things then I hope I would have stood up and told what I knew.

I have cried enough today, you would think, but there seem to be more tears available to me. Industrial quantities of tears. I bet I could beat Beth in a crying competition today. The skin on my face is drying out with so much salt water streaming down it. I know Mandy was disgusted with me, but she doesn't know what a backlog of tears I had to dispose of. I could set off the third Sheffield flood, I think to myself, with the part of my brain that isn't feeling like a poor, mournful, inconsolable wretch.

I stop eventually. One does, I've found.

My phone must be charged by now. I venture back to the kitchen, where Mandy and Nev are sitting at the table, apparently waiting for me.

'I'm sorry,' I say. 'I should have thought years ago, I should have said something. Honestly, I am truly sorry that I didn't speak up when I should have done.'

I stand there, wondering what to do next, and they look at each other, probably wondering the same. Mandy nods at Nev. You say something, she means.

He thinks for a bit, then says, 'Apology accepted. Is that right Mand?'

'I think she means it,' she says.

'I'm going now,' I say. 'Thank you for everything, you've really helped. All sorts of ways.'

'Where are you off to then?'

A good question. I begin to tell them, making it up as I go along. 'The bank first. I've got some money in the bank, I'll be fine for a while. Then I need to go back to Annie's to get some stuff – my passport mainly, and a better set of clothes.'

Mandy's face seems to stiffen slightly and I can see her thinking that I'll see Troy.

'If I see Troy,' I say, 'I'll just tell him how good you were to me. Or maybe I'll just tell Annie and she can tell him. You'll like Annie, she's great.

'Then I think I'll go up to Scotland to sort things out with James. I've never talked to him about all this. I think he needs to know.'

'So does the other one,' says Mandy.

'I know. His girlfriend is having a baby any day now. But when the time is right I'll go and see him too. I really will, I'm not just saying it.'

'And then?' says Nev. 'Will you be coming back up here?'

I haven't thought that far ahead but my words come out without me even knowing what I was going to say. 'Not yet,' I say. 'I'm thinking I might find a way of seeing my old boyfriend. He's in New Zealand you know, but he says I'm welcome to go there and see him.'

'Worth a try,' says Mandy. 'Good luck.' I can't tell if she's being sarcastic.

'What about your mum?' says Nev.

'No,' I say. 'I don't want to see her. Maybe never again.'

He says nothing to that, only, 'And your dad?'

'Tell him I've gone,' I say. 'And tell him I'll stay in touch.'

I put my bag on my back and go out into the rain. My phone, working again, buzzes, and I have a text from Tricky. 'Roisin, born this morning. All well. So happy.' I have a niece to go with my nephew. I can send them postcards from wherever I am.

As I walk past the bungalow on my way to the bus I do not look at it. I should probably have gone into it, to prove to myself that my Nana and Grampy are really not there any more, but I have had enough emotion for one day. So, no, I don't look at it. But my hand makes a little wave, a little involuntary sign, an acknowledgement, a goodbye maybe, or a thank you.

Also by Susan Day

THE ROADS THEY TRAVELLED

What did happen to Marcie?

Four girls set our one wartime morning, on a day that will bind them together for years to come. Work and marriage, children and divorce, change and death.

Many years later they are still in touch, and still trying to resolve the tragedy that has been a constant in their lives.

Ordinary is made extraordinary by the intricacies shared in this beautifully woven tale of lives shaped by the forces of history… The reader is drawn into a skilfully painted picture of lives, changed forever by war.

Bryony Doran, author of *The China Bird*

Offers fresh new perspectives on lives lived – its pages are filled with moments and stories that are a pleasure to take into the imagination.

Docs and Daughters Book Group, Bristol

WHO YOUR FRIENDS ARE

It's the 1960s and you may recognise some of the characters from *The Roads They Travelled*.

Rita – clever, determined, ambitious.
Beautiful too.
Pat – none of the above.

Rita is the oldest of five children.
Pat is the only child of a widowed mother.

Rita gets her education against the odds.
Pat has a more conventional life.

Rita achieves success and money.
Pat has a family.

They say history is written by the winners, but in this case it is by Pat with time on her hands.

What conclusions will she draw?

What judgements will she make?

THE CHILD WHO FELL FROM THE SKY
Stephan Chadwick

Untold secrets of a post-war childhood.

A true story of a child born in war-torn London soon after the Second World War whose early memories are of the care and security given to him by his grandmother and a guardian angel who watches over him. At six he finds out a devastating secret that changes his life. He withdraws into his own world, searching for understanding and meaning. Isolated from his family and children of his own age he turns to his angel for love and guidance but even she cannot save him from what is to come.

'This is an extraordinary, raw, and powerful book.'
James Willis, *Friends in Low Places*

A LIFE GUIDE FOR TEENAGERS
Lucinda Neall

There are many things teenagers need to know to navigate their way through adolescence: from information about drugs, sex and alcohol; through how to deal with stress and peer pressure; to how to negotiate with parents and avoid being nagged! This easy-to-read book covers all this and more with quirky illustrations, lots of colour and buckets full of wise advice.

HOW TO TALK TO TEENAGERS
Lucinda Neall

If you have teenagers in your life – at home, at work, or in your neighbourhood – this book may stop you tearing your hair out! It will give you insights into how teenagers tick, and strategies to get their co-operation.

- ➢ Explains how teenagers see the world
- ➢ Packed with examples from day-to-to life
- ➢ Focuses on what to say to get them on board
- ➢ Includes 'maintaining boundaries' and 'Avoiding conflict'
- ➢ Gives tips on how to stop the nagging and shouting
- ➢ Encourages adults to see the positive in teenagers
- ➢ Concise chapter summaries for easy reference

'Has captured the art of dealing with teenagers in a fantastic, easy to use guide.'

John Keyes, Social Inclusion Manager
Arsenal Football Club

ABOUT OUR BOYS
Lucinda Neall

A Practical Guide to Bringing the Best out in Boys

This book looks at what motivates and de-motivates boys and how to help them navigate the journey to manhood. Written at the request of parents and youth workers who had read Lucinda Neall's book for teachers, it is packed with practical examples from everyday life.

'A really accessible, practical and useful handbook.'
Sue Palmer, *Toxic Childhood*

The TOM AND JAKE Series
Helen MccGwire

Six charmingly written and illustrated little books about Tom and Jake, two little boys who live with their family and animals in an old farm-house in Devon. The stories are based on the experiences of the author's five children during the 1960s, whilst living in the countryside.

Tom and Jake

More About Tom and Jake

Tom and Jake & The Bantams

Tom in the Woods

Tom and Jake & Emily

Tom and Jake & The Storm

Ideal for reading to children, and for revisiting a 1960s childhood.

THE VERY SKINNY WHIPPETY DOG
Kate Tomlinson
Illustrated by Sue Luxton

An engaging picture book about a skinny whippet who finds joy playing hide and seek in the English countryside and comfort in a loving home.

The delightful illustrations make this a perfect book for dog lovers, or to read to small children.

www.leapingboy.com

Lightning Source UK Ltd.
Milton Keynes UK
UKHW010737200722
406119UK00002B/449

9 780993 594786